MY FATHER'S CHILD

MY FATHER'S CHILD

Diane Roblin-Lee

byDesign
MEDIA

byDesign Media Publishing
Brechin, Ontario Canada *www.bydesignmedia.ca*

My Father's Child - 2nd Edition - Paperback ISBN 978-1-896213-81-1
epub ISBN 978-1-896213-82-8

Copyright ©2016 Diane Roblin-Lee
All rights reserved

Publisher: byDesign Media – www.bydesignmedia.ca
Brechin, Ontario Canada L0K 1B0

Library and Archives Canada Cataloguing in Publication

Roblin-Lee, Diane, 1945-, author
My Father's Child: the journey to faith in the home of clergy / Diane Roblin-Lee.
-- 2nd edition revised.

Issued in print and electronic formats.
ISBN 978-1-896213-81-1 (pbk.). -- ISBN 978-1-896213-82-8 (epub)

Roblin-Lee, Diane, 1945-. 2. Families of clergy.
3. Baptists--Canada--Biography. I. Title

BV4396.R62 2015   253'.22   C2014-908498-6
C2014-908499-4

All rights reserved. This publication may not be reproduced, stored in a retrieval system, or transmitted in whole or in part, in any form or by any means, electronic, mechanical, photocopying, recording, or otherwise, without the prior written permission of the Publisher.

CONTENTS

FOREWORD by David Mainse
INTRODUCTION
PART ONE
My Story
PART TWO
The Preachers' Kids – Introduction
    Chapter 1 – Are They Really Perfect?
    Chapter 2 – Congregations
    Chapter 3 – Developing a Self-Concept Beside the Pulpit
    Chapter 4 – Reverend Daddy
    Chapter 5 – A Minister's Wife for a Mother
    Chapter 6 – Relating to God
    Chapter 7 – Preacher's Kid to Preacher's Kid
    Chapter 8 – Preachers' Kids to Parents
PART THREE
The Preachers Speak – Introduction
    Chapter 1 – The Problems and Advantages of Raising Children as a Minister
    Chapter 2 – The Minister's Role as Dad
    Chapter 3 – Life and Rules in the Rectory
    Chapter 4 – The Rebellious Child
    Chapter 5 – Pointers from Pastors
PART FOUR
God's Answer...
    Speaking Victory Through Faith

An important note from the author...

This book was first published in 1980. Because the circumstances of my life have changed drastically since that first edition, I considered adjusting the text to reflect a deeper understanding of my situation and an awareness of realities which were, at the time of the writing, unknown to me. However, upon deeper reflection, I have changed little, because the message of the book is as true now as it was in the beginning. The progression of my journey is the stuff of another book ... someday.

Dedicated
to my sons, Tim and Todd

to Mom and Dad
with love and thanks

to my husband, Morgan Sharp,
for his love and long hours alone
while I reworked this manuscript

and
to God be the glory.

FOREWORD

You will find, as I have, that Diane Roblin-Lee has a delightful and compelling writing style. Because of a busy day time schedule I found myself reading My Father's Child late into the night and, even though tired, I was forced by the very power of the words to delve very deeply into my own life and feelings as a preacher's son, a father, and a preacher myself.

Diane has given to the people of God a precious gift. Every clergyman – woman – wife – father – mother – child – should prayerfully, carefully and humbly read this book. In fact, I would recommend it to members of every congregation. All should know what this book says. Congregations will learn how better to understand their pastor and his family; and pastors and families will better learn to understand each other and their congregations.

Diane's own life story is a powerful one. I've not drawn any conclusions concerning the reasons for her rebellion. I know her minister-dad personally. We pastored in the same city. I worked together with him on numerous projects. I always found him to be a joyous person of complete integrity and total dedication to God. He has had an influence for good on my ministry.

Finally, Diane interviewed my eldest daughter and me as two of her "preachers' kids." I can't escape a feeling of embarrassment because it makes me and my family out to be better than we are. Believe me, we are far from being the model family. We've made our share of mistakes and only God's grace has brought our children to Jesus and caused them to serve God faithfully.

Rev. David Mainse
Toronto, Ontario
Summer, 1980

INTRODUCTION

"I DIDN'T BRING YOU UP TO BE A HEATHEN!"

Years of effort appeared to be resulting in futility for my father as he exploded in the frustration of not being able to control his daughter's development.

"You have been raised in a Christian home! We did everything we could for you. Now look at you. You should be reflecting the Christian training you've had, but instead of that, all you care about are your friends, yourself, and having a good time!" His face was red, every nerve in his body stretched taut, crying for release from the tension.

But where was release? He was much too civilized and refined to slap me (although I felt he would have liked nothing better). I was twenty-two-years-old and untouchable. He was sixty and at a place in his role as a parent where he had tilled the land, planted the seeds and done what weeding he could. Now he had to stand by and watch as uncontrollable influences shaped the growth of his seeds. Helplessly.

Like a stone, I sat and looked at him as, furiously, he berated my attitudes and actions. What could I say? I was wrapped in guilt about being such a disappointment to him, but how could I shape myself into a mold into which I didn't fit, and in which I felt terribly uncomfortable?

Bitterness and resentment surged and boiled. Other people liked me. They all laughed with me and accepted me as a worthwhile individual. I had made it through university, had landed a good job as a social worker, and really felt that I was 'making it' as a person. Would nothing ever please this man? I just wanted to be accepted as myself – not as a perfectly molded clone.

My father is a minister – a Baptist minister. He is a man called of God to be a spiritual leader. A minister cannot be an ordinary parent. As a person selected to do a highly conspicuous work for God, he is expected to have standards higher than, or different from, the rest of the community. He is the embodiment of so much that is intangible and dependent on belief.

Consequently, when one says, "My father is a minister," he places his life in a glass box before his audience, most of whom assume that they clearly see the contents. As they look in the box they imagine they see a stuffy, oppressive home, a father who is either less or more than human, a mother who is all understanding and never tiring; and scrubbed children who all get good grades, play the piano, and win public speaking contests. It's a pretty heavy box.

Is it surprising, then, that when you hear someone say, "My father is a minister," you generally hear him expand a bit further on the subject? He is probably trying to clarify some of the contents, and so attain a degree of individuality. If he doesn't, he feels people will assume that he accepts the whole box, as is, with the inherent belief system.

I did a lot of expanding and clarifying. It usually went something like this: "My father is a minister. He was going to be a doctor, but he changed his mind." That statement generally served to get my point across rather well. It demonstrated the probability that my dad did, in fact, possess a degree of intelligence in spite of the fact that, in my superior opinion, his beliefs were sadly antiquated. As I said it, I always tried to give just the right tone of condescension, to convey the impression that we put up with the poor old dear, even though he was a bit dotty. There was always that need to explain my dad's profession.

The reason for that need to explain to other people, was that I could not understand the ministry. To me, the Bible was a history book. No one could know for sure whether or not there was really a God. The church was a stuffy place where people went once or twice a week and acted self-righteous. Many of the so-called Christians I knew, walked around looking like they had tired blood – great ads for Geritol. They all seemed so hushed and sad and phony and uptight. I, on the other hand, wanted to laugh freely, to spread my wings and run with joyous abandon. I was high-spirited and needed to be where I could feel alive!

The hypocrisy I saw bothered me. I despised phoniness in any form. But why did many of the church people seem to have so much fun away from the church – and then act so pious in front of my dad and our family? I wanted to be part of the fun life too.

Why did my dad become a minister? Why did he devote his whole life to something so intangible, so unlucrative, so thankless? He seemed to have everything going for him when he was young. He was good-looking, brilliant, witty and a champion athlete. Before going to university, he had had a rapidly climbing career in sales. What had happened? What happened to make him throw away all that potential earning power for the ministry? In the back of my mind, I vaguely concluded that at some point he had gone a little weird and blown it.

But now I'm thirty-four, and I understand. The understanding has not come easily. A lot of pain resulted from my struggle to flee the God of my father. But I'm thankful for all that I've endured because it brought me into a deeper understanding of people, a real appreciation of honest happiness and, most importantly, an absolute knowledge that God is real, that I really matter to Him, and that He has a valid purpose for my life.

These and other revelations were so mind-boggling to me and have effected such a profound transformation in my life, that I feel compelled to share what I discovered. Hence this book. My prayer is that it will help other ministers' children to understand their situation, to capitalize on their advantages, and cope with the problems involved. I pray too, that the ministers will read carefully, that they may gain greater insight into their children, and become more aware of the pitfalls that need to be avoided in raising children in the parsonage. Many of the principles involved can be effectively applied to any Christian home.

My discoveries brought not only a treasure of enlightenment to me, but also a barrage of new questions. What about other preachers' kids? Why did some just continue to grow spiritually, while others went through such heavy rebellion? Were my problems with my dad's profession unique, or were they generally universal? How could parents present spiritual matters so that the kids would listen? How could they listen so the kids would talk? What are the factors essential to the growth of spiritual understanding? What are the unique problems involved in being a preacher's kid? What are the advantages?

It seemed to me, that the best place to get the answers was directly from the P.K.s and their dads. With that in mind, I compiled two in-depth questionnaires – one for the offspring and one for the ministers. Then I set out, armed with a new tape recorder, the excitement of curiosity, and lots of prayer. One contact led to another and soon I was up to my ears in interviews. I travelled through a year of researching my questions and found that as I talked with all sorts of people, patterns were forming in some areas, while other situational experiences were without form and totally individualistic.

The interviews were conducted on a random sample basis. I wanted to talk to people from all age groups, from all walks of life, Christian and non-Christian. I talked with famous people, some not famous at all, and a few who were downright infamous! The ministers' children interviewed included housewives, musicians, students, television personalities, dope addicts, teachers, secretaries, an evangelist, and the list goes on. The ministers included famous evangelists, small town pastors, and many in-between, some active and some retired. I wanted the picture to be as comprehensive as possible. Some were thrilled at the prospect of having their names appear in a book; others preferred to remain anonymous for their own reasons.

Some of my experiences in gathering information were rather humorous. For example, I had heard that Hugh Hefner's (owner-editor of Playboy magazine) father was a minister. Since he was definitely a catalyst for cultural change, I decided it would be valuable to discover whether or not early influences in his life as a preacher's kid had any bearing on his choice of lifestyle. I spent a whole morning carefully composing a letter – something which would arouse his interest in my project without offending him. I included a blank cassette tape and a questionnaire with a return envelope, all conscientiously pre-stamped. A couple of weeks later, my post office box yielded a crisp white envelope emblazoned with a silver bunny in the corner. Now in our little town where everyone knows everything about you before you know it yourself, a silver bunny tends to stimulate whispered speculation. It was a courteous letter from Playboy's Special Events Coordinator, Barbara Bums. She thanked me for my request re Mr. Hefner's possible participation in my upcoming book, but sent regrets that they would be unable to comply because, "Mr. Hefner's father was not in the ministry."

It just goes to show you can't believe everything you hear!

This is a book for, and about, ministers and their children. I share my own story with hopes that my experiences and their consequences may bring the experiences of others into clearer focus and shed new light on the direction they are taking. The responses to my interviews give fly-on-the-wall insight into the inner feelings and experiences of those who have been raised in parsonages, manses, and rectories, and of those who have raised them.

Before I begin, I must make something abundantly clear. I have a tremendous love for my dad even though our relationship was not good for many years. I did not agree with many of the things he did in raising me, but now that I'm a parent, I don't always agree with everything I do with my children either. I do the best I can and so did he. Where I expose difficult situations it is never with the intention of hurting anyone, but in the hope that by reading my story, someone else will find the way to avoid unnecessary problems and pain.

PART ONE

My Story

My Story

IT WAS DARK OUTSIDE. The little old church was dimly lit for the evening service, an island of warmth and security sitting solidly amid the sea of snow and cold hearts outside. Everything seemed to have a golden glow of mellow richness as the minister guided the people to the climax of the meeting, to the place of personal confrontation. A solemn hush enfolded his words.

"Perhaps there is someone here tonight who has never accepted the Lord as Saviour. If you have never asked Jesus to come into your heart, why not do it now?"

Quietly, reverently, the old hymn, "Softly and Tenderly," emanated from the organ. Expectancy hung in the air as the minister spoke again. His words were gentle, beckoning.

"If you feel Jesus calling you tonight, just raise your hand in acceptance as we pray. That's all you have to do. He loves you and is waiting, with arms outstretched, for you to say 'Yes' to Him."

He began to pray. Over on the right hand side of the church, about six pews from the front, sat a four-year-old girl with long ringlets and a yellow bow in her hair. With brown eyes full of innocence and trust, she listened seriously to her daddy who was up at the front of the church, talking about Jesus.

"Just lift your hand. Accept Him into your heart tonight."

She loved Jesus. Every night, Mommy read stories to her about how much Jesus loved the little children, and how He made sick people well. Jesus was a nice, gentle man who would take little children, just like her, on His knee and pay attention to them just as though they were the most important people on earth. He used to tell people not to send the children away from Him.

In a moment of triumphant independence, she lifted her chubby little arm, and held it up in mute testimony of the most monumental decision of her whole life. In quiet jubilation, knowing that she was doing something very right, she waited for her Daddy to see her arm – and for his sure approval.

"Yes, I see your hand," he said. But he was looking at someone else; someone on the other side of the church. His eyes scanned the audience. He didn't see her. Her arm was too short. She stretched it higher; as high as it would go and waited. His head was turning in her direction. He stopped. "Yes. I see your hand. God bless you."

That scene, in the little old church in Toronto, happened thirty years ago. I was the child. My father was the minister. I am yet the child; just older, more seasoned, but finally with the decision intact, and firmly rooted.

It has not always been so. I went through years of agnosticism and near rejection of God in my search for reality, purpose and truth. But the Bible reads, "I will never leave you, nor forsake you."* Those were God's own words. It is my firm belief that He has had His hand on me since that time when I accepted Him in the trusting faith of early childhood. But He allowed me to explore other roads so I would know with surety that my greatest desire was to follow His single narrow way. In the things I tried, and the philosophies I explored, there were so many elements which could easily have led to disaster, but He was there and He sustained me, oblivious as I was to His presence.

Why did it take so long for the understanding to come? Why did my parents have to suffer so many sleepless nights on my account? As we explore some of the steps, perhaps you will see and understand some of the things which God has not yet illumined to my understanding.

I am five. It is Sunday. My sister Dona (who is ten years older than I), and Mom and I, are in the church basement.

"But Mommy there is nobody left to play with."

Everyone else has gone home after the morning service. We are unwrapping the first of the two meals Mom has packed for the day. The afternoon looms long. The big old Sunday School room feels boring and unyielding. Finally the hours have passed and it is time for the evening service. Mom and Dona and I go up and sit in a pew. My mommy feels so snuggly and I love her so much. Daddy is standing in the pulpit talking, talking, talking, talking. I guess he is the most important person in the whole world. Mommy is wearing her fox collar with the real head and the mouth that bites the tail. I play with it for a little while, snapping and unsnapping the moth from the tail. Mommy's hands are so nice. I love her dearly. Her hands are rough from all the hard work she does and that makes me love her hands more, because I know she works hard for me. I trace each finger in minute inspection of every vein and bone. Then I put her leather glove on her hand, and take it off again, and on and off, again and again.

"As we close, will you turn with me in your hymn books to number 366, 'Shall We Gather at the River.'"

Dona and I were raised in the church, almost as much as we were in our home. The sound of a squeaking pew takes me back to the shapes and smells of childhood. Churches have always evoked a sense of safety and security in me, because that is where my parents were when I was a child. Dona and I endured a lot of boredom because children are not capable of appreciating adult teaching; but generally we learned to cope with the tedium. It taught us patience and forbearance.

But there were drawbacks. We had so much church that we became saturated with its organization and lost sight of its significance in our personal lives.

I am six. Daddy and I are on our way down to the jail. He parks the car where I stay and wait and wait. I heard Mommy and Daddy talking and I think Daddy is getting a man out of jail. I watch the people pass by. Finally, I see Daddy coming. There is a man with him. The man looks unhappy. He is big, but not very old, and he has curly blond hair with grease in it. His face is sort of square and there are a lot of scars on it. He is getting in the back seat. I say nothing as we drive home, but I feel safe because my Daddy is here and he is the strongest man in the whole world. I wonder what that man did?

We are finally home. He is coming in the house with us. A young girl is here. She is slim and pretty and has short dark hair. I heard Mommy say she is his wife. Oh! They are hugging and kissing.

Mommy says they'll be staying with us for a while because they have a lot of problems. They are going to be sleeping in our guest room.

It is night time and I am sleeping. Suddenly, I am awakened by a terrible scream and a lot of yelling.

"Mommy! Mommy!" I call.

At last she comes. No one is yelling anymore. "What was all that noise, Mommy?"

"It's alright, darling. There's nothing for you to be upset about. Why don't you come and get into bed with me tonight?" She tucks me warmly under her covers and hums softly as she strokes my forehead.

It is morning. I am in the kitchen. Mom and Dona don't see me. They are talking about how the man from the jail tried to stab his wife last night. They say Daddy took a knife away from him!

This type of situation would seldom arise in an average home. However, Dad took his ministry seriously and seemed to derive great stimulation from the most difficult challenges. Perhaps he felt a certain invincibility, knowing that God was with him.

Dad had come to know Whitey, (the fellow who tried to stab his wife in our home) through his work with a street gang in the area of our Toronto church. One night after a meeting, Dad happened on three young fellows who were trying to break into the church. He startled them and they ran. What they hadn't figured on, was a young minister who not only was a champion runner, but who also held a Canadian inter-Collegiate boxing award! He pursued them doggedly, as they gave him a frenzied chase over fences and through alley ways. With a mighty lunge, he catapulted himself forward and grabbed one of the young hoodlums!

Out of that initial contact, evolved a ministry with the whole street gang. Whitey was a member of that gang. He had many psychological problems, among which was an intolerance for confined places. He went to Dad one day and asked him to perform the marriage ceremony for him and his girlfriend. As it turned out, the girl was a doctor's daughter who had run away from home and had become involved with the gang. Neither she nor her parents, who were vehemently opposed to Whitey, were Christians. The boy was non-Christian as well.

Dad set up a meeting and, in the presence of Whitey, he laid out all the boy's problems before the girl. In detail, he described what marriage to this person would be like. Then he asked Whitey to evaluate what he had said. Was it all true? Was it a fair description? Yes, Whitey agreed it was all true. Now Dad turned to the girl. Did she still want to marry this person in spite of his character and his problems? Yes, she still wanted to marry him. Knowing that if he refused to perform the ceremony, they would simply go to someone who was not familiar with the situation, and who would not be in a position to help later on, Dad agreed to perform the ceremony.

And so they were married. A young, rebellious girl who would listen to no one, and a young psychopath who needed treatment and care rather than the responsibility of a wife.

In spite of all Dad's counselling, the situation was tempestuous from the beginning. It wasn't long before Whitey was in jail. On his release, Dad felt it would help them get things together if they could stay with us for a while; that there was hope for them if they could be in an environment more conducive to positive growth.

But their churning, undefined needs were inadequate tools for coping with the pressures of their relationship and reality. The screams that awoke me in the night were predictable.

The battle that ensued, as Dad fought to disarm Whitey, was a tense struggle of will versus frustration, fear and anger. They battled until Dad managed to calm him and something in Whitey began to subside.

At the first possible moment, the girl (dressed only in a robe and slippers) ran out to our car. Dad followed her. He quickly yanked the door open and jumped in beside her before Whitey would change his mind. Suddenly he realized – no keys. An icy knot cracked in the pit of his stomach. He jumped out of the car and ran back to the house, mutely calling on God for divine help. And God was there. Whitey made no attempt to oppose him as Dad returned to the house for the keys.

Backing out of the driveway, the situation almost took on an air of surrealism for Dad. Here he was, driving a half-dressed girl across town in the middle of the night, leaving his wife and two daughters alone with a psychotic criminal. The distance increased between him and his family as he pressed on toward the girl's parents' home. The true meaning of dependence on God was so real to him that it almost took tangible form. It had taste and odor.

The obvious question is, why did he not just call the police, stay with his family, and let the law deal with the problem? After all, he was taking a mighty big risk acting without them. The stakes were high. I guess from his point of view, all his efforts with Whitey would go down the drain if he abandoned him to the cold machinery of the law. He had a lot of confidence in his own abilities, and knew that God was there to protect his family. He also knew that the boy's only chance at life was dependant on him accepting the Lord as his guide.

As I look back, that whole episode could have been a fantastic object lesson for Dona and me, about the keeping power of God. Too often, ministers just take God's grace for granted, thanking Him privately, but failing to point out to their children exactly how greatly God has worked. If children are to grow in true understanding of God, then the reality of His existence must be demonstrated to them. Had Dad taken the time to sit down with us and discuss the situation in which he had involved us, in the light of God's grace and love for us, perhaps later on we would not have questioned so painfully whether or not He cared for us. But Dad was very busy, and probably so preoccupied with the urgency of the situation, that our spiritual growth was just assumed as intact by him at the time. It's understandable.

In situations of this sort, both father and child need to become more sensitive to the deep needs of the other. However, the children are generally too young to be able to comprehend the father's needs without mature coaching; and the father is too preoccupied with the visible work at hand, to involve himself with the less visible growth patterns of his children. Here is one area of major concern to the minister's wife. She is generally more sensitively aware of the needs of both the minister and their children, and should therefore be able to more effectively draw them together.

What happened to Whitey? Well, he stayed with us for a couple of weeks, during which time he managed to keep things interesting by demonstrating his skill at picking locks and so on. But generally, he behaved himself. He pled with Dad to intercede for him with his wife, but Dad refused because he felt it would be futile until Whitey himself had changed.

Finally, Whitey could stand the separation no longer and just had to talk with his wife. He made his way across the city and reached her parents' home. Her dad spotted him walking up the pathway. Whitey had no idea what awaited him in that house. Ever since the night of the stabbing, ever since the girl had returned home, she and her parents had known Whitey would come. By this time, their hatred, fear and anxiety had become totally irrational. Adrenalin had been building for days. Whitey knocked. The door flew open and, before the boy knew what was happening, the father grabbed him, pulled him into the house and proceeded to beat the boy with all his pent up fury and frustration. He had lots of help. His wife joined in with the heel of her shoe and his daughter grabbed an empty coke bottle. The gentility of the doctor's home was nowhere to be seen as the four of them flailed at each other in a life or death struggle. By the time Whitey managed to get out of the house, four colors of hair littered the floor. Blood was splattered all over the hall. The once-gracious entry way was an ugly mess of broken glass, mirrors and plaster. All four were badly beaten.

It was a sad story, from beginning to end. The last we heard of Whitey, he had joined the military in search of order in his life. But he stepped out of line again and was placed in solitary confinement. There he went berserk. That was the last we heard of him.

I am seven. We have just moved from Toronto to Peterborough, Ontario. This big, old house belongs to the church, but they let us live in it. Our other house was our very own. This one is creaky, but it feels good. I love the way the two staircases meet at the top. I can run up one staircase and slide down the bannister of the other one! The ceilings are so high. Dona's room even has one part of the ceiling that slants and a balcony in front. I wish I could have that room. The bathtub is really funny. It has legs that look like lion's paws! I love this big old house.

Mr. and Mrs. Wicks are people who go to our new church. We are having dinner at their home. They have two little girls. Mr. Wicks says that Gloria, the oldest girl, will come to our house and walk me to school tomorrow, because she goes to the same school as I do. Boy, I'm sure glad I'll know someone there. My tummy gets all squiggly inside whenever I think about going to that new school.

Generally, ministers move fairly often. We seldom stayed anywhere longer than five years. Dad used to say that both the church and the minister needed a revitalizing change after about four years. The moves were exciting times. I always looked forward with eager anticipation to moving into a strange house. It was always fun running through strange rooms, exploring things which were now ours for a time, and would soon be so familiar.

The worst thing about moving was always the first day at a new school. In one new place, I was so shy and felt so totally alone that I spent the entire lunch hour in a stall in the washroom eating my lunch and crying. It was horrible and I hated it. But all these situations, where I was forced to adapt to new people and new surroundings, were good because, as a result, I became easily adaptable.

When the average family moves to a new location, it is common to go through a period of perceived isolation, when everyone around is a stranger. But when a minister and his family moves, they move into a whole new congregation of people who welcome them with open arms. From the beginning, they are sought after and invited into every sort of group imaginable. That is a big help in getting to know people.

I am eight. Betty Johnston is my very best girlfriend. She and her sister, Yvonne, live right across the street. Sometimes Carole Ball plays with us. We are walking home from school. The three of them are just up ahead, walking slowly, whispering. I run to catch up.

"Don't tell her. She's a minister's daughter."

Carole's words whip across my heart. Something inside is wizening up. I want to hide where no one can see me. I think my insides are going to fall out.

The girls walk on, giggling together. I let them go. My steps are slow and heavy. So what if I am a minister's daughter? What does that have to do with any old secret? I'm not any different than they are.

That little episode began a twenty-five-year struggle to prove to the world that I was okay. It was just the first episode in a long road of discrimination. People in the church held me up to their children as an example, simply because I was the minister's daughter. They looked at me through eyes of prim approval, and I hated the dishonesty of it all; because inside, I knew I was not really good. People outside the church held me at arm's length, because I had a label and was supposedly different. I always felt on the edge of the circle, but somehow never quite able to get inside.

Is it any wonder that many minister's children go through rebellion? They are fighting for honest acceptance of themselves as individuals. They have had a label fixed on them that is not of their own choosing. The problem with this label is that it presumes to tell what is supposed to be on the inside. If the label is wrong, then they have to fight to prove it.

My problem was, that while I had accepted Jesus as my Saviour, I hadn't made Him Lord in my everyday life. I didn't really understand what it meant to be a Christian. I thought it just meant being a goodie-goodie, and I was finding out fast that goodie-goodies didn't have much fun. I didn't know anything about living a victorious Christian life. I felt like a pretty chocolate with poison inside. I hated the dishonesty. These feelings became more pronounced in my late teens.

I am ten. It's our summer holiday. Daddy is away working in the Air Force for a month. He often does this in the summer to relieve another chaplain. Dona is twenty-years-old now and she is away on a trip. Mommy and I are at the church. No one else is here. Vacation School has finished for the day. We're getting the craft materials set out on the tables for tomorrow's activities.

What was that loud being? Someone is running down the stairs! Mr. Brown (false name) just came in. He looks so mad! He has a letter in his hand and he seems really mad at Mommy. I'm scared. What can I do to protect my Mom? I feel so helpless! He is throwing the letter at her.

"Go into the primary room Diane, and shut the door, darling."

I don't want to leave her, and I'm scared. Closing this door seems so final. I wish there was another door out of here so that I could run and get someone to help us. I sit down at the table and wait and wait. My mind is racing and my heart is thump, thump, thumping. Maybe he will kill her and then come to kill me. The whole scene, detail by bloody detail passes before my eyes. Oh Mommy, Mommy I love you so much.

I hear him marching out. The door bangs behind him as he runs up the steps and out of the church. I open the door and peer out. What will I see? Mom is sitting at a table with her head buried in her arms. I run to her and put my arms around her.

"What did he want, Mom?" *There is no sound.* "Why are you shaking, Mom?"

She is shaking more and more. What am I going to do? She won't say anything. How can she shake so much?

"Do you want me to go and get someone?" *She seems to be shaking her head, no.* "How are we going to get home? You can't drive the car when you're shaking so much."

"You get my purse and things, and we'll be alright." *She is shaking so much that she can hardly talk.*

I am helping her walk across the room to the door. We make it to the car and I help her in.

"Get the keys out of my purse, dear." Her voice is so shaky I can hardly understand her words.

I find the keys and hand them to her. "Do you want me to try to drive, Mom?" The fact that I was just a little girl who had never driven a car was not even a factor to me. I would do anything to fix my precious mom.

"No, dear, you just pray."

"Oh, God, God, help us!" I scream silently.

We move out into the street. One block, two blocks, three blocks, four blocks, home. "Oh God, thank you. But don't go away. Help us. Oh please make Mommy stop shaking!"

I help her into the house. She is leaning on me as I lead her to the couch. Oh no, she is starting to cry! The only time I ever saw her cry before was when Grandma died.

"Can I phone Daddy long distance and get him to come home?"

"Not right now, sweetheart. I'll be alright."

"But Mom, you're shaking even harder!"

Finally, the next day, Daddy is on his way home, Mom says. She has stopped shaking, but she seems so quiet and sad. Why won't she tell me what Mr. Brown said?

A couple of days later, Mom says Mr. and Mrs. Brown are coming over to our house to talk with her and Dad. "When they are here, we would like to talk privately and so I would like you to go down to your friend's house for the afternoon. You must go at two and you can come home at four o'clock."

"Okay Mom." I know I must not ask any questions. But it feels so weird. No one has ever told me not to come home before. Sure wish I knew what was going on.

Finally it is four o'clock. I hurry home. It's rather quiet but it seems as though things are somehow right again. I wish I could ask about what Mr. and Mrs. Brown wanted, but instinctively I know I must not.

For five years, I wondered what had happened that summer. One afternoon, Dona and I were talking in her room. I asked her whether or not she knew the story. She opened up and finally I learned the answers to the questions I had harboured for so long.

The letter which had been the cause of so much pain and turmoil, was a love letter which Mr. Brown had discovered in a waste paper basket in his home. It was written in his wife's hand, and was signed by her. It was addressed to my father.

The Browns had been having many problems, not the least of which were marital problems. Mrs. Brown and the children went to our church. Dad had been doing a certain amount of counselling in the situation, trying to help in any way possible. Mrs. Brown was so starved for understanding and care, that she imagined herself to be in love with Dad because he showed her genuine caring. She mistook the Christian concern for a romantic type of love on his part. She imagined that he could not tell her of his love because he was a married minister. She wrote him a letter, pouring out her feelings. For some reason she threw it out instead of sending it. And that's where her husband found it – discarded in a waste paper basket.

What eventually happened to the Browns? I don't know. But I do know that this is an old story. It is one that has happened often to doctors, ministers, psychiatrists, and people in other professions of help where they show loving concern for emotionally deprived people. Depending on how the situation is discovered and handled, it can result in a myriad of difficulties.

As far as I was concerned, I believe that when a child is involved to that extent in a situation, he should be given some explanation. A child must be taught about the hard parts of life. If he is wrapped in cotton batting all through childhood, the sun will burn when he or she is finally exposed to it. Honesty and a little bit of self-exposure to a child at that age goes a long way. If a parent won't ever confide in a child, the child may not confide in his parent later. Trust puts wild imagination to rest.

I am eleven. Today is Saturday – preparation day. Today we have to get everything ready for Sunday. Usually, Mom and Dad invite someone from church home for lunch and so everything has to be prepared ahead of time. The house has to be spotless. I am sitting at the table polishing silver. It is all spread out before me on newspaper. I have soft flannel rags and a toothbrush for the fancy work. I like rubbing the dried cleaner off and seeing the mellow shine underneath.

"Diane, don't forget to polish the shoes when you're finished your job. I'd like you to do the dusting in the living room and the dining room, too. Don't forget to do the bottom rungs of the chairs and the tables."

"Aw Mom, nobody will notice if I do all that underneath stuff."

"Perhaps not, dear, but they'll notice if you don't."

Finally the last rung has been rubbed with lemon oil. Mmm, I love the clean smell. I wander downstairs. Mom is ironing with her Bible open on the end of the ironing board. She is memorizing Scripture as she irons.

"Here, dear. Take my Bible and correct me if I make a mistake." *I take the Bible and settle down on a pile of cushions.*

"I will lift up mine eyes unto the hills, from whence cometh my help. My help cometh from the Lord, which made Heaven and earth. He will not suffer thy foot to be moved: He that keepeth thee will not slumber. Behold, He that keepeth Israel shall neither slumber nor sleep. The Lord is thy keeper: the Lord is thy shade upon thy right hand. The sun shall not smite thee by day, nor the moon by night. The Lord shall preserve thee from all evil: He shall preserve thy soul. The Lord shall preserve thy going out and thy coming in from this time forth and for evermore.[1]" *She speaks gently as though she is tasting the words.*

"That's good, Mom. You got every word right. Can I go over to Betty's house for a while?"

"I guess so, but don't be long, because supper is almost ready."

It is getting dark now and the dishes are almost done. I am dawdling along with the last few pans in the greasy water. Yuk. I hate doing dishes. Why does Mom have to use practically every dish in the house for every meal?

[1] Psalm 139

Dona is rushing around getting ready for her friends to pick her up. "Hurry up, Diane. I'll help you wash your hair as soon as you're finished. Mom wants me to put it in rollers for you and I'm going out, so let's hurry and get it done."

I am asleep. The house is spotless, ready for Sunday. I am awakened by a noise in the hall outside my room. "Clickety-clak, clickety-clak, clickety-clak...." I roll over and look at my clock. It is 1:30 a.m. Dad is doing the church bulletin for tomorrow. The old Gestetner heaves and chugs as it churns out copies of tomorrow's order-of-service.

Memories of home. The threads that dominated the warp and woof of our lives. There's a lot of security in routine for a child. It feels good to know that some things happen, rain or shine. It feels good to know that there's a dependable pattern to follow. The most mundane things of life sometimes turn out to be the most important. No routine is complete without complaints, and I had plenty of those. But there is a certain comfort in feeling free enough to complain, too. And I did with Mom. But never, never with Dad. His word was law, and never, never to be questioned.

To me, Dad was all-powerful. There did not seem to be anything that he could not do. He had built a house for us from scratch in Toronto, including all of the electrical work and plumbing. He was terrific at carpentry work. He did most of the repairs on our cars by himself. He was a crack shot with a rifle. People came to him with their problems. Whenever we attended an official function, he was generally on the platform. But I remember sitting on his knee only once – the night I asked Jesus to come into my heart.

It seemed that Dad was always leaving to go somewhere. One of the most frequent memories of him is that of him leaving, going out a hundred different doors. But that was okay. I was more relaxed while he was away, relieved that for a while I need not fear falling into his disfavor. It wasn't that I was afraid of physical abuse, or anything like that. As a matter of fact, I only ever really remember being spanked about a half dozen times.

It was my constant fear of incurring his anger. I never knew when it would come, nor what might spark it. I was terrified of falling into his disfavor. At the time, I didn't realize that his anger was often more a result of the pressures he faced, than of my actions. As a result, I often lied about little things that I thought might not meet with his approval. Then there was the guilt of the lie and the fear of discovery to deal with. Some of those lies got pretty complicated.

He very honestly, I believe, tried to give us all, the very best home that he could, and the greatest comforts within his grasp. One Christmas, he gave me the most exciting gift I've ever received – my very own little black puppy. Another year, despite the fact that money was very tight, he surprised me with a brand new 120 bass accordion, for which I had longed. He bought a cottage for us where we spent a great deal of time every summer. It was a beautiful place to grow up and I dearly loved it.

In retrospect, I believe he was under a great deal of pressure and needed a release valve. So many people came to him with their problems, and he was the epitome of patience with them. There were political hassles that had to be dealt with in the church, and he was the man. There were sick people to be visited, old people who needed his attention, organizations that all expected him to give them a certain degree of leadership. There were sermons to prepare, Bible studies to conduct, prayer meetings to lead. There were people to marry, people to bury, and people to baptize. And there were unsaved people all around him in the community who needed to be reached with the message of salvation.

Beneath all of these responsibilities lay his greatest obligation. He was required by God to maintain a deep spiritual life of his own. People expected that to be the very foundation of his whole ministry. But when there are so many demands on one's time from too many different directions, it is not easy to spend a lot of time reading the Bible and praying. There is a temptation to forget personal spiritual needs and one's own hunger for God. When in the position of leading people spiritually, one may find oneself using the Bible as a tool for the benefit of others, rather than as a personal guide. It is hard to make the transition from using it as a textbook to using it as a devotional guide.

As I look back, the pressures were great. Dad had everyone else's problems to handle as well as his own. He was expected to be nice and wise and courteous all the time. I guess home was the only place where he could let his humanity hang out. He was not perfect. He was not one of God's completed projects; he was just under construction like the rest of us.

But I had needs too. I needed time to spend with him when he could concentrate on nothing but me. I needed to be able to take my problems to someone who would have patience with them. I needed to be able to take my joys to someone who would truly appreciate them and delight in sharing them with me. I needed someone who would not shatter my dreams with disapproval. I needed to be valued as a unique individual who could be trusted with a certain degree of decision making. I needed a love that was tolerant of my imperfections. I needed to see God's love reaching out to me through my Dad.

The dilemma was spawned in the early days of time and has appeared insurmountable to countless individuals in countless circumstances. How can a person possibly cope effectively with all the external and internal pressures and needs of life?

There are answers. As I went around interviewing people who have lived in homes like ours, I found clues in both negative and positive responses to my questions. I will deal with these later in the book.

I am still eleven. Mom and Dad and I have moved to Winnipeg. Dad was a senior chaplain in the R.C.A.F. during World War II, and now has been asked to return for a year. I am in grade six. The teacher is a stern old lady who has the seating of the class arranged in order of test results. The dumbest kid sits in the front seat on the far right hand side of the class. The smartest one sits in the front seat of the far left hand row. All the others are in between, according to their efforts and abilities. I have to sit in the dumbest seat because the Manitoba school system is six months ahead of the Ontario system and so I'm way behind. I have never felt such shame. I don't know how to handle it. These are new, horrible feelings. I have always been good in school. I have always been treated like a smart kid. Now, whenever the teacher asks me a question, I have to stand up beside my seat and say I don't know the answer. Her face gets all red and mean and she yells at me. I start to cry and then she tells me to sit down and learn the answer. I wish I could die.

"Mommy, I have the most awful pain in my stomach. I feel like throwing up. I can't go to school this morning. Oooo, it hurts so much."

"Well, I guess you'd better go back to bed dear."

It worked! Thank goodness I don't have to go back to that awful place.

It worked yesterday. I'll try it again today.

"Mom, I still feel terrible this morning. Oooo, my stomach really hurts."

"Let me feel your forehead, dear." *She puts her hand on my head and looks closely at me.* "I think you'll be alright to go this morning."

"But Mom it really hurts."

"You go this morning and we'll see how you are this afternoon."

Oh no! I have to go and face that horrible old Miss Nisbett. Now my tummy really is getting all squiggly and upset inside.

Mom was wise. She knew I was able to handle only a certain amount of pressure. But she knew too, that properly handled, duress produces strength and confidence. She never gave any indication of not trusting my integrity. There were times when I was not worthy of her trust, but it was very important to me.

The average minister moves fairly often. With regional differences in educational standards, moves can present real problems for children. However, the cloudiest day can have the best sunset. In this case, I was finally able to muster a little of my Irish heritage and managed to make it to the front seat of the left hand side of the class by the end of the year. It took a lot of work, but now I remember that year in Winnipeg as my finest year in school and Miss Nisbett as the best teacher I ever had.

I'm thirteen. We're living in Sudbury, Ontario. We're on our way home from church. Mom and I were working in the nursery while Dad preached.

"Diane," Dad calls me to attention. "You've never been baptized, have you?"

"No," I reply.

"Well, I guess we should get some baptismal classes going."

It was as simple as that. The decision had been made for me. Believing it would naturally be my desire to be baptized, Dad planned baptismal classes, and about eight other young teenage girls and I were baptized by immersion at the conclusion of the course. As far as I was concerned, it was part of the natural course of things. I had not felt any particular need for it, nor did I feel any aversion to having it done. It was just a ceremony as far as I was concerned.

To me, the whole church structure at that time was basically an arena for ceremony. I had no real personal relationship with Jesus. I vaguely wondered what a man, dying two thousand years ago, had to do with me. As far as the Holy Spirit was concerned, 'It' (not He) was just something vague and dusty. I had no real understanding of Him and His function in our world.

I am fourteen. My friend, Helen Dixon, and I are listening to records at her house. I feel so free here. Helen's family doesn't go to church. It feels really neat to be able to turn the music up loud and groove on the freedom.

"Teach me how to jive, Helen."

I jump off her bed and we start to move to the music. I feel something new and strange about my body as we twist and turn and allow the music to possess us. I feel so good and different somehow. I want to keep on and on. But too soon, Helen has had enough. We go out to her living room. Her dad comes in. He banters back and forth with Helen in an easy give and take. They are close and comfortable with each other. I am jealous of their relationship. How I long to have a relationship like that with my dad.

I feel so relaxed here; accepted just because I'm me. Helen doesn't have to prove anything. She knows who she is and nobody demands anything different.

As I became involved in High School, the things that were missing in our home; like dancing, going to shows and playing cards, took on an aura of glamour. At school, I wanted to be able to join in the conversation about dances and boyfriends and all of the things that were so foreign to my world of church activities. My social life felt musty in comparison with what everyone else was doing.

One day, I said something rather witty to one of the girls. Laughing, she said, "Hey, you're really funny!" I began to capitalize on that, because I thought maybe humour could be my conduit to acceptance, even if I was unable to take part in normal activities. As a result, I failed grade eleven and had to repeat it. Although I was bright, I did poorly in High School, simply because my focus was on acceptance.

I felt as though everything I said to Dad met with either an alternate proposal (which he considered superior to mine), or with his disapproval – and so I stopped trying to communicate with him. For four years, I sat at the kitchen table and stared out the window during meal time. Generally, I spoke to him only when he spoke to me first. That seemed to save a lot of hassles. The sad thing was that he had no idea what was happening. He had no idea what was going on in my head. He simply thought I had become a rather quiet girl. But inside I was a seething mass of bitterness and resentment.

I am seventeen. My closest girlfriend, Chris (an assumed name), is home for the Christmas break from university. We have been at a Young People's Christmas party, and she invited me to sleep at her home tonight so that we could have a good gab and catch up on each other's lives since we were together in the fall.

Her home is gorgeous. I love this place and feel like a princess sleeping here. Even the sheets feel rich. The house sure seems funny without Chris' mom here though. She died of cancer in the fall, just before Chris and her brother Mike left for Acadia University.

We talk and giggle as only best girlfriends can, on into the wee hours of the morning. She is bubbling over with her adventures at university, and I can't get enough because I'll be going there next year too. She tells me about all the boys she has gone out with and what residence life is like. I can hardly wait to get there! It sounds so exciting.

We get onto the subject of her dad. He has been terribly depressed since her mother died. He wanders around their huge home all alone now, except for Johnny, Chris' twelve-year-old brother. Sandra, her sister, is married now and living in a distant city. Chris and Mike are both away at Acadia University in Nova Scotia, and that leaves their dad suddenly with no one except young Johnny, rambling around in this huge home. Chris is worried about her dad and tells me how he cries and cries. She says that he can't stand to be alone. It is especially hard for Johnny. She wonders if she should forget about university and stay home with her dad and brother. It's hard to decide. We hope this is just a normal period of grief that will pass with time. Finally, her words blur together and I drift off to sleep.

I am jarred suddenly out of my sleep by Chris' screams as she comes running into our bedroom. She is laughing wildly, running into the room with blonde hair flying. I wonder what fantastic thing has happened. She flings herself on the bed, trying to tell me something, but she is laughing so hard that I can't understand what she is saying. No, wait; she's not laughing; she's crying!

"Chris! What happened? What's going on? Tell me again; I didn't understand you!"

"Dad is dead!" she cries, convulsed in heaving sobs. "He hung himself! He's downstairs just hanging there! Oh what are we going to do? We've got to get him down from there! We've got to get him down!" She jumps up off the bed and runs into Mike's bedroom.

I sit in bed for a moment, stunned, trying to make some sense out of my scrambled thoughts. Morning light is filtering through the drawn drapes. I can't believe night has passed. Things don't seem real. I feel like an actor in a play, waiting for my cue; but I don't know the script. I am trying to absorb something that won't register. Part of me won't come together with the rest of me.

Chris must have had a nightmare. That's it! She has had a nightmare, wakened in the middle of it and still thinks it really happened. I jump out of bed, grab my robe and throw it on, running to tell Chris that she was just dreaming. Sounds of desperate sobbing are coming from Mike's room. They stumble, clutching each other, out into the hall. We three meet just at the top of the steps. Mike looks dazed, as though he has no idea what is happening. None of this is really happening.

"Chris," *I start to speak, but my voice sounds unforgivably fake.* "I'm sure you've been dreaming and just woke up in the middle of your dream."

"No, no it's true. It's true. I really saw him. He's hanging down in the furnace room! I heard a noise and I got up and looked for him and I couldn't find him anywhere. I knew he hadn't gone out because his coat was still here, and so I just kept looking for him and that's where I found him." *She is becoming a little more controlled.*

I begin to shake. "If he really is down there, one of us should go down just to make sure."

We sense something behind us, and turning, see twelve-year-old Johnny standing in the doorway of his bedroom. He has no expression on his face. He says nothing, but we know that he has heard every word.

"I'm going downstairs." *Mike speaks hesitantly.*

In the instant, I know what I have to do. "No," *I hear the strange words coming out of my mouth.* "I'm going." *I am the only one here who is not family. Why do I feel I can handle it better than they can? Maybe it's because this whole scene cannot be real, and something that is not real can't touch me. But if this is not real, then why am I shaking like this? I look at the three of them. Their eyes are all filled with the same hollow horror. Unspeakable.*

I turn and start down the steps. This is silly. It is just all an act and there is no one down there. I round the landing. Beautiful mural of birds in flight on a vivid blue background. How often have I looked at that mural? It feels different against my eyes. Hollow. I am at the door of the family room. Chris said the furnace room, didn't she? Everything is so quiet, but pregnant, on the edge of exploding. I continue, step by measured step through the family room. There is the furnace room door, and there is a light on in there. Gingerly, I pull the door further open, and peer inside. Where shall I look? Slowly, fearfully, my eyes turn to the right of the room. Nothing there. Relief. Deliberately, I continue. More to the left. Okay so far. Further to the left. I knew it was a dream. I turn my head further. Still okay. Further.

There he is. Lock of iron grey hair falling across his forehead. That looks so strange. He is usually so well-groomed. Neck tied so tight. How can it be so skinny? Tongue hanging out the side of his mouth. Not real. Stool kicked over, on its side on the floor.

I'm in the kitchen, making coffee. Chris, Mike and Johnny are sitting in the living room. No one is talking. The coffee is ready and I take it in. Cream? Sugar? Does it really matter? We sit watching the large flakes of snow fall, waiting for the ambulance and my dad, sipping coffee. Words sound ridiculous. We sit here in velvet comfort and he is hanging down there. I wish someone would get here.

Dad arrives, then the ambulance. Again we sit in silence, imagining all that is happening downstairs. The ambulance leaves with its cargo. Relief. Dad comes upstairs. It feels good to have someone in control.

Chris stays for the next couple of days at our house. We spend a lot of time in my room, discussing every awful detail of our imaginations. It's good to be able to speak openly and honestly with each other. The doctor has given us sedatives for sleeping at night. Our discussions help us to purge the horror, rather than having to store it all up inside. We are worried about Johnny, because he is not talking to anyone about how he is feeling. He has not asked any questions about anything, and we've never seen him cry.

As I look back, I think perhaps Johnny was more prepared for that terrible morning than anyone else. He had lived alone with Mr. Lawford ever since his mom's death in the fall. He had seen the terrible toll grief had taken on his dad. Perhaps Johnny knew, in some undefined way, that there would be an ending to the grief. When it happened, it was almost a relief.

That was my first personal encounter with death. Mr. Lawford was a very close friend of Mom and Dad's. He sang in our church choir, was a member of the church board and was generally a very active member of the congregation. People in a congregation become almost like members of a minister's family. Often, as in the case of Mr. Lawford, the bond is deep because people tend to take their deepest burdens to the minister. More than once, Mr. Lawford called our home in the middle of the night threatening suicide. Dad would speak peace and assurance to him until he got to the point where Dad could hang up the phone, jump into his clothes, and speed over to his home to talk with him. Ministers deal with the deep spiritual needs of people and therefore tend to become closer with them personally than do doctors or secular counsellors. If and when a loss comes, it is often a lot closer to home, and felt more personally.

It is September of 1963 and I am eighteen-years-old. About three minutes ago, I left home never to return as a permanent resident. Mike is driving Chris and me to Acadia University in Wolfville, Nova Scotia, about two thousand miles from home. A couple of tears well up in my eyes, in spite of my excitement, as I think of leaving Mom. I am grateful to Dad for using some pull to get me into University. As it was, I made it by the skin of my teeth, because I fooled around so much in High School. I am proud of his ability to pull strings and override the system. It makes me feel somewhat above the ordinary people who have to accept institutional directives with no recourse.

As Mike drives the car further and further from my home, I feel tremendous exhilaration and freedom. For the first time in my life, I can do exactly as I please. I am my own decision maker; I can set my own standards. I don't have to fear rebuffs from anyone. I do feel guilty about wanting to get away from Dad, and my heart aches to be close to him, but bitterness covers the ache, because every time I have tried to expose my heart to him and get close, something has happened to make him stomp all over me with his disapproval. I want to feel adequate.

This is the third and last day of our journey to Acadia. We are on the Bluenose ferry which we boarded at Bar Harbour, Maine, early this morning. It is a magnificent fall morning. The sky is bluer than I've ever seen it before. The ocean air is crisp and deliciously salty against my cheek. I feel exquisitely sophisticated and independent. Nothing can stop me now. I lean against the ship's rail and my imagination soars with the gulls as they swoop and glide, soar and dive, calling, screeching, "I am alive! I am alive! Look at me world! I am alive and I can fly!" Just a speck on the horizon at first, land is becoming more visible ahead of us. On through the foaming blue waves we surge toward my dreams.

A lighthouse; the very first lighthouse I've ever seen – a materialization of my daydreams, so simple and beautiful against the fluffy white clouds and the blue, blue sky. My future is there, on that shore, in that land. I am so thrilled and excited that I can barely wait to step on the soil of Nova Scotia.

It is time to get into the car. Mike follows the line of cars as he drives out of the ship's hold into the sunshine. It has been a six hour crossing, and it feels odd to be on solid land again. We drive up Route One from Yarmouth to Wolfville, along the ocean coast. We pass quaint old fishing villages, harbours, jettys, lobster traps, Cape Islander fishing boats, seining rigs and more light houses. The reality is so much better than the dreams.

Almost a hundred miles later, we reach Acadia. It is a beautiful University campus nestled in the Annapolis Valley right on the Bay of Fundy. I love it. Chris and I are to be in Seminary Residence. Mike drives us around to the front and we go in. It is a huge Cape Cod style structure, all white frame with a flat black Plymouth roof. Inside everything is gleaming and mellow. An elderly lady is walking toward us. Chris calls out a greeting and with outstretched arms, embraces her.

"Diane, I want you to meet our housemother, Mrs. Hopkins."

I shake her hand as Chris introduces us. A round face, and lots of smiley wrinkles. She's a cross between Aunt Helen and Miss Nisbett, my Grade six teacher. She goes to a desk near the door and takes a list from a shelf underneath.

"Chris, I guess you've got Julie for your roommate this year and Diane, you're upstairs with a girl from Montreal named Diane Marshall. I'll show you to your rooms. You girls are the first ones here this term. I'm not expecting anyone else until Saturday, so you two will have the run of the place for about three days."

We follow her down a long, wide hallway with shiny wooden floors and great high ceilings. We turn a corner, and pass what Chris calls the "common room." We continue past about twenty great high doors, all double rooms awaiting their next occupants.

"Here we are," she says. "This is your room, Christine."

"Wasn't this Sue's room last year?" Chris asks.

"Yes, and she is just across the hall this year with Wendy Woods. Now if you'd like to come upstairs, I'll show you your room, Diane."

Wide steps, freshly varnished, gleaming handrails and waxed wood everywhere. I'm glad no one else is here yet. It will give me a chance to become familiar with my surroundings before I have to cope with meeting a lot of new people. Mrs. Hopkins opens a door at the head of the stairway, across the hall. Here is it. Home sweet home. A twelve-foot high ceiling, two single beds, two desks, two dressers, and a great long window overlooking the Bay of Fundy and the University Chapel with its maritime spire. The view is magnificent, even awe inspiring – but a chapel? I came two thousand miles to get away from that, and now every time I look out of my window, there it will be. Oh well, it really is pretty.

It is the afternoon of the second day. Chris and I are unpacked and settled in. I am beginning to feel as though I belong here. Her old boyfriend Ed, is coming to pick us up in a few minutes. He is bringing a friend, Frank, with him, and we are all going to the Lunenburg Exposition. They are here. We are introduced all around and go out to the car. Frank is gorgeous. I have only been here for a day, but I'm in love already! Nothing could be better than this. The boys take out their cigarettes and offer them to us. Frank and I are in the backseat and I shake my head "no." I think smoking makes a girl look cheap. Hey, wait a minute; Ed is lighting a cigarette for Chris.

"When did you start smoking?" I ask in amazement. I am shocked at her wickedness.

"Oh, last year sometime I guess," she replies with a nonchalant wave of her hand.

I can't believe this. It upsets me. I feel deserted, disappointed in her. I suddenly feel very young and naive, foolish, left out.

The residence is full of girls now, laughing, chatty, bubbly girls. Living here is great. My roommate is gorgeous and has more clothes them I can believe. She is going to be a super roomie. We get along famously. I am sitting in Wendy Woods' room gabbing with a few of the girls. Most of them are smoking.

"Wendy," I say, "if I ever ask you for a cigarette, don't give me one." I am already feeling drawn toward trying one, and yet I don't want to.

"Okay," she laughs easily.

It is two days later and Wendy and I are alone in the common room. "Wendy, let me try one of your cigarettes."

"But you told me not to give you one, even if you asked, Robbie."

Before the rest of the students arrived, I told Chris I was changing my name to "Robbie," short for my last name, "Roblin." Supposedly this was just to keep people from getting my roommate, Diane, and me confused. In actual fact, it was another step toward my independence, a further separation from my former life. I was "Robbie" to everyone now. A new name gave me more freedom to create a new image, a more sophisticated personality.

"Oh, just forget about that Wendy. Give me one and show me how to do it." This is exciting. I feel so daring.

She extends the package toward me, and I draw one out of the package. "What do I do with it now?" I ask, laughing.

"Okay, just do what I do." She puts hers in her mouth and lights it. The end glows red. She extends the flaming lighter towards my cigarette. "Just suck in on the end of yours." I draw air in through the tobacco leaves, but suddenly there's smoke coming with the air and I begin to choke. But I persevere and seem to be getting the hang of it. I am beginning to feel nauseated, and decide to go to my room. As I climb the great staircase, I have to hold the bannister for support. Everything is spinning – but I'm rather pleased with myself.

That night was the beginning of a fifteen-year bondage to cigarettes. I practiced alone in front of my mirror until I felt polished and suave enough to attempt it in public. It didn't take long. And then there was liquor. Robbie was not a prude. Diane might have been a little naive, but Robbie was game to try anything.

I had never been taught anything about alcohol except that it was sinful. Now that sin was of no particular interest to me except in what measure of fun it could afford, that aspect of liquor seemed no longer relevant. Consequently, my first few experiments were disastrous. I had no idea that mixing drinks was dangerous. I didn't know how to tell when I'd had enough and had to learn my lessons from experience. More than once, I began an exciting evening, only to end up in the bathroom at some party, sitting on the floor with my head spinning.

But as with smoking, I persevered until I found out how to do things the 'right' way.

And there were boys, lots and lots of boys. Everyone needs love, and I was no exception. I wanted someone to pay special attention to me, to make me feel special and to want to understand me. And I needed a person on whom I could pour out my love. I had so much inside to give. Not yet sure of who or what I was, I depended on responses from others for clues to my identity. No one had ever made it clear to me. I guess they all assumed I knew what it was. I thought someone who wanted to be close to me could teach me.

It's incredible to imagine how innocent I was that first year of university. Being so naïve, I was not on my guard and believed everything anyone told me. When someone would tell me I was the most beautiful, most amazing girl he'd ever met, I believed every word and lapped up the approval like honey – like sweet honey. Apart from my High School graduation and Young People's group outings, I never had been on a date. I hadn't been allowed to go to any of the places people normally went, like shows and dances. Put all of that together with a girl who is hungry for masculine approval and love and you know there will be problems. And there were. I was not promiscuous, but when I believed words of love, I was afraid to say no too much for fear of incurring disapproval. I was sure if I didn't please whoever it was, his 'love' would be withdrawn. The stakes were high.

That attitude did not last too long. I learned the ways of boys through experience, but not before a certain amount of damage had been done. I learned to distinguish between sincerity and cunning to a degree, but painful lessons taught me that even when you are very sure of a person's sincerity, you can be fooled.

I had been taught to trust people. For the most part, the people who came into our home were genteel folk, often devoted Christians. When they made statements about their feelings or actions, we didn't question their words or their motives. I was accustomed to believing whatever people said, unless they were being obviously sarcastic or facetious. I never experienced anyone in our family lying to me, but always felt secure in trusting whatever they said. Thus I did not have any experience in either the need for, nor the art of, weighing words.

I went with one fellow for over a year, all the time trusting in his love and sincerity. We had a lot of fun doing beautiful things – going for drives, planning our lives together for hours on snowy nights, skating, feeding the ducks at the town pond, studying together, playing the guitar, singing, laughing, crying, loving. I was sure we were meant to be together. Over the following summer, the relationship began to deteriorate. I began to see a side emerging that I never knew existed. One night, we were at a house party and he had had quite a bit to drink. We had a disagreement and he became physically violent. I couldn't believe this was the same tender, beautiful person I had cherished so dearly. He kicked me and pushed me and told me he had never loved me. He spilled revelations of going to Kentville to visit prostitutes after taking me back to residence at nights. I was shattered. Insight into the duplicity of someone I had trusted hurt me far more deeply than any physical abuse could ever have done. Suddenly, he was contrite, realizing he had said too much. He apologized profusely and walked me home. As we walked, he cried and said he was so sorry. It was raining hard as we approached the residence. He stopped and knelt in the rain before me, kissing my calves where he had kicked them. I looked down at him and quietly said goodbye. I walked on, through the rain, into the residence. The result was that I found it increasingly difficult to trust anyone.

Without realizing it, I was learning deeper lessons. Although I would not have admitted it at the time, I was taking my first steps on the road to discovering that God was real and I needed Him to direct my life. Without allowing any harm to befall me beyond what I could handle, He was showing me that the kind of life which I had coveted was not all pretty. I needed Someone who would never let me down. I was learning that some of the things I had thought were so wonderful, were really only shams, covering the emptiness and pain underneath.

By the time I went home for Christmas that first year of university, my relationship with my mother had undergone great changes within me. We had been exceptionally close up to the time I left home. Until then, I told her about most of my activities and ideas. But really, there hadn't been a whole lot of things not to tell. On the outside, I had conformed almost perfectly to her standards, and so I felt a freedom of expression with her. However, by the time I went home at Christmas, my internalized longings had become externalized realities. I was a heavy smoker, a social drinker, an avid bridge player and had become sexually aware. I had not been in church since leaving home. My poor little mom couldn't have handled all that and I knew it. I still felt tremendous love and tenderness toward her but it was all overshadowed by a great sense of guilt. The honest communication that had existed between us was no longer possible. I shut myself off from her in an attempt to spare her the knowledge of what I had really become.

Some people might say I was really not so bad, that I was just going through normal development; but some things are relative and this was one of those things. In our home, the standards were high. I felt the standard for me was perfection and no matter how I tried, I was never able to attain that standard.

I knew Mom went to bed every night praying earnestly for me. Although I didn't smoke or drink in front of her, she saw the tremendous changes in my attitudes and it hurt her deeply. I hated myself for being the instrument of her pain, but felt helpless. I couldn't see the harm in the things I was doing and believed the problem was with her. I thought if she could just loosen up and be rational, things would be fine.

I am nineteen. Mom and Dad are living in Sudbury, Ontario, and I am home from university for a few days before going to Toronto to work for the summer. My boyfriend, Barry, is here with me. Tonight we're very busy; because tomorrow, John Diefenbaker, the Prime Minister of Canada, and his wife Olive, are coming to our house for dinner! It is so exciting that I can hardly believe it's true. Mom is nervously giving us all jobs to do and we're giddy. Barry is polishing silver and I'm skewering pork and veal for "mock chicken."

This afternoon, we all stood around the Big Nickle, with the wind whipping across the barren rocks, as Mr. Diefenbaker dedicated the giant symbol in an INCO ceremony; then the city of Sudbury presented Mrs. Diefenbaker with a huge bouquet of roses.

Tomorrow morning, they'll attend our church for the morning service and come to our house for dinner. Mom is fussing around the dining room table. Crisp white linens, white napkins, silver, silver, silver on white. Everything looks lovely. She calls us all into the dining room.

"I thought it might be a good idea if we had a rehearsal. Let's pretend the Diefenbakers are here and we'll practice where we'll sit and so on."

"Mother! Are you serious?" Barry and I laugh.

"Excuse me, Madam," Barry taps me on the shoulder. "may I escort you to the table?"

"Why of course," I reply with a regal air. "My, you really are a rather handsome young fellow, aren't you." I peer at him closely, taking his proffered arm.

"Yes, Madam and my manners are impeccable." He extends his hand daintily toward a bowl of nuts, suddenly grabs a whole handful, and stuffs them in his mouth. "What did I tell ya?" he chortles wickedly. We collapse on the chesterfield in gales of laughter.

Now we are on our way home from church. Following our car is a sizeable motorcycle escort surrounding a long, black limousine. We arrive home and Mom and I go in the house. Barry and Dad wait for the Diefenbakers. Mom and I take our coats off and nervously fuss with each other's hair.

They are at the door! The moment Olive Diefenbaker enters the house, she puts us at ease. She is the most charming woman I have ever met. She follows Mom into the bedroom to take her coat off, all the while admiring this and that, commenting on the bedspread Mom made and telling us how delighted she was with our invitation. She makes us feel that we are special people and we have a truly charming home. I feel like hugging her.

"Mrs. Diefenbaker, would you sit here beside Barry, and Mr. Diefenbaker, on this side with Diane." As Mom graciously indicates where we are to sit, we all settle at the table and Dad asks the blessing. We were all so worried about the conversation, that it would go smoothly, and now we don't have a chance to get a word in edgewise. Mr. Diefenbaker is doing all the talking. He tells us all about his exploits in Cuba with Castro and the issues in Canada topping his list. I really don't understand a whole lot about what he's saying, but I love sitting here listening.

I glance out the window. I think every kid from two blocks around is here, chatting up the R.C.M.P. and checking out all the gadgets on their motorcycles. They're even peering in the windows of the limousine, trying to get the driver to talk to them.

Finally it's time to go. The visit has gone so quickly. The Deifenbakers graciously thank us for our invitation and say how much they enjoyed themselves.

There they go, gliding up the hill in the long black car, flanked front and back by the motorcycle escort. Did it really happen? Did the Prime Minister of Canada really eat dinner at this, now messy, table?

It's Monday morning. There is a knock at the door. The florist is delivering a magnificent bouquet of spring flowers in a tall green vase. Attached is a charming 'thank you' note from Mrs. Diefenbaker.

Mom still has that vase, and she has always called it "Olive Diefenbaker's vase." But the Deifenbakers left us with more than that; they gave us a fine memory.

Often, ministers' children find themselves in positions where they have opportunities to meet interesting people. These serve as great benefits in broadening and developing the personality. This particular experience helped me to overcome, to some degree, my tendency to be a "respecter of persons." I used to hold important people in awe, but the Diefenbakers taught me that even the greatest people in the world are flesh and blood, human and approachable.

I am twenty-one. It is fall in Yarmouth, Nova Scotia. My friend, Wayne, and I are going deer hunting. We come down here from the university most weekends and stay with his parents who live here in Yarmouth. Wayne is their only son and they make me feel like their daughter. I love it here. They are very plain folk who accept me in spite of my smoking and other faults. I don't have to pretend anything here. They expect me to take them as they are and they take me as I am. We have a lot of love for each other. We don't talk about it much, but we know it's there. I value their love tremendously.

Bus, Wayne's father, is a big, gruff fellow with a fat cigar seemingly implanted permanently at the side of his mouth. I don't think I've ever seen him light it, but constantly chewing on it keeps him occupied. He's helping us get all the hunting gear together and outfitting me in overalls, rubber boots and warm plaid tops. When he and Wayne complete my makeover, they stand back and laugh uproariously. This is hardly the usual attire of a well-dressed university girl. Bus has never said anything about his fatherly love for me, but he doesn't have to. I can see it in the way he acts. He plans all sorts of interesting things for Wayne and me to do on the weekends and loves to surprise us with things like a sack of fresh lobsters. When we are around, he is happy. I feel like a little girl here, a special little girl who is loved just because she is herself. Sometimes I wonder who I love more, Wayne or his family.

The two of us are in the woods, walking along a forgotten woodland road. The day is crisp and clean. The leaves crunch under my feet. Wayne shows me how I must walk in the woods if I am to be a cunning hunter. Everything is gold and orange and red. My world is beautiful and I am secure.

Always in the back of my mind, lived my constantly nagging guilt about not living the kind of life my parents wanted me to live. I was drinking, smoking, using unacceptable language, never going to church, and building all my goals on the material things of life. In order to alleviate some of the guilt, I adopted new parents. I transferred my affections to them and paid only lip service to my own parents.

How cruel I was. Mom always tucked some money into her letters. I know she sent me every spare penny. She and Dad lived frugally so I would not have to go without. When I would get the money, I would often blow it on clothes, cigarettes and pizza. Thoughts of my parents were like a great, heavy sack of guilt. I longed for things to be otherwise, but they couldn't accept my lifestyle and I couldn't accept theirs. There seemed to be no solution.

During this time, I developed a close relationship with my sister, Dona, who felt essentially the same way I did. We commiserated together about the impossibility of our relationships with our parents. Our common problems were the glue that cemented the bond between us. In spite of the miles that separated us, we became best friends through the mail. Neither she nor I understood the truth of the Gospel. We took great security from knowing we were not alone in our guilt and attitudes. We upheld each other in love.

During my visits home at Christmas and in the summer, I used to try to explain to Mom how antiquated her beliefs were, in light of my studies in philosophy. I outlined various schools of thought to her which, to me, made a lot more sense than the Bible. I told her she was not being rational. It was frustrating, because in spite of the fact that she was not always able to give me any tangible evidence of the validity of her beliefs, she never wavered. In spite of my eloquence and well-researched arguments, she remained unshakable. But she never tried to shame me. She listened. When she was alone, she prayed.

During those visits home, I was expected to go to church on Sunday. I remember walking down the aisle, one Sunday morning, feeling the eyes of the congregation on me. I hated the dishonesty of the whole thing, because I knew those people imagined me to be good and pure – but I knew what I really was. Their warmth and acceptance made me feel hypocritical and guilty, but I imagined myself to be far superior to these people with their primitive beliefs and stuffy lifestyle. They were simple, gullible and irrational. I told myself they needed a crutch in life. They were social misfits who couldn't make it in the real world. I could. I was smart, young and educated. I pitied them and imagined them to be envious of me.

I am twenty-two. Miss D. Roblin, B.A., Social Worker at the Ontario Hospital for the mentally challenged in Orillia, Ontario. I have my own car, an apartment, my own office and I am on my way. I travel all over Ontario in my big car on an expense account and answer to no one for my private life. I am taking a modelling course in the evenings and I am number one.

When I look in the mirror, I feel brave and superior – but what is this gnawing thing inside of me? I can't get rid of it. Now that Wayne is so far away, our relationship is falling apart and I can't get the ends of my life together. I need people around me constantly.

There is a knock at the door. It is that fellow, Warren, from the ski shop. He has a set of skis and poles with him. "I thought I'd bring over the skis you ordered," he says.

"I didn't order any skis." I was in his shop about a week ago and he fitted me for a ski outfit, but I hadn't ordered it.

"Yes, you did. I have the ordering instructions in my book."

"That may be, but I did not give you a definite order." I am perturbed, but decide not to make a big fuss. I really do want a pair of skis anyway. "Oh well, now that you're here with them, you might as well bring them in."

He stamps the snow off his boots and comes in. He really is pretty terrific looking, dark and rugged ... but I put the thought out of my mind. I'm still involved with Wayne and not looking for anyone to date. I'm concerned about what is happening to us. If we do split, there goes not only my boyfriend but my adopted family. I'm on the edge of losing my chosen parents. My neatly constructed world is falling apart.

Warren seems to want to say something more. I sense his visit has an ulterior motive.

"I have a cousin who met you at a party a while ago and he wants to go

out with you," he begins. "He owns a mink ranch. You might remember his silver Corvette."

"No, I don't remember."

"He comes up here on weekends from Woodstock. Can I tell him he can call you when he comes the next time?"

"I don't know. Maybe."

Wayne was a long way away and I had been dating occasionally, just for something to do. I was getting sick of the whole dating thing with its phoniness, role playing and rules of the games. I wanted some security, reality, permanence. I was ready to settle down, but all my dreams of a home and a husband were falling apart. I wanted to be looked after, but Wayne and his parents were two thousand miles away. Letters and phone calls weren't enough.

As it turned out, I flew down to Nova Scotia to spend Christmas with Wayne and his mom and dad, and we broke up. I flew back shattered. The man on the plane sensed my sorrow I guess, and kept me supplied with Manhattans all the way back to Toronto. I had lost everything that was important to me. After two years of working hard at building a fabricated family, it was all lost. No one else had any idea of all that was involved in that breakup.

I was empty, alone and without an anchor. Through a set of funny circumstances, I went out with Warren, the fellow who owned the ski shop. The whole cousin routine had been a set-up to get me to go out with him because he was too shy to ask me directly. It all backfired on him and, much to his dismay, I actually did begin a relationship with his cousin. Finally, in February, Warren asked me to represent his sports shop in a snowmobile race at Penetanguishene.

"But I've never even been on a snowmobile, let alone raced one!" I argued.

"That's okay," he assured me, "the race isn't until next weekend, and I've got all week to teach you. We'll go out on the lake and practice on the ice in the evenings."

And that's what we did. Saturday morning dawned windy and cold. We loaded the machines on the truck and set out for Penetanguishene. When we arrived at the lake where the meet was to be held, it seemed as though the whole world was into snowmobile racing. Machines were roaring and whining and billowing blue exhaust smoke. An atmosphere of rough camaraderie and keen, but wholesome, competition filled the air. Warren unloaded his machines and I felt nervously out of place. This is not who I was.

"Here, why don't you try out the track so you know where you're going before the races start?" He pulled the starter of the machine I was to drive and motioned for me to get on.

I settled myself on the seat as the machine vibrated beneath me. The accelerator was at my right hand, and the brake at my left. Ever so slowly, I squeezed the accelerator and moved away toward the flags and the track. It was bumpy, so I explored the course gingerly. I was to be racing against a girl named Joanne, Ontario's top female driver. This was an impossible situation. Absolutely ridiculous!

When the time came for the Powder Puff race, Warren showed me where to line up. Slowly, I maneuvered the machine toward the starting line. There were about nine of us competing. We lined up with our eyes on the starter. The flag went down and the race was on. The track was no longer just bumpy, but now filled with deep ruts and holes from the previous races. I had to hang on for dear life to keep from bouncing off the machine. In order to do that, I had to squeeze the accelerator as tight as it would go.

I didn't even notice as I flew past machine after machine in the whirling snow. My snowmobile flew up and down as I hit one hole after another. Every nerve in my body was keenly alert as I held on to the handlebars for dear life, madly steering through the course. I couldn't think about anything except staying on the wildly bucking machine. As I rounded the final curve, I spotted a fellow waving mightily at me with a flag. I figured he wanted me to stop and that I'd come in last, because I now could see that all of the other machines were in front of me. I thought the race was over, so I steered over to the side and stopped. Warren and some others came running over to me. I felt dumb about coming last ... but then I realized they were smiling and laughing.

"Great race," they shouted.

"What do you mean, great race?" I asked. "All the others were ahead of me!"

Warren and the others laughed. "You lapped them all!"

And so I won my heat; but there was still a final race to face. Joanne was to be in this one, too. Warren told me later that, right from the start, it had appeared to be a royal battle between Joanne and me – a battle of which I was not even aware, as I fought to stay on my machine. The only time I really remember seeing another machine was once when I was going into a corner and another person started to go in front of me ... but right at that moment, I hit a great hole, and my snowmobile flew way up in the air, right over hers, and landed – hard – in front of her. I never noticed that machine again. After rounding the final curve, I was exhausted. Fifteen feet from the finish line, I hit another hole and that was it. I bounced off. My boot caught in the stirrup and the machine dragged me. I became vaguely aware of the people in the crowd yelling and screaming, but I wasn't budging for anyone. It felt so peaceful to lie there in the snow and let the machine slowly drag me along toward the finish line. One machine flew past, two machines, three, four. By the time they could wave me across, I was fifth. A very peaceful and tired fifth. I could have cared less.

Joanne came over and congratulated me on my driving skill and told me that I'd given her one of the most difficult races she'd ever had. She said something about my fantastic nerve. I didn't want to disillusion her, so I didn't say a whole lot about how I'd just been holding on for dear life.

After the race, we drove back to Orillia and dropped in to Warren's home for a few moments. He introduced me to his parents. I really liked them. Like Wayne's parents, they accepted me with open arms. I was ripe for another family. I didn't fit with my own parents and had just recently lost my adopted ones – but here was a couple who seemed eager to include me in their lives. It was the start of an unusually close relationship.

They seemed to approve of everything I did and that was exactly what I was looking for.

Before long, I had replaced my parents with a second attempt at a happy family. The only problem was, that in order to keep this family, the price of my package was Warren. We went out for the first time on February twenty-eighth. He gave me a ring March eleventh, just two weeks later. I didn't pretend to share his feelings and told him I didn't love him. He said it was okay, that I would one day. On that condition, I accepted the ring because I didn't want to lose his family and I didn't want to hurt his feelings. I thought later on, when it wasn't such an emotionally-charged moment for him, I would be able to give it back.

But fantasy has a way of becoming reality, whether positively or negatively, and that is what happened to our 'let's pretend' engagement. Suddenly, everyone was wanting specifics. What was our date for the wedding? How many guests were we planning on inviting? Who would the attendants be? Suddenly the parents on both sides were pressuring for details. We set a date far enough in the future so as not to be real, but everyone started giving us reasons why we should move it closer. My parents were moving again and wanted us to be married in the church where they were at that time. So we moved it ahead a bit. Then Warren's mother wanted it moved ahead again so that her sister, who was going on a trip, could be there. Finally, the wedding date was set for June twenty-first, just four months after our first date.

And I did not particularly care for my fiancé. He was two-and-a-half-years younger than I and our interests were widely divergent. There was no love on my part and I made it no secret to anyone. I told Warren, and he just said, "That's okay, you'll learn to love me." I told his mother, and she said, "Well you know, if you marry Warren, you'll always be well looked after and this house," she said with a wave of her arm, indicating their gorgeous home, "will be yours someday." That was pretty heavy bait for someone as immature and insecure as I. I told my roommate, and she said if I married Warren, he would probably treat me like a queen all my life and keep me on the pedestal he had me on. That sounded pretty comfortable to someone who had recently experienced a great loss. Little did we both know that the pedestal would be tossed aside as soon as the wedding ceremony was over.

In spite of the advice, I couldn't marry someone I didn't love, and so left Orillia after writing a goodbye letter to Warren. I went into seclusion for a couple of days, but between Warren and my Dad, they found me. Dad called my sister's, where I was staying, and I tried to explain to him that I didn't love Warren. He said, "You get back up there to Orillia. Neither Warren nor his father are going to put up with your foolishness for very long." He had no idea that I really did not love Warren, and interpreted my change of mind as pre-marital jitters.

Disapproval. Rejection. It pricked me inside somewhere where it hurt a lot. It was like physical pain. And so I gathered my things together, got into my car, and drove back up the highway to Orillia.

I am twenty-three-years-old. My birthday was two days ago. Tomorrow I will be a married lady. Yuk. We had our wedding rehearsal tonight and I am still upset about it. When it was just about over, I ran out of the church with Warren running behind in pursuit. He caught up to me in the parking lot. I was crying that I couldn't marry him because I didn't love him. He put his arms around me and said that it was okay. I would learn to love him. He is so patient. He never gets angry with me or gets discouraged. He is so determined. Maybe I will learn to love him. But right now, I feel like I'm caught in a trap and there's no escape. Everyone is here at Mom and Dad's house from the rehearsal reception. They are merrily chatting and laughing. This is insane. I can't stand it. I've got to get out of here. I've got to talk some truth to somebody.

"Dona, you've got to come for a drive with me." I can always count on my sister for love and support and understanding and truth.

"What's the matter?" she senses my agitation and is immediately concerned.

"I've got to get out of this crazy place. I have to talk to you."

It's raining. We run out to my car. It's about eleven o'clock and very dark. We drive around the city of Toronto for hours and I pour everything out to her as I manoeuvre the car through street after street. I am crying but have to keep driving. I can't stop. I have no idea where we are and I don't care. She listens and sympathizes but doesn't try to impose her feelings on me. I know that no matter what, this person is constant in my life and will stand by me just because I am me and she is my sister. I don't have to do anything to earn her love or approval. I drive until my tears have run dry and everything has been said. I am drained, exhausted, but resigned. I want to go to bed.

"Where are we, anyway?" We strain to see the street signs as the windshield washers struggle furiously to foil the rain. We continue until we find a vaguely familiar sign and work our way home.

It is morning. This is the day. It is to be a candlelight ceremony at eight p.m. My bridesmaids have spent the night at Mom and Dad's with me. They will all be going out later this morning to their hair appointments. I didn't make one for myself. I just want to look like me. If I can't be me, at least I'll look like me. Funny, I always imagined that on the day of my wedding I would have a milk bath. Now it doesn't interest me in the least.

The girls have gone. I'm wandering around the house like a robot in my housecoat. The cake is sitting in the kitchen waiting to go to the hotel, where the reception is to be held. Dad is spending an absolute fortune on this wedding. The cake is magnificent. He iced it himself. Mom made it and he decorated it to look like a frothy white dream, complete with roses and intricate swirls. Each layer is a masterpiece of care and design. He hunted in all the specialty shops until he found the perfect bride and groom for the top of the cake. He is trying to give me everything I could possibly want for this wedding. It was always true: my daddy could do almost anything – except understand me.

I wander downstairs. Mom is giving my gown a final pressing. It really is beautiful. She made it herself. Meticulously, she has covered each tiny button with peau de chéne, and formed all those tiny loops for the buttons. Very simple, very elegant. I know she is worried about this wedding, but I dare not confirm her fears. I don't want to hurt her.

"Don't you think you should start to get ready, dear? You know the photographer will be here in an hour and a half."

"Mmmm. There's lot of time, Mom."

I wander back upstairs. I am sad. Here they are, doing all this stuff for me, and I can't relate to them. I am always disappointing them. What this whole thing really boils down to, is that I am going through this wedding so that I will have another set of parents to keep. My parents do everything for me except accept me, and my chosen parents have to do nothing for me except accept me.

With Warren's parents I am comfortable. With my own parents, I have to constantly play the goody-goody. It puts me on edge all the time, and I just about go out of my mind for a cigarette. I can't concentrate on any subject they try to discuss, because I'm throwing a nicotine fit. While I'm at home, my thoughts constantly revolve around how I'm going to sneak the next cigarette. Even if I could smoke in front of Mom and Dad, I wouldn't, because I know how much they disapprove of it. How could I sit there and enjoy a cigarette knowing what they would be thinking?

I pour a bath and step in. My stomach is squirming. I can't stand this. I've got to get those tranquilizers Warren's Aunt Dora gave me. I get out of the tub, grab a towel and rummage through my purse for the pills. There they are. She gave me two in case of emergency that night I was crying for no reason and couldn't get stopped. Well, if ever there was an emergency, I think this is it, Aunt Dora. I pop both of the pills and swallow them. I step back in the tub and sit in the warmth, waiting for the pills to do their thing.

Well, I suppose I'd better get dried off and get ready. It seems I have a wedding to go to. Things are beginning to feel better. Now I'm strong and independent and beautiful. I can handle things. I'm like a starring actress, preparing to go on stage. I have an audience waiting and my performance will be superb.

"The photographer is here."*Dona runs into the room, carrying my veil.*"What shall I tell him?"

"Mmmm, I'll only be about five minutes. All I have to do is brush my hair and put this veil on. Tell him I'm almost ready."

I feel good on the outside. Mom has done a fantastic job on my gown. It fits like a glove. It feels like me, unpretentious and simple. Everyone is fussing around, adjusting my train, checking buttons, picking things up. I am calm.

The church is full of perfect guests. The decorations look perfect. The candlelight is perfect. The bridesmaids are perfect. The little ring bearer and the flower girl are a perfect match in their perfectly matching outfits. Warren looks perfect. I look perfect. And inside I feel perfectly empty, and thanks to my little red pills, perfectly calm. Uncle Ted comes up to me and says "Everything okay?"

"Marvellous," I reply with a smile befitting a radiant bride. Everyone else has gone down the aisle. Only Uncle Ted, who is giving me away, and I remain at the back of the church.

Aunt Jessie begins to play, "Whither thou goest, I will go. Wherever thou lodgest, I will lodge. Thy people shall be my people, my love. Whither thou goest, I will go."

One step. Two steps. Lights, cameras, action. We're on our way. Act one, scene one. The bride progresses demurely down a centre aisle. I smile for effect, a certain crowd pleaser. My mouth is dry. Oops, my top lip is stuck on my dry teeth. I can't stop smiling now. Everyone thinks I'm so happy. I don't suppose anyone has any idea that my wide smile is nothing but a stuck lip.

We kneel on satin cushions at the front. I try to effect the most angelic appearance I can, as Dad conducts the ceremony. He has put a lot of preparation into his sermon. He compares our lives to a chess game with Warren as the black king, and me as the white queen.

We are at the hotel in the reception line. Everyone is smiling and cordial. My pills are still hanging in there. No one would ever suspect that anything is amiss. They all think we are deliriously in love. Oh well, there will be a lot of security with Warren. I know he would never, ever cheat on me. He puts me before everything else in his life, and does everything I want him to do. He tries to be with me every moment he possibly can. He seems to practically worship me.

Warren's attention lasted for about two days after we were married. Having known him for such a short time, I hadn't realized that his habit was to desire something desperately until he had it. The novelty would wear off fast as soon as it was his, and from that time on, he would cast whatever it was, aside in neglect. I was just another toy to be left in a heap of once important possessions. But I was expected to perform. I was to keep his house spotless and his clothes all ironed and delicious meals on the table every night. In short, I was to take his mother's place.

As the days went by, I would try to talk to him, and often he simply would not reply. He never wanted to discuss anything with me. If I would suggest that we go somewhere, he would just say no. If one of my friends dropped in to chat, he would stay if the girl was good-looking; otherwise, he would simply not speak to her. He made no attempt to help with any of the household affairs, in spite of the fact that I was teaching High School Physical Education and Guidance, full time, by then. He left all the bills and finances to me. Where he had put on a phenomenal act of friendliness to my parents before we were married, he ignored them afterwards. He gave me no emotional support whatever. His whole life was working, television, sleeping and eating.

I couldn't believe the change in this person. From someone who had vowed that I would love him, he had become totally uncaring. It wasn't that I displeased him, or so he said, it was simply that he had me and didn't have to put out any more effort on my behalf. He didn't care. I was an object. I belonged to him now.

A year and a half after we'd been married, little Timothy came along. I poured out my love on that child. He was beautiful and wondrous. When the nurse brought him to me for the first time, tears of joy and love and tenderness rolled down my cheeks. This wee babe was a miracle, so soft and tiny and perfect. He was part of me; born from my body. For the first time, I felt the wonder of the human body. This little person had lived inside me for nine months, and had been totally sustained by my body. Now he was independent of me, yet my body was equipped to feed him totally for as long as necessary. This child and I were two, but we were one. Never, never, had I experienced the depth of love that I found at that moment.

Tim became my life. I devoted my time and thoughts to him. He was my delight and my treasure. I loved it when he would waken in the night and I could hold his little body close to me. Often I would sit much longer than necessary with him and just watch him sleep. By focusing my love on him, I was able to cover over the huge hole in my life.

Warren's parents lived close by, and they were very supportive during that time. In some respects, they took Warren's place with Tim; for while Warren thought Tim was cute, he never wanted to be bothered with his care. He basically left the baby to me. His parents, on the other hand, liked to be involved in Tim's growth and development; consequently, I really even closer to them.

Warren began to travel a lot with his job, so Tim and I were alone during the week. Often, Warren even stayed away on weekends. He had never had a time of growing up away from home. He had moved directly from his mother's care into my care, so now he was testing his wings. He began to feel his oats. His business trips were a series of one night stands and experimentation.

At that point, I had no idea he was being unfaithful to me – even with my best friend. All I knew, was that our marriage was a bad joke. We had nothing in common, and all of my endless efforts to establish a relationship ended in futility. He simply didn't care. Nothing was important to him except his own physical comfort. Otherwise it seemed to me that he was an empty person, devoid of feelings and emotional needs. I couldn't understand that, and searched my psychology books for clues to his psyche. Naturally, I found bits and pieces of answers that sounded reasonable – but nowhere could I find solutions to our problems. Even if someone had told me at that time, I could not have understood the answer; that Warren was empty because he had a great big God-shaped hole inside of him that needed to be filled before he could become a real, total person. I was not yet ready to understand that answer. God knew that He had to let me go the full length of my own efforts before He could step in, in a way that I would know that He was real, and we needed Him.

Another precious baby came along. We named him Todd. Again I was filled with the wonder of life and birth. My days were filled with the constant cares of motherhood, but underneath the busyness, my soul agonized in its isolation.

Ripe for disaster, I fell prey to a man who was in a position to take advantage of the situation. Once I had allowed him a tiny toe in the door, the dye was cast. What was done could not be undone and I was now in the position of having to enter into the secrecy upon which a predator depends – or risk losing my family. I took the guilt upon myself, imagining the situation to be my 'fault.' At that time I had no insight into the strong spirit of manipulation that governs the heart of a seasoned predator (which he later proved himself to be). While I continue to take responsibility for allowing the toe in the door that set my course, in those days I didn't understand the dynamics of victimization or predator control and so was unequipped to move forward in strength. Today I understand and would have responded differently. However, that was then and my lack of recognition of selfish manipulation resulted in me allowing the 'relationship' to last for over a year, until the trauma ran its course and I began to come out of my stupor.

During this time, Warren was travelling constantly and came home only long enough to have his laundry done. When he was home, we didn't fight, but we were miserable. Had we fought, I would have seen that he cared enough at least to fight, but there was nothing there.

Although the deceit was abhorrent to me, the emotional interaction I was able to give and receive helped sustain me through the despair and loneliness. Subconsciously, I wanted Warren to know I was involved with another man, as dysfunctional as the involvement was. I wanted him to claim me as his, but he cared so little, he didn't even notice that anything was amiss. Finally, he admitted, much to my surprise, that he was having an affair. I was stunned.

We decided to split and divided our possessions. When our lists were complete, in a total about-face, he fell on his knees before me and told me that, until then, he had not realized how much he loved me and wanted me to stay. After much turmoil, I decided to give him another chance.

And then, one day while he was at work, I called him to come home and told him about my so-called 'affair,' even though it was over. He was calm and said he had had no idea. His lack of emotion following the disclosure would have been crushing in a normal relationship, but I was already so accustomed to emptiness that I hardly questioned it. At least the secrecy was broken.

Only God kept us together through those days. There is so much that happened but it is too painful to recall. I have never told this story before, and tell it now only to demonstrate God's keeping power, and to give hope to anyone in a situation of despair.

Not long after the revelations I have just described, we moved from Montreal to a little town in Ontario. By that time, Tim and Todd were getting old enough that I was able to afford a little more freedom. In an attempt to fill the emptiness in my life (but determined never again to become involved with another man), and hoping to attract Warren's attention, I became immersed in several aspects of community life: I contacted the Board of Education, which agreed to support me in the formation of evening fitness classes for ladies; I developed a program in which I alternately taught grooming, exercises, jazz dancing, Estonian Rhythmics and individual diet counseling; I became involved in the local Little Theatre group; I became the commentator and a driving force behind the local beauty pageant. Warren still didn't pay much attention. I decided to run for Town Council, and stayed awake until two and three o'clock in the mornings, studying the Regional Plan book. He still didn't seem impressed. After discovering that politics bored me anyway, I decided not to run for office.

We started to go out a lot to the dances in the town and took out tennis memberships at the golf club. Our home was nice. Warren was in business with a successful partner. Our children were intelligent, healthy and well-behaved. We had a big garden, a lovely yard for the children to play and two dogs and two cats. We had nice clothes and a certain degree of social prestige and life was hell.

I began to see the futility in all of my efforts to get my husband to appreciate me. The harder I tried to impress him, the more he ignored me. I knew I was batting my head against a brick wall. We had a tremendous amount of illness that year, and our home became a depressing place. It seemed that one of us would get sick the moment another of us would get better. I began to feel that life was an endless merry-go-round of antibiotics and thermometers. I felt I was coming to the end of something. I could find no purpose in anything.

I began to feel that there was no point in getting up in the morning. When I would awaken, I felt like crying because I had to face another day. Deep inside I was in pain, not the pain of physical starvation, but of starvation of my soul.

I was so empty in there and I couldn't find anything to fill that aching void. I had gone the whole self-help route, exploring things like transactional analysis, transcendental meditation, behavior modification, age passages, communication skills and on and on. Everything required me to pull up my own socks and I was getting too tired to do that anymore. I needed Someone to help me tug.

I began to think a lot of death thoughts. I imagined what it would be like to just keep driving into a tree or into a lake. But I loved my children too much to leave them. And although death thoughts sometimes promised a release, I was afraid of death. It terrified me to think of what would become of my children if I died. The possibility of having Warren raise them nauseated me because he was so detached from all of us. My children needed the love that only I was giving them. I felt terrible anxiety about that and wrote a homemade will stating that I did not want my children raised by him in the event of my death. I knew that cigarettes were killing me and I was experiencing a lot of chest pains resulting from them, but I couldn't quit. I tried Smoke-Enders, acupuncture, pills to lessen the craving, hypnosis, cold turkey, special filters, cutting down, switching brands and every stop-smoking fad that came along. Nothing worked. I just smoked more. I felt as though I had a self-destruct button pushed and I couldn't deactivate it.

And then the tears came. They were not ordinary crying tears. They originated way down inside of me and I never knew when they would appear. I could be sitting talking normally to someone and, with no warning, great tears would start to roll down my cheeks. It was very embarrassing. I always made a feeble excuse about something being in my eye. I never felt like sobbing with the tears. They were their own. I had no control over them.

I knew I needed help. I went to my sister to ask her advice about where to go for help. She suggested a Christian therapist in Toronto, whom she knew well. For some reason, the fact that he was a Christian appealed to me and I made an appointment. On the day I was supposed to go, Dona accompanied me to his office and introduced us. He had one of the kindest faces I had ever seen and I felt an immediate rapport. I knew I could trust him with the inside of me. He took me to his inner office, and there I laid everything out. I held back nothing that I considered to be important to the situation, because I knew the only way he could help was by knowing the nitty-gritties. It was exhausting to let everything out, but I left that first appointment with a ray of hope that perhaps there was some chance for me.

By that time, Warren and I had been married for ten years. I was thirty-three-yars old. In my mind, I had tried everything to bring us together. I had really given it a good shot.

The illnesses continued and my only bright spots were the two week interval appointments with the therapist. For some reason, I dug out a Bible that had been given to me by a family friend on the occasion of my university graduation. I had never opened it except to read the inscription. It was a J.B. Phillips translation of the New Testament in modern English. The only Bible I had read before was the King James Version with English that confounded my understanding. I read a few verses and it really surprised me that I could understand what I was reading. I left it beside my bed and, once in a while, I would pick it up and read a few verses.

Warren was ill at that point, and was totally insufferable. No matter what I did for his comfort, he complained. Nothing was good enough. If I fixed something for him that I thought he would like, he wouldn't eat it. If I asked him what he would like before I fixed anything, he would get impatient because I was "not nursing him properly." At one point, he wanted fruit, and so I went to the grocery store and got a wide variety of the freshest fruits I could find. I took them home to him but he wouldn't eat any of it because I hadn't gotten grapes. Then he decided he wanted escargots. I had to order them from out of town, because they didn't have them in our little village. The next thing was pork tails. Those too, had to be specially ordered. Finally they came in, and I went to pick them up. I put them in the oven, went up to tell Warren that they were cooking and he said he didn't want them after all. By that time, my patience was running thin. I was disgusted. I went down to turn the oven off and he called me to get something else that I didn't have. When I told him that I didn't have any, he called me a dummy. That was it.

I packed a suitcase with all of the necessities for the children and myself. It was February. I got the children all bundled up and into my car. By the time I went back to the house for the suitcase and my little dog, he was in the hall.

"Just make sure you're back in a half hour," he said.

I looked at him, picked up the suitcase, called the dog after me and left, thinking, "Good luck, fella."

I started the car and drove down the highway, having no idea where I was going. I felt good; absolutely peaceful. A song from way back in my past started to roll through my mind, "God will take care of you." I sensed I was truly being cared for. The night was dark and my car was not working properly, but I knew that we were safe. I had no fear nor anxiety. I found myself on the highway to Dona's house.

When we arrived, she and her family welcomed us with open arms, but found it hard to understand why I was not upset. We tucked the children into bed and I chatted easily about the situation. When I went to bed, a very strange thing happened. I had not heard the Twenty-third Psalm for about fourteen or fifteen years, but line by line, as each line was made personal to me, the whole Psalm came back to me in a vibrant, relevant way. I had such happy peace, and fell asleep feeling loved and special. It was strange.

Little did I know, that several weeks before, Mom and Aunt Jessie had made a covenant between them that every Monday, they would pray and fast for me. Aunt Jessie is a bubbling, joyful Christian, whom I have always loved dearly and admired. She and Uncle Harvey have raised their six children on Christian principles in a beautiful way that anyone would have to admit worked. She shared Mom and Dad's concern about my emotional situation and knew the most constructive thing they could do was pray. And pray they did. As they took hold of God, He began to work very fast in my life. I believe that my life was saved as a direct result of those prayers.

After a week of separation from Warren, I agreed to return to the house on condition that he accompany me to the therapist in Toronto. During those sessions, a lot of things were aired that had been mildewing beneath the surface for years. Having an impartial third party was invaluable. We found we were able to bounce our feelings back and forth onto the therapist without directly hitting each other.

I became very aware of two totally distinct forces at work in my life. I was conscious of an evil force, almost in tangible form, pulling at me from the lower right side of my body. I felt that it was trying to force me down, pulling, pulling from my right side. On my left, God was waiting in a position slightly above me. He was not trying to coerce me in any way, but was just there, gently loving me and longing for me to love Him. I felt torn and desperate. There was such pressure and pulling from the evil force. The problem was I couldn't understand God. I didn't know how to reach Him.

The therapist told Warren that my description of the two forces worried him somewhat. I knew it sounded ridiculous; nevertheless, they were absolutely real to me.

I began to read the Bible more and to ask a lot of questions.

One day when Dad was over, I asked him what Jesus' death had to do with us. I couldn't understand what a fellow dying 2000 years ago could possibly have to do with me. He said the significance of Jesus' death was wrapped up in the old system of Jewish sacrifices. In order for people before Jesus' death to be forgiven for their wrongdoing, and thus to be able to get into a right relationship with God, there had to be innocent blood shed. Satan, the lord of this world, was the author of death and the only way to cross over into the light and life of relationship with Jesus was via the shedding of innocent blood. The only innocent blood was that of animals, because all men were inherently sinful. But by sending Jesus, who was God's Son and who had no sin in Him, God provided the perfect sacrifice for all people for all time. People could take Jesus' shed blood as their sacrifice for their sins simply by believing in Jesus. Now, the only way we can become acceptable to God, is by accepting Jesus as our payment for right standing with God, and asking Him to remain within us via His Holy Spirit.

That made sense to me. Over and over, I had heard about being "saved" and the need to be "born again," but really didn't know what those terms meant. I picked up a book by Hal Lindsey called The Liberation of Planet Earth. In it, he explained from Scripture, that Satan was originally the archangel Lucifer who led a revolt of some of the angels to overthrow God. God had put him in charge of Earth. The result of the revolution was that Lucifer and one-third of the angels were banished from Heaven to Earth, where the war continues.

When God created man in his own image to glorify Him, and for the pleasure of His company, Lucifer, or Satan, as he became known, tried to cause separation between God and His creation, and thereby gain control over man. God had given man the gift of free will. He didn't want puppets who had no choice but to glorify Him and worship Him. He wanted people who would commune with Him in love because they chose to. Satan's plan was to present the choice to man as silly and trivial. Men fell for the trick and thus chose Satan as lord of the Earth. Man made the choice, and being absolutely just, God was not about to snatch the lordship back without paying the legal ransom price. The price was the shedding of the innocent blood of God's Son. The whole presentation of the law of Moses and the system of animal sacrifices, was God's method of preparing man for the understanding that he was indeed in need of a Saviour. At this point in history, since man's acceptance of Satan made him lord of the this world, Satan is the incumbent ruler, as it were – even though the true God is Yahweh, the Creator of all. The sobering fact is that we are automatically bound to the incumbent ruler, Satan, unless we make a conscious step to take out citizenship with God. If we don't accept God's plan for us, we automatically accept Satan's plan for us. Satan's desire is to destroy everything God has made.

The whole revelation stunned me. It was like suddenly having the lights turned on. There was purpose in life! There was meaning to my struggles. I was not going crazy. The two distinct forces I felt at work in my life were a fantastic reality. No wonder I felt I had a self-destruct button pushed. There was an evil force within me, trying to destroy me. But there was hope. The price for my freedom had been paid. All I had to do was accept it.

But become a Christian? Everybody would think I was crazy! I considered myself to be a sophisticated, wordly-wise person. I had fought too hard for what I had achieved. I could accept the truth of the purpose of my life, but I couldn't accept the lifestyle that I thought had to be part of the package. I wanted to be happy and joyful and the thought of living a stuffy Christian existence just depressed me more.

There was one person, besides Mom, I knew who was joyful and honestly happy and yet a Christian and that was my Aunt Jessie. I truly envied her happiness with her husband and family and wished I could have what she had. I thought it was probably just her temperament that made her so radiant and shiny. I knew that I was incapable of turning myself into that sort of a person by my own efforts.

One day when Mom was visiting us, I asked, "Mom, what is it that makes Aunt Jessie different from other Christian people? What is it that makes her so happy?"

"It's the baptism in the Holy Spirit," she replied.

"What's that?" I had never heard of that before. To me, baptism meant a ceremony where you were immersed in water and the "Holy Spirit" was just some vague ghosty thing tacked on to the end of the Trinity. I had a concept of God as the Father and of Jesus as the Son, but the Holy Spirit? I had absolutely no concept of Him whatsoever.

"I have a book," she said, "that you might be interested in reading. It describes the whole thing."

More hope! Perhaps there really was a way I could get what Aunt Jessie had. I could hardly wait to get my hands on that book! The name of it was *Nine O'Clock in the Morning* by Father Dennis Bennett, an Anglican priest. I had always had expensive tastes, and had never been satisfied with anything but the best. It was no different now. If I was going to be a Christian, I wanted the whole package and the best package possible.

The book arrived and I devoured it practically in one sitting. The things I discovered in that book made Christianity come alive for me. I found that when Jesus arose from the dead and went to be with His Father in Heaven, He did not leave us alone. He left His Holy Spirit on earth to comfort and guide and protect us. The Holy Spirit is God's active force in the world today. When we accept Jesus as our Saviour, His Holy Spirit comes to us as our guide, protector, comforter and counselor. When we reach the point where we are ready to make Jesus the Lord of our lives, to let Him take complete control of us, He fills us with His Holy Spirit which then works His power and love through us, to reach other people and save them from destruction.

Wow! That was heavy stuff! I became desperately hungry to know more. I scrounged everywhere I could for Bible commentaries, Bible dictionaries, theological encyclopedias and anything I could get my hands on to learn more. I was thrilled to find this wealth of truth.

Where Dad and I had been distant, we began to have a lot to discuss. All my life he had been there with the answers, but I had not been ready to receive them. Suddenly we were spending a fortune on telephone bills and he was making many trips to bring more books. I began to appreciate him, and to see the depth of his love for me. He was tremendously excited by my interest. My father was, for the first time, truly connecting with his child.

I came to the point where I knew that I had found the core of life. Intellectually, I knew that this was it. And so one day, I knelt down by the side of the bed and, in spite of the fact that I could see no one in the room, I began to talk:

"God, I need you. You know how I've messed up my life. Father, I am sorry about all of the things that I have done to displease you. Please forgive me. I accept your Son as the sacrifice for my sins. Thank you for sending Him. In Jesus' Name I pray, amen."

I waited for something earth-shattering to happen. I waited for some sign that something was different. Nothing happened. I got up from my knees and felt exactly the same as I had before. I was puzzled, but not totally discouraged. I wasn't ready to give up yet. I simply figured that it hadn't taken that time. At that point, I was not aware that our emotions cannot be relied on in spiritual matters. God promised in his Bible that if we accepted Him, He would come into us; but I didn't realize that all I had to do was claim that promise and believe that He had come in as He said He would. And so, day after day for about two weeks, I tried to give myself to God. Nothing different happened. I begged Him for the joy and the abundant life that He said He came to give us, but I didn't feel anything different.

Until one day, I was talking with a friend who had been a Christian but had fallen away from communicating with God. During that conversation, I suddenly realized that there was a power within me that was reaching out to her. I was stunned at the realization. At once I was filled with a "joy unspeakable and full of glory." Had it been my imagination, it would have left after a day or two, but it has never left, and it has been two years now since that day. I am not saying I have never felt any sadness or pain in those two years, but I am saying that even in my times of sadness there is a feeling of fullness within me, a well of strength and beauty and hope that I have to draw on. That place inside where I felt so empty and hopeless has been filled up, and I feel like a complete person. The only thing I did was open myself up to Jesus and allow Him to pour His Spirit of strength, power and comfort into me. It is a totally supernatural thing.

There are parallels between this story and a work of science fiction. The war is between two extra-terrestrial armies, the good guys versus the bad guys. Each alien force has the power to possess the bodies of earthlings. The battle is fought through the people on earth who generally have little understanding of the strange war. Often they do not know why they act as they do, nor why they harbour uncomfortable thoughts, nor why there are strange struggles within them. The planet is the battleground of its Creator and His arch enemy. The pivotal point of the war is man's free will. Which army will he choose to support and fight for?

In the real story, while the battle was won at the Cross when Jesus conquered sin and death, the skirmishes will continue until all the good guys (God's people) are accounted for.

The thing that makes this story more astounding than science fiction is that it is science-fact. There is a greater wealth of material available to support the veracity of the Christian account of life than there is the secular account. There is more historical evidence to prove the life, death and resurrection of Jesus, than there is to prove the life and death of Napoleon. People seem to feel that they can arbitrarily either accept or reject Jesus, but everyone accepts the fact of Napoleon's life. It is because the acceptance of the fact of Jesus requires a personal commitment. The life of Napoleon does not have to have a personal impact on us, but the life of Jesus does.

Some people say Jesus was a great moral teacher, and in that way they try to explain Him away to themselves; but that is an impossibility. Either He is the one He claimed to be, the Son of God, or He was a lunatic. Great moral teachers don't go around calling themselves Sons of God. Jesus said:*"Do not believe Me unless I do what My Father does. But if I do it, even though you do not believe Me, believe the miracles, that you may learn and understand that the Father is in Me, and I in the Father."*

Eventually Jesus was locked up because then, as now, He was a threat to the self-righteousness of people. He made them uncomfortable. And He was sentenced to the most humiliating method of execution used in His day: crucifixion. But even death could not put an end to Him. His body was buried in a tomb, but three days later, He came to life again!

After Jesus came to life again, He continued His ministry on earth for forty days. He was seen by many people, on one occasion by over 500 people at once. His body was not just ghostlike, it was real. He ate and drank with people. Thomas actually touched the wounds inflicted on His body during the crucifixion.

As far as the Bible was concerned, people have said for centuries that it was God's Word. To me that was very difficult to understand, because it was written by men. It claims to be a supernatural, God inspired, God given book. It claims that the writers of Scripture wrote, not of their own will, but only as they were moved or controlled by the Holy Spirit, to write not their own words, but the very words of God Himself.

That claim was incomprehensible to me until I got into the science of Theomatics. It has proven, in an absolutely fascinating study of the Hebrew and Greek languages, which both incorporate their numerical systems into their alphabets, that the entire Bible text is underlaid by a mathematically precise code. A Russian scientist by the name of Ivan Panin went back to the early manuscripts and, by applying the mathematical values of the Greek and Hebrew alphabet letters to the script, he discovered that the whole Bible is constructed on an amazing numeric design. The facts are indisputable. They are overwhelming evidences of divine inspiration which shatter all the arguments of non-believers in relation to the supernatural origin. Albert Nobel of the Nobel Research Foundation, said of Panin's work, "The material is accurately presented and will withstand a thorough scientific investigation."[2] He concluded that the discovery was a valuable contribution both to science and to religion. The sixty-six books of the Bible were written down by thirty-three different men, over a period of 1600 years, in various countries. Even if they had all been able to meet, it would have required thousands of years to carry out such profound numeric schemes. No human minds could possibly have devised such a means of binding the whole of the Bible together into one body.

That revelation to me was a magnificent confirmation of the purity of the Bible. It meant I could trust every word in it to be God-breathed. What it really boiled down to, was that our Creator gave us an operator's manual. In it are answers to the complexities of life!

During the time that I was involving myself in so much research, and becoming so excited with my discoveries, Warren was watching me closely. One night, I felt that I had to come out of hiding and kneel down by my bed to talk with God – in spite of the fact that Warren was in the room. I climbed out of bed, and knelt. My heart was racing with nervousness and I couldn't concentrate on talking with God at all. My only thoughts were of Warren watching me, probably thinking I'd finally flipped out.

When I got up, I told him I'd become a Christian. He was calm about the whole thing and said I had my "thing," and he had his, and that he wouldn't pressure me, but that he didn't want me to pressure him. I sweetly promised not to push him, but in secret, I started to put the pres-

---

[2] *Astounding New Discoveries*, by Karl G. Sabiers, Robertson Publishing Co., Copyright 1941, page 6.

sure on where it counted – with God. I prayed and prayed that He would show Warren that He was really real.

I came across a book that listed five or six steps to follow in praying for the salvation of non-believers. One of the steps was to speak directly to the devil and to demand that he release the person because Jesus had paid the ransom for that person. Speak to the devil? You've got to be kidding I thought, with shivers running up and down my spine. But that night, with the book in front of me, I knelt down by the bed. It had taken the whole day for me to get up the courage to confront him face to face. But God gave me the assurance that He was stronger than the devil, and that He would be with me, and so I dared to do it.

"Satan," I said, "I'm talking to you. I come to you covered by the blood of Jesus Christ, and you cannot touch me. I am here to demand that you let go of Warren, my husband, because God paid the legal ransom price for him when He sacrificed His own Son Jesus. Now you creepy old liar, you let go of him right now!"

About a week later, Warren came into the bedroom on a Saturday morning when I was making the bed and watching *100 Huntley Street*, a daily Christian interview show. Just as he walked in the room, the host said to one of the girls on the set, "Julia, I think this is a moment for a miracle. Would you pray a prayer that those in the viewing audience could pray with you to receive Jesus?" Warren flopped down on the bed as Julia began to pray. A few minutes after she had finished praying, he shyly said, "Y'know I prayed that prayer with her."

"You're kidding!" I exclaimed in jubilation.

"But nothing happened," he continued.

"How do you know?" I asked.

"Well, I don't feel any different." He picked up a magazine and left the room. The discussion was closed.

About two weeks later, he awakened me early one Sunday morning. He said he was now a Christian. During the night, in a vision, Jesus had taken him to experience Heaven and Hell, and He had shown him the devil. Warren began to describe to me the wonder of the things that had been revealed to him, but it was too far out for me to absorb. Privately, I wondered at the truth of his story; I thought He was putting me on, until ... Jesus began to speak to me – through him. It was an experience that is difficult to describe. There is no way to convince anyone of what happened. It just happened and we know it did because we experienced it. It was as though Warren was a transmitter. At first, I didn't realize it was Jesus. I thought Warren was just describing things he had seen, but as I questioned him, I realized he was not answering of his own wisdom; but rather was waiting for each answer to come from another source Who was giving him the answers. Each time he gave the answer purely, as it was given to him, he said he felt a smooth, creamy sensation in his stomach. If there was something he did not have quite right, he would say, "No, that's not quite right," and wait for the correction. What he told me was beyond Warren's natural understanding. Jesus explained to me about His true church; saying that it was not a building, but that it was the union of all those who believed in Him. Each believer is a temple within which He dwells, and the union of the believers is His church. He reminded me of my constant need to feel important, and then Warren laughed.

"Why are you laughing?" I asked.

"It just seemed so funny," he said. "I was feeling sorry for you because I thought Jesus was being a little bit hard on you, but He said, "Oh it's alright; she knows I love her."

He talked to us of many things and each thought He expressed was like a precious, glistening jewel. There was so much I wanted to ask, but I was afraid to ask too much, because I knew I was on Holy ground. I didn't want to push too far. I felt that by asking too many questions, I could burst the bubble, or tarnish the majesty of the moment. We are not sure how long that Holy time lasted. But too soon, the power ebbed and we were left, but not left, to marvel at the wonder of God's presence and revelation to us.

God deals with each person in a special, individual way, tailored precisely to fit the needs of each one. With me, He knew He had to let me get to the end of myself, to the place where I discovered that my efforts at fulfillment brought me nothing but increasing emptiness. He allowed me to discover for myself that I truly did need Him. Warren, on the other hand, needed to be hit over the head with a demonstration of God's power. He needed to experience the truth of His reality and the consequences for non-believers.

The change in Warren was phenomenal. He was so different. I hardly knew how to talk to him. Our relationship before had been distant and strained without any common ground except for the children. Now we had God with us, and everything was new. A fragile shyness emerged between us; a whole new time of discovering each other as changed people. Slowly, God began a healing in our relationship, a new building on His principles and teachings. Our marriage is still under His construction, and occasionally there are problems, but out of the ashes of ugliness and hatred and bitterness and resentment is unfolding a thing of gentle beauty, strong reality, and cherished caring. Where I often wished he would be in an accident and die, I now entrust Him to God's care and pray for his safe return.

Gradually, step by step, God worked at cleaning up our home. The swearing left. We lost all desire to drink alcohol. We lost all desire to go to dances. The pornography stopped coming into the house. It wasn't that we made any big effort to stop any of these things; God simply took away our desire for them.

(Second edition note: This story had some tragic, unexpected turns many years after the publishing of this book. For those who know what happened and may wonder about the veracity of the previous paragraph, I need to explain that, while the pornography stopped coming into the house at that point, Warren didn't deal with the root of it. I realized, much later, that he had applied Jesus like a bandage to his life, covering the darkness that still existed underneath, rather than inviting Him to be the scalpel that could forever dig out and expel the darkness. Consequently, when a strong temptation showed up, Warren let the bandage fall off and partook of an evil that would have destroyed us all, had God not proved Himself greater than any evil. See *The Husband I Never Knew* by Diane Roblin-Lee - available at *www.bydesignmedia.ca* or on Amazon.com.)

To continue ...

One thing was really bothering me. My smoking habit seemed to be increasing, if anything. At night I would kneel down by my bed and pray; and then get into bed, light up a cigarette, and read my Bible. It just didn't feel right. When I spoke at meetings, I couldn't wait to get out to the car for a cigarette. I felt like such a hypocrite, but I couldn't stop. I had already tried all the gimmicks, and they hadn't worked. I began to pray about it. In altar services, I went forward several times for special prayer, but nothing happened that I could see.

One day, I decided to call the counselling service at "*100 Huntley Street.*" I was thrilled with what the Lord had done in our lives, and so shared it all with the counsellor. I went on to tell her of my problems with smoking. Rather than share in my enthusiasm about what God had done with us, she simply said, "You haven't humbled yourself."

Inside, I was thinking, "Who does she think she is, telling me I haven't humbled myself? How does she know what has gone on between the Lord and me?"

She continued, "When you get off this phone, I want you to kneel down by your chair and tell God how sorry you are for your sins."

Well, alright, I thought; but as far as I was concerned, I'd already done that. Nevertheless, I hung up the phone, went over to my favorite chair and knelt down beside it, feeling rather silly. I was definitely not feeling the least bit emotional; certainly not at all sad. There was a certain element of contrition present, but only as a rather obedient response to the counselor. But as soon as I began to pray, something broke within me. A flood of anguish suddenly erupted deep inside and I felt myself to be lying on the ground with my arms wrapped around the cross. I lay there with my head on the ground and wept all of the tears of my past. I was at Calvary with all the old hurts and feelings of bitterness, rejection, and sorrow. Great heaving sobs poured forth. As I wept, I cried out to God from the innermost depths of my being, "Oh God, I am so miserable. God, I need You. I need You. I am so miserable." My face and my neck were streaming with tears. My nose was running. I felt like I had come finally to the very end of myself. "Oh God," I cried, "take over. I can't do it. I want you to take over my whole life. You do it. I don't want it anymore. Oh God, I just want you." Softly, gently, the anguish ebbed, and in its place came an exquisite peace. I continued to sob, but now there were tears of comfort. I wanted to stay right where I was because there was such beauty in the comfort, but I didn't have any tissues with me, and I couldn't stand the mess I was in. And so I got up, blew my nose and washed my face.

Only God really knows what happened inside me that day. I know it was not a natural thing; certainly not anything I worked up myself. I believe it was a time of cleansing, forgiveness and emotional healing – and being wrapped up in the righteousness of Christ.

About a week later, I was sitting in the living room, reading Catherine Marshall's book, Beyond Ourselves. The Lord began to deal with me about my smoking habit. I lit a cigarette and raised it to my mouth to take a puff, but a voice said, "Put it out."

It was not an audible voice, and yet I knew it was not something that had originated within me. It was in my mind, but it had not come from me. I thought, "This is ridiculous. Now I'm starting to hear voices." And so I raised the cigarette again to take a puff.

"Put it out," came the voice, more firmly this time.

"No," I thought. "I'm not going to put it out; I'm going to smoke this cigarette. I'm becoming compulsive about thinking I have to obey this voice that I'm just imagining." I put the cigarette to my lips.

"Put it out."

"No."

"Put it out."

"No." But I could not take a puff from that cigarette. I wanted to smoke, but the Holy Spirit was stronger than my physical and mental desires. Finally, the cigarette had burned right down to the filter, and there was nothing left to smoke. I had to put it out. I got down on my knees, and said, "Lord, if this is really You wanting me to quit smoking, then You'll have to take over and do it for me, because You know how often I've tried to quit before and I've always failed." That was July fifth at 4:36 p.m. a year and a half ago, and I haven't had a cigarette since! True, I went through all of the withdrawal, and my body screamed for a cigarette, especially on the fourth day, but it was as though the decision to smoke had been taken away from me. I did not have to decide whether or not to have a cigarette. I just knew they were no longer a part of me.

Warren's experience with smoking was different from mine. Again, God tailored the experience to fit the needs of the individual. Warren was driving home from work a few days before Christmas, singing the Hallelujah Chorus along with the radio. Right there in the car, God's Spirit moved on him, and he began to speak in another language. Not having been involved in any Pentecostal fellowship, he was puzzled about what had happened. When he arrived home, he sat at the table with me, and said, "Sweetie, I don't know what happened in the car on the way home, but while I was singing, I began to sing strange words!"

From all the reading I had been doing about the baptism in the Holy Spirit, and from what we had heard about "tongues," we assumed he had been given the gift of tongues. It wasn't until one night, when he was feeling ill and thought I was sleeping, that I actually heard him use the new language. I lay quietly, listening to him speaking softly to God in a language totally unknown to us, and yet with a definite syntax and sound organization. I marvelled at God's power.

Three days after Warren had received the new language, God simply removed his desire for cigarettes! Like me, he had been a chain smoker, and totally miserable if he were deprived of cigarettes for any longer than about a half hour. But with Warren, God not only took away the desire to smoke, but He also took away any withdrawal discomfort. When he said he wasn't going to smoke anymore, I said, "That's fantastic!" but inside, I was thinking, "Oh brother, do we have to go through this again?" because he had tried to quit many times prior to that and had practically driven our whole household around the bend with his nicotine fits! But not this time. I kept waiting for the snappy irritation, but it never came. That was just over a year ago, and his lungs are getting pinker every day!

For months, I had been feeling a great longing to be re-baptized, by immersion in water, as the Scriptures described. I felt I had not really understood the implications of my baptism when I was thirteen-years-old. I may have understood in my head, but heart knowledge is very different. I knew I could not be satisfied until I went under the water again. I had no peace in accepting my original baptism as sufficient.

But there was a problem. I knew Dad did not agree with anyone being re-baptized. He held that there was no example of it given in the Bible and therefore it was unscriptural. I knew that no amount of talking would change his mind, and the thought of it was so precious that I did not want to tarnish it by getting into an argument. To me, it was not something that required a scriptural precedent, but only a leading of the Holy Spirit. I knew what I had to do.

Another reason I could not discuss it with Dad was that our relationship was beginning a healing that was very precious to both of us; but it was so fragile and new, that I didn't feel it could withstand the pressure of a dispute. Not yet. His views were firm and I knew I could not change. If I were to give him space to advise me and then didn't take his advice, it would be much worse than as if I were to go ahead and did what I had to do.

Warren and I were attending a little country church at the time where God had led us by another series of supernatural events. The pastor, Bob McLellan, was a marvellous help to us. When he asked us if we would like to be baptized, we said yes. The service was to be held in two weeks on the bank of a river. That thrilled me, because Jesus was baptized in a river. But still I felt torn about Dad.

I phoned Aunt Jessie and told her about the service and she said she and Uncle Harvey would be there. We told Warren's parents about it too, hoping they might come and see the beauty of God's work. Two days before the service, I told Dad what I was going to do. He said very little, but his brittle tone of voice revealed his disapproval. There was nothing left to say. We hung up. I felt horrible. More guilt.

On Sunday morning before we left for the service, Dad called and stated that he did not agree with what I was doing. He sounded as though I was greatly disappointing him. When he had stated his message, he simply said good-bye. Turmoil gripped my heart. All my life I had wanted a close relationship with Dad, and now by my own action, I was destroying it. With my Bible before me, I sank down on my knees and asked God to give me an answer. I have heard people say you should never just let your Bible fall open expecting God to choose the proper page, but I did it anyway that day. It fell open at the eighth chapter of Acts, where Phillip was talking with the Ethiopian official:

"Then Phillip began to speak; starting from this passage of scripture, he told him the Good News about Jesus. As they travelled down the road, they came to a place where there was some water, and the official said, "Here is some water. What is to keep me from being baptized?" The official ordered the carriage to stop, and both Phillip and the official went down into the water, and Phillip baptized him."

To me that was a direct answer from God. It was a confirmation that I was to be baptized, as evidence of my new life in Christ.

It was a beautiful service. Warren's parents and Aunt Jessie and Uncle Harvey were there, and we saw God's hand working through the whole service. It was a magnificent day. About two hundred people gathered at the bend of the river as fifteen believers were taken into the waters of baptism. I will never forget the sight of my big husband walking resolutely into the depths of the river toward the minister. He was walking away from all the misery in our lives into beauty and truth. Our old lives were washed away; we were fresh and new. The old hurts were meaningless and gone in the light of God's healing power. Now we were truly married, one in Christ as our Creator intended marriage to be.

The relationship between Dad and me shattered again, as I had feared it would. He felt that in rejecting my first baptism, I was rejecting him as a minister, because he had been the one to baptize me. He went through a difficult time wondering how many people he had baptized felt as I did. He could not understand that I was in no way rejecting him. To me he was only the instrument in my first baptism and had absolutely nothing to do with what did or did not happen between God and me on that day.

It appeared that from Dad's perspective, my relationship with God in my early years was wrapped up in my relationship with him as my minister. My spiritual depth was a reflection of his ability in ministry. It seemed that in recognizing the inadequacies of my early relationship with God, I was pointing out inadequacies in Dad.

To me, that was not true at all. Dad was my dad. Aside from teaching me about God, he had nothing to do with what happened between God and me. He was torturing himself needlessly, in my opinion, and there seemed to be nothing I could do about it except pray that God would continue to heal our relationship and release us both from any hurt or bitterness.

And He is doing that. Now Dad is being healed inside too. He seems to be no longer strained and defensive. I feel a new, more mature, warmth beginning to emerge between us. He is trying less to control my growth and trusting God to work out my wrinkles. I am more appreciative of him. I feel more comfortable in his presence and can more easily tolerate our differences.

By meeting our difficulties head on, and trusting God to sustain us and carry us through to the other side, we are growing as a family. By recognizing our differences and allowing them to surface, instead of constantly trying to deny them, we are getting to know each other better. Often the things we try to hide are made more plain by our denials of their existence. Dad told me not long ago that I hurt him more by trying to hide things than I would have by just being open about them. But it's hard to reveal something that you know may hurt someone else. Also, you don't always know how others are going to react to what you do. Sometimes, the things that you think will hurt them terribly, are received with understanding. Other things, which to you are rationally acceptable, are devastating to them.

Where there is growth, there is generally pain. Dad and I have not been plopped suddenly into a fantastic relationship. We have a long way to go in trust, understanding and tolerance. But the love and appreciation of each other has grown tremendously, and love is the surest foundation on which to build. If the foundation is strong, then the whole structure is more likely to survive. God is at work in both of us, and it is His Spirit within us that is drawing us together.

As far as this book is concerned, I think that if I had a child writing a book about his or her relationship with me, I would have some measure of nervous apprehension. But that has not been in the least evident with Dad. On the contrary, he has been tremendously encouraging and helpful in procuring contacts and interviews for me. He has shown tremendous dignity, selflessness and gentility in the whole matter.

If the truth were known, few people could stand to have their lives examined at close range and emerge unscathed. Most people try to hide every little imperfection for fear that people will find out that they are not flawless after all. That may be terrific for self-protection, but who can it help? Who can relate to perfection? Who is perfect? Jesus said, "Be on guard against the yeast of the Pharisees – I mean their hypocrisy. Whatever is covered up will be uncovered, and every secret will be made known. So then, whatever you have whispered in private in a closed room will be shouted from the housetops."[3]

In these days of anxiety and turmoil, there are a lot of people hurting and in need of hope. Surface solutions are of no lasting value. They need hope that comes from the depth of honest experience. If our experiences in despair, that have blossomed into beauty, can help others, then why not shout them from the housetops? Jesus said the time when they'll all be uncovered will come anyway, so why shouldn't we uncover them now, while we still have a chance to help someone else? I believe our trials are pieces of a patchwork quilt given to us by God. As we grow in Him, He helps us to work these experiences into a blanket of understanding and love with which to enfold others.

After all of these years of trying to deny God's place in my life, and my place in His family, I have come full circle. I humbly and gratefully thank Him for choosing me to be raised by my real parents. They are two beautiful, strong people who have contributed so much to the lives of so many. They have been selfless and untiring in their work for God. I pray that when my boys grow up, they can say something like that about me.

---

[3] Luke 12:1-3

PART TWO

The Preachers' Kids

PART TWO

Introduction

WAS I SO STRANGE? Were there factors leading to my rebellion that were common to the homes of other ministers' children? Why did so many children of clergy have the reputation of being the wildest kids in town? Could the rebellion in ministers' homes be prevented? How? Why did some preachers' kids develop in strong faith with no apparent signs of rebellion? What were the differences between the homes of the rebels and the 'good' kids? I had many questions.

And I was so excited with my discoveries about the purpose of life and the reality of the living Jesus, that I was burning to share my fabulous treasure with everyone possible. I wanted to tell them! I wanted to shout, "He's alive! He's alive!" I yearned for everyone to grasp the true beauty of life.

Another of my concerns, was that ministers and their families should be made aware of the possible psychological implications involved in the child's development in the home of a minister. I wanted to warn them about the insidious pitfalls of the parsonage. I felt such tremendous love for people that I wanted to spare everyone from any unnecessary hurt, to help them to understand that Jesus is the answer to life!

Where ministers' children were experiencing difficulties, I wanted them to take a look at the fantastic opportunities and benefits they had in their positions. As I look back now, there were so many advantages I had being raised in a minister's home; but I didn't experience the benefit of them at the time, because I didn't always recognize them.

With these questions and purposes in mind, I prepared two in-depth questionnaires; one for ministers and one for the people who had been, or were presently being, raised in a minister's home. I made no attempt to compile wide-range statistics, but only to explore the feelings and understanding of a widely divergent sample of people who all shared the common denominator of having experienced life in a manse, parsonage, rectory, or vicarage.

The minister's offspring interviewed ranged in age from fifteen to forty-eight. They were from many different denominations including United, Anglican, Presbyterian, Pentecostal, Associated Gospel and Baptist. Their spiritual situations ran the full gamut from the avowed atheist, to people who were deeply committed to the Lord. Some were wealthy and influential; some were very plain folk; and two were in jail. All were raised in North America.

I have included here a copy of the interview given to each respondent, for the general interest of the reader.

PREACHERS' KIDS INTERVIEW

STATISTICAL GENERALITIES

1. Name - phone - address - age

2. Occupation

3. Denomination

4. In regard to the publication of this book, may I refer to you by name, or do you prefer to remain anonymous?

5. Number of brothers and sisters?

6. How often have you moved?

7. How do you feel generally about being a minister's child?

    a) positively b) negatively – why?

CONGREGATIONAL RELATIONSHIPS

1. What is your general attitude towards congregations? Do they consist generally of sincere people, hypocrites, or what?
2. Does your attitude toward congregations affect your attitude toward your parents?
3. Do you feel that congregations have helped or hindered

    a) your relationship with your parents?

    b) your relationship with God? If so, how?
4. Do you feel that your problems are of greater or lesser importance to your parents than are those of the congregation? In other words, do you feel you come first or second?
5. In your opinion, what could individual members of the congregation do to help to strengthen the spiritual development of preachers' kids?

PEER RELATIONSHIPS

1. Do you generally feel well liked by the other people at school or work?
2. Do you feel this has been affected by your dad's profession? If so, how?
3. Do you generally feel that people a) ridicule or b) respect the fact that your dad is a minister?
4. As you grow older, do you find this attitude changing? If so, how?

RELATIONSHIP WITH SELF

1. Has your own personal attitude toward your dad's occupation changed significantly as you have matured? How?

2. What are the major problems involved in being raised in a minister's home?
3. What are the major benefits?
4. Did you go through a period of rebellion? Why? Please enlarge on this.

PATERNAL RELATIONSHIP

1. In your opinion, what is a minister?
2. What are the responsibilities of a minister?
3. Is your dad measuring up to your ideal standards for a minister? Discuss.
4. Should a child be expected to go to church every Sunday?
5. Does your dad have a public face and a private face? – or is he the same all the time?
6. Which face do you like best?
7. Can you discuss your problems with your dad? Why?
8. Do you and your dad spend any time together doing non-religious activities? i.e. sporting events, camping, etc.?
9. Would you like to spend more time with your dad? What is his reaction to that? What would you like to do with him?
10. Do you feel that he would still love you if your views about life and God differed somewhat from his?
11. Do you feel that your dad has a deep personal relationship with God?
12. Does he enjoy his relationship with God, or do you feel he is tense much of the time?
13. What are the things that make your relationship with him good?
14. What things does your dad do to make it easy for you to take your problems to him?

15. If you have an unsatisfactory relationship with your dad, do you see any chance of it improving? In order for that to happen,

- How would he have to change?
- How would you have to change?
- Are you anxious for things to change?
- Is he aware of these things?

MATERNAL RELATIONSHIP

1. What are the responsibilities of a minister's wife?
2. Does your mother measure up to your standards for a good minister's wife?
3. Do her church responsibilities interfere with her relationship with you?
4. Does she spend enough time with you?
5. If you were ill, would she stay home from a church meeting with you?
6. Does she expect you to be an example to the other kids in the church? How do you feel about that?
7. In what ways could she improve as
- a minister's wife?
- a mother?
8. Do you see a conflict between those two roles?
9. Do you feel comfortable enough to discuss your problems with her?
10. Is there much laughter in your home? What is your most humorous memory in relation to your position as a P.K.?
11. Do you feel that your mom has a deep relationship with God?
12. Does she show a lot of joy in Jesus, or is she somewhat tense and worried much of the time?

SPIRITUAL SITUATION

1. Do you believe in God?
2. What is your concept of Jesus?
3. What is your concept of the Holy Spirit?
4. Have you made a spiritual commitment with your life? If so, what was your conversion experience?
5. To what degree has this affected your life?

- little
- somewhat
- greatly
- profoundly

6. Do you feel you are now growing spiritually, or are at a standstill, or are going further away from the Lord, or what?
7. What is the most important thing in life to you?
8. Have you seen the power of God at work in your home? How?
9. Do you feel that being raised in a minister's home has

- speeded
- slowed down
- hindered

your acceptance of the Lord?

GENERAL COMMENTS

1. What would you like to say to other preacher's kids? Please expand.
2. Do you have any advice for their parents? Please expand.
3. Do you have any advice for congregations? Please expand.

As I share the responses to these questions, you will see, as I did, definite patterns emerging in many areas. On the other hand, there are developments which are totally unique to individual environments and temperaments.

Allow me to introduce you to the Preachers' Kids.

PART TWO – CHAPTER ONE

Are They Really Perfect?

OF THE PEOPLE INTERVIEWED, 83.3 percent had positive attitudes toward their position as offspring of clergy. 13.3 percent responded negatively, and one was simply resigned to his parentage. These results, however, differed with their attitudes as children growing up in the homes of the clergy. In their developmental years, only 40 percent were glad their dads were ministers. 13.3 percent had mixed feelings, while 46.6 percent reacted negatively.

Why did the feelings of so many undergo a reversal from negative to positive? Generally, it was a result of the transition into maturity and spiritual peace. They came to a place in their lives where they were able to look back on the situation from a more objective, removed position.

Often, they recognized that many of their problems had been simply results of the conflicts they had within themselves. These conflicts were often of a spiritual nature, and once they were at peace spiritually their other problems dissolved.

Bob Wells, crew chief at *100 Huntley Street* says, "As a child, my feelings were more negative; but as I've matured, I've become my own man. I have reassessed myself and found that I'm following Christ, not my dad anymore. Now I appreciate my dad for what he was. Unfortunately, when I lived at home, I didn't understand fully, and there was a bit of resentment."

A twenty-one-year-old guitar teacher, who recently came out of the drug scene into a vibrant relationship with Jesus, says: "I resented being a

P.K. because I felt I was given more restrictions than I would have had in a normal home. I hated church because I was told that I had to go until I was seventeen. Before I went to church, I predetermined not to like the services. I hated it because I was forced to go there. I didn't have a personal relationship with Jesus, and my relationship with my dad was almost non-existent. Now I am a Christian, and I love my parents. My whole perspective at the time was negative. That's where my memories are from. Now my perspective is positive."

As they matured, things once seen as negative factors, were often viewed as positive. For instance, a high school teacher says: "In the church, if no one else will lead a particular group, as the minister's daughter, you're expected to do it. At the time, this seems to be a negative aspect, but later on, you see it as positive, because you've had to develop your leadership abilities."

A middle-aged social worker says, "I remember being upset about other people having a lot more material things than we had. Dad certainly did not make much money as a minister. But things like that all helped to strengthen my character. Now I feel that the experience was a real benefit; but when you're in the middle of the situation, you often don't see it quite that way."

When we remove ourselves from areas of concern, we are usually able to see things with a more balanced perspective. When enmeshed in certain situations, it can be difficult to judge accurately what is going on. In all instances where the attitudes were reversed, a period of time removed from the immediate situation was involved. This was not necessarily a physical removal, but was a separation of at least psychological involvement. It was a time of balancing and evaluation. Often it was a time of pain and heartache for both parent and child, sometimes involving a time of doubting God. But in each of these cases of reversal the temporary separation resulted in a reaffirmation of the reality and wisdom of God.

Unfortunately, not all of the respondents who had negative attitudes toward their minister dads in childhood changed their minds as they matured (by the time of the interview). 13.3 percent remained adamantly opposed to being raised in a minister's home, while one simply resigned himself to the situation.

The young boy who resigned himself felt hopeless about the situation. He did not understand the Gospel and therefore could not relate to his dad's work or position. His dad was a United Church minister who claimed that the institution of the church was "really not much different from any other social club." The boy sounded rather lost as he said, "You get to meet a lot of people, but you sort of live in a fishbowl, because everyone watches everything that you do."

One middle-aged woman who experienced a very disturbing life in a manse said, "I had no choice." She reminded me of a wounded bird, whose wings were just beginning to heal. Her parents had both been so involved in ministry, that they had taken little time for her. As an only child, she had simply tagged along through life, sitting quietly through meeting after meeting.

A young boy who was raised in a legalistic, extremely restrictive atmosphere, was bitter and resentful toward his parents who had forced him into an outward show of religion. Recently, they had been filled with the Holy Spirit and their lives were changed. The boy turned around and came to the Lord. He, too, was filled with the Holy Spirit. That family has been revolutionized by the power of God. They now travel around together ministering in schools and Full Gospel meetings. Although the bitterness the boy felt has been healed by God's love, he retains his negative memories of life in the parsonage because he and his parents were different people in those days.

A few years ago, through an experience at a Christian summer camp which his children attended, a 47-year-old P.K., who had fallen away from the Lord, became a Christian. He now finds great satisfaction in travelling around with his family as a Gospel singing group. In recalling his childhood and adolescence as a minister's son, he says: "I got irritated at how people took advantage of my dad. He was always worried about not having enough money to retire. He worked beyond 75-years-of-age and we couldn't get him to quit, because the church had such a lousy pension plan. In those last years, he was earning more than he ever had in his whole life, and it wasn't much. There he was; a university graduate who had been the top in his class. When I was growing up, there was so little money that we could barely afford the necessities of life. Dad had no money for an education for me. At that time, there were no such things as school loans. As a result, I felt that there was no point in my continuing high school, because I knew there was no hope of going on to university anyway; so I quit high school with no preparation for my life."

This person feels very strongly that as a well-educated man, his dad should have received a better salary. In his opinion, the fact that his dad was a poorly paid minister resulted in limited work opportunities for his own life, and consequently little job satisfaction.

A minister, who was himself brought up in a vicarage, retains tremendous frustration in his childhood memories. He went through a period of tremendously violent and aggressive rebellion against an ineffectual father and a domineering mother who insisted that he must not bring any disgrace on his father, while she herself was of no help to the father's image.

There is no doubt that there are many problems involved in being raised as a minister's child, but there are also a great number of benefits. First we will take a look at the problems encountered by the respondents, and then we will see how they are balanced to a large degree by the many benefits.

P.K. ISSUES

Frequently, ministers' children feel isolated in their difficulties because they seldom have the opportunity of associating with other ministers' children. In a church where there is only one minister, there are no other P.K.s. Thus there are no other children with whom the minister's children can relate on a common basis. They may feel that no one understands them; that they really don't fit in anywhere. By bringing the thoughts of my respondents together, I hope to show P.K.s that they are very much part of a group of people who share common difficulties and benefits. What are some of the main problems?

One very common complaint was, "You're not accepted as an individual and you're not allowed mistakes. You need more freedom to be treated like any other child."

A high school teacher says, "A minister tends to move quite often, and it's pretty hard for a P.K. to be liked right off the bat in a new school, particularly in a small town, because everybody knows that your dad is a minister, and they tend to shun you. Consequently, in order to gain approval, many P.K.s go way overboard, and do things they shouldn't to prove themselves normal. In a lot of cases, they end up worse than the other kids. I remember doing a lot of things – like swearing. I would never have sworn at home, but the first day I went to school in one new place, I heard the kids up the street say, 'Oh, here she comes; watch your language!' So I thought if I threw in the odd swear word, I would be liked. Those pressures lasted only during childhood and adolescence, but as a child, you knew right away that people expected you to act differently than them. That pressure came mostly from peers."

Another girl, discussing the problems involved in moving says, "If the family disagrees about a move, it's like you're fighting with God because the preacher feels that God is telling him to move."

In tabulating the results of the questionnaires, I discovered that the average number of moves in my sample group was five point five moves, while the median number was four. Moving often was cited as a problem for some, while for others it was a benefit. This was seemingly dependent on temperament and circumstances.

In Bob's case, moving was a very difficult thing, because just as he was beginning to establish roots for himself, it would be time to move again. Considering his great need for security, this was often traumatic for him.

Wendell Fisher, an assistant school principal, expressed similar feelings. "The reaction of people to me, as a result of my dad's profession, differed according to what town we moved to. There was always a certain degree of ridicule involved. This made me feel sort of a collective uneasiness for the whole family. That led to a feeling of insecurity, which was heightened by the ever-present possibility of another move. I never knew whether we would move again next year, or the year after, or what. I hated moving. We were always on display, and vulnerable, and open to the criticism of people. The social pressures are the greatest problem. Ministers' children are always either devils or angels, and there doesn't seem to be any in between."

A teenage boy, known in his town as a rebel, comments, "Sometimes you have to work a little harder at proving you're a normal person. I have to work at being an individual instead of just being known as the 'minister's son.' Everybody looks you over and thinks you're going to be an angel."

A charming fifteen-year-old girl, whose father was a Presbyterian minister, has not yet made any commitment to God in her life. She is puzzled about the church, and says, "It's hard to understand about the church. It's hard to accept when you're young and everybody thinks that just because your dad believes, you should believe everything too."

If a child is not firmly entrenched in a personal knowledge of God and His place in life, he is bound to be confused about the ways of his family. He will feel isolated from the believing members of his family, from the congregation of the church, and from society in general.

Whether or not the child believes and understands, however, he is regarded as an important part of the community of believers. He is a conspicuous symbol; and could, at times, be compared to a church mascot.

A teenage girl observes, "When I was little, I used to think I was better than everyone else because I was the minister's daughter."

Charles Vickerson, who is himself now a minister, expanded somewhat on this same thought. "Prior to high school years when I entered the time of social awareness, I had the feeling that I was very important; more important than anyone else in the church. Other people made me feel that way. There was also a feeling that I was supposed to act in a certain way, and I didn't want to act that way. My early years were spent trying to break out of the mold of what a minister's son was expected to be. I knew that I didn't fit that ideal picture, and that I never could. With that combination of despair and frustration, I looked for something else that I could be or do. I became the kid at school who sat at the back of the class and made trouble. I Was determined not to be a goodie-goodie. I used to get a big charge out of saying, 'Sure my dad's a minister, but look at me and what I'm doing.' It was a big kick for me. The whole area of legalism was another problem. I felt tremendous pressures to produce and be useful. I saw poverty and huge problems all around me, and I felt great pressure to change things. The people in the church always talked about reform, but it was always, 'bla, bla, bla,' and I just didn't see them getting the job done.

When the chips were down, the bucks weren't there. My dad would have to go around begging to get a milk program going for poor kids. I saw my father, a well-educated Harvard man, with very little materially, being used and unappreciated by these people. It really bugged me as a child."

Ministers' children generally feel a great pressure to be examples to others. This pressure may come from all sides; parents, peer groups, congregations and the society at large, it is difficult for them to feel relaxed because they are almost constantly aware of being watched and judged.

Elaine Mainse Stacey is the married daughter of David Mainse, the well known host of the Christian T.V. talk-show, "*100 Huntley Street*;" but for most of her growing-up years, Elaine's dad was a Pentecostal church pastor. Her only real difficulty was the fact that she always felt the pressure of being an example to other people. She says the problem is, "always being aware that whatever you do will be a reflection on your parents."

Janice Crump Rempel is the daughter of Bill Crump, who founded and directs Fairhavens Christian Conference, in Gamebridge, Ontario. She too, felt the pressure to protect her dad's position. "I was always very conscious of how my behavior would reflect on my dad's position. I suppose that certain kids in other families feel protective of their dad's role as well; but in a pastor's home, the pastor is expected to be guiding people morally, and if his own children are acting morally irresponsible, it can have a bad reflection on his position. Scheduling of the family life is another very real problem. It's hard to have regular times together."

As a child, Karen Gamble was ridiculed in school. They knew she was a Christian and what she stood for. If she made a wrong move, they let her know about it. She felt a lot of pressure. Karen says, "I never really felt a part of the group at school, because I was a Christian. Sometimes, I wanted to be a part of them, and do the things that they did, but my conscience wouldn't let me. Other kids point their fingers at P.K.s, and they say, 'I can do that because she's a P. K. and she does it.' I didn't join in the dances and the drinking parties, because my conscience wouldn't let me. It was a self-imposed restriction. My parents would have felt badly if I had gone, but they are very understanding people. I think that's why all five of us kids are born-again, Spirit-filled Christians."

Bob Wells' healthy, athletic appearance is accompanied by a persona of inner strength and assurance. But as a young boy in school, Bob was plagued by an inferiority complex. He feels his problem was greatly due to the fact that he was a minister's son. He says, "I was always a little bit afraid of the P.K. label. Whenever I did anything wrong, it was the 'Preacher's Kid' who did it. Whenever any other kid did something wrong, it was just plain Johnny who did it. We were always poor, and didn't have much because Dad was always a pioneering pastor. We didn't have the clothes, and trips and things that the other kids had. It was not just my parents who expected me to follow all of the rules and regulations that were set down; everyone else expected me to follow them too. I could set goals and achieve them, but there was always that shadow of the inferiority complex."

Sylvia Oldenziel is the wife of a school teacher and has two young daughters. Over the past four years, she has been working on a university degree on weekends and in the evenings, as part of an extension program. She has worked very hard and is getting close to graduation. Sylvia appears to be a very strong person, but she admits there were a few problems as she grew up in the manse: "When I was a teenager, the kids were often a little embarrassed to come to our house for the first time. They shied away from it, I guess because they thought that we were on our knees praying all the time. Boys were very reluctant to show up at our door for dates! A lot of people expected that since we were minister's kids, we were blessed with a super portion of goodness. That is ridiculous. The lack of money was a problem. Also, never being able to live in our own home, but always in a manse was sometimes hard, because we could never fix things up as we would have liked."

Despite Sylvia's difficulties, her strong personality sustained her. However, the reaction to her by her peers was always intertwined with their reaction to her father. She was never 'just Sylvia,' but was always the minister's daughter. A P.K.'s feeling of identity can be tremendously overpowered by the position of the minister-father.

Jennifer Holmes (an assumed name) has a difficult relationship with her dad; she finds it impossible to relate to him. She feels he considers her opinions to be inferior to his own. She has felt inadequate all her life because her dad incessantly imposed his superiority on her. He never instilled in her a knowledge of her own worth. She says: "During my preschool years, I felt that everyone respected my dad. After school started, I met people who were not part of the congregation. Some taunting occurred then. I discovered that only a unique segment of the population held respect for my dad's occupation and therefore for my dad, because he was essentially his occupation. During my adolescent years, my dad's occupation had a fairly great influence on the opinion of my peers. As I have matured, I have fortunately found that the people around me are more concerned with my accomplishments than they are with the accomplishments of my father. The major problem associated with being a minister's child is the inability to be oneself."

Tanya Marshall (an assumed name), like Jennifer, has an inadequate relationship with her dad. Her father has no idea of her true feelings about him, and she loves him too much to hurt him. She desperately wants a warm, honest relationship with him, but she can't get past his pride and his theological ego, without risking deep hurt to him. In spite of the fact that she has now devoted herself to the Lord, the walls remain. She says: "People don't really understand what it's like to be a P.K. Please retain my anonymity for me. Please camouflage things that would identify me specifically. I hope you can disguise them for me somehow, because it would really devastate my father if he heard me telling it like I think it is now. He would be deeply hurt, and what trust we have would be just shattered. He couldn't handle this as my position. So, until he's freed – until God frees him, and until we can work out a lot of these things; until he's not threatened by my perceptions and my statement of perception, I don't feel I can let you use my own name. I hope that anything that hurts parents in this book will eventually be freeing; enlightening and freeing. The truth will set us free. Praise God."

Last week, I went to visit a minister's son in jail. The boy is 21-years-old. We sat and talked for two hours. I had security clearance to do an interview with him and he had agreed to do one, but as we started to chat, I set the interview aside and we simply talked. He said it was the first time in about ten years that he had really talked about the Lord with any interest. I attribute that to the amount of prayer support that preceded my visit with him. He said he had been his father's pride and joy, but had gotten fed up with his dad always expecting him to be just like him. He insisted that he was a person – not just a copy of his dad. He was very defensive about how others viewed him. He sensed their disapproval of his lifestyle and resented it deeply.

Tim Crookall is also 21-years-old. He too, was deeply into the drug scene. Two years ago, he was at the point of suicide, but just in time, he turned to the Lord, and now is a strong Christian, playing the guitar and singing his songs for Jesus. Tim says: "I got really sick of people expecting me to be just like my father. Friends of my parents and other people used to come up to me and witness to me about things I had already heard a lot of times before. I felt them condemning me."

If a minister's child does not conform with expectations, he receives more condemnation than the average person, because he supposedly 'knows better.' The very fact that he does 'know better' makes him all the more sensitive to the condemnation. The antidote is loving and true caring; not criticism.

But in a minister's family, time for special caring and concern for each other is often at a premium. Laurie Brady says: "There is more pressure on the minister and his wife to fulfill the demands outside the home than the demands within the family. It takes very special people to fulfill both areas adequately. There are too many demands on the minister's time."

Some of the respondents remembered feeling that they would get into Heaven if they were to die, because their dads were ministers. And generally, people expected that they were Christians, and accepted them as such, simply because they lived with the minister. But as Dave Lawrenson put it, "Just because you've been born and raised a P.K. doesn't make you a Christian. It doesn't give you any inroads into the Word of God, or into the presence of God."

And so, in spite of the ridicule they may have to endure because of their close connection with the church, P.K.'s are no different than anyone else in God's eyes. Without a personal commitment of their own lives to God, they have no special passes into Heaven. God has no grandchildren. Each person has to be spiritually born in the family of God, as a child of the Father, if he hopes to inherit eternal life with Jesus.

THE BENEFITS OF BEING A P.K.

So far, the picture looks pretty negative. The preceding few pages could be enough to scare any young minister and his wife into forgetting about baby booties and Fisher-Price toys. But they shouldn't despair. There is a bright side to this issue. Remember, 83.3 percent of the respondents are now glad that they were raised in the homes of ministers, despite the problems.

Why? What are the benefits?

Joan had a lot of problems when she was growing up. She did not understand the Gospel at all; but now she is a joyful Christian and says, "You're made aware of God. As I was growing up, I learned a lot of hymns, and later on, when I began my search for God, I started to remember bits of those hymns and they really helped me. It was marvellous to have them to draw on."

In my own experience, I found that to be very true. In my time of deepest despair, the Holy Spirit used the teachings of my childhood to strengthen my awareness of His Presence. The words of hymns and Scripture passages that I had not heard for years were brought forth once more to my conscious mind.

This background of Christian teaching proved valuable to David Harris. Wistfully, he says: "I wish my Dad had really been on fire for the Lord, and then I could have said so many good things. One benefit was that I went to Sunday School and therefore got a fair background in God's Word from the stories."

Appreciation of early Scripture teaching was prevalent among the P.K.s. Although Tim Crookall went through difficult times away from the Lord, he never regretted his early teachings. He says: "I was taught the Bible when I was really young and I think that has helped me all through my life. Even when I wasn't serving the Lord, it helped me with some of my attitudes. Besides all the rottenness in my life, there were some good character traits that wouldn't have been there, had I not been taught the Bible."

A high school teacher says: "During childhood, you concentrate more on the problems involved; but as you mature, you look back and you can see more of the benefits. There is great opportunity to develop your leadership abilities, particularly as you watch your parents being leaders."

The opportunities to develop leadership skills are plentiful as a P.K. The way the minister and his wife, and the congregation, approach a P.K. in this area is crucial. Service for God is a privilege, and a child should be helped to feel that stacking chairs, or picking up hymn books is a delight – as service for Jesus – rather than a dreary chore. God's work is exciting.

As well as developing leadership skills, there are many opportunities to develop personal skills in areas such as music, public speaking, counselling, teaching and organizing activities.

Diane Osborne is eighteen-years-old, the daughter of Don Osborne of *100 Huntley Street* fame. She says: "Dad's profession was a family involvement. We all ministered together and it was a family profession. Dad wasn't alone in his pastoring. We all felt it together. We learned things as a family. We had to go through a lot of things on faith; praying things in, like money and food. You remember those things. When my Dad was in evangelism, things were pretty tight, and we just had to pray the food in, as a family; and then when it came in, we thanked God for it as a family. I really remember those things, and seeing God at work in our home. It was an exciting way to grow up."

Karen Gamble loved it when she was a child and found out about some of the church affairs before the rest of the congregation did. It made her feel special. She adds, "When your Dad preaches a good message people love it, and you feel very proud, and very fortunate."

If you ever watch *100 Huntley Street* and the "*100 Huntley Street* Singers" happen to be singing on that day, you'll see Chris Kirby. She is the pretty blonde girl with the big happy smile. Chris is now the assistant music coordinator for the program. She says: "Being a P.K., you become more outgoing because you're involved with other people from the time you're a baby."

Expanding on this thought, Tanya Marshall says: "If people like your mom and dad, they usually like you. I learned to speak to people on all levels of society through the constant entertaining and open houses.

I became articulate at an extremely young age. I became poised and sympathetic to people. I learned early to listen to the fine points of what was being said. Consequently, talking to people at any level really doesn't phase me now, and this ability has helped me tremendously in my work with the public."

Bob Wells outlined three advantages which he considered to be major benefits in being raised by a minister. "The first thing I would say is that the lack of material excess in our home actually turned out to be a benefit. What I thought to be a disadvantage then, has actually turned out in the reverse. The whole experience led to a strengthening of my character. It was a tremendous learning experience for me. We were forced into learning how to budget our money. The second thing I would say, is that I've made many friends in many places. I could go to practically any city in Ontario now, and I would know someone, and I would have a place where I would be welcome. And thirdly, there is so much potential if pastors and their families could come to grips with it at the right time in life. They could be the best families in the world."

Jean Windatt is a well-known and much loved person in her community. She says: "Ministers' children are very fortunate. I wouldn't have missed the experience for the world, and I feel that I am a better person for it. I feel that I have a fairly good understanding of people as a result. I have learned to take people as I find them, not just as other people describe them. I believe that this is a result of my upbringing."

Wendell Fisher says: "The kids I became good friends with in High School were a result of the environment in which I was raised. When you move into a new area, there is a great body of people waiting for you with open arms, who are ready and willing to help you get to know the new community. Not everyone who moves has hundreds of people ready to help him out. Having well educated parents is a real benefit. You are taught to be discreet in what you discuss outside the home. It has given me a good background from which to draw."

Elaine Mainse Stacey enjoyed her childhood. She says: "We had a lot of fun. We used to have the visiting singing groups home, and we met a lot of interesting people. We used to have a lot of people home for dinner.

All of the people in the congregation were so good to me. Every Christmas we got extra gifts from the people in the congregation. We had a lot of special attention in the church. Some of the people treated us like their own grandchildren."

Elaine wasn't the only P.K. who received a kindly dose of spoiling from the congregation. Many remembered little old ladies slipping them candy and nickels.

Paul Holbrough is seventeen-years-old, just at the age between childhood and maturity. He too, enjoyed all of the special attention and says: "You get to meet a lot of people you might not meet if your father was just an ordinary person. When I was a kid, I liked my dad being an important person in town. You get involved in the community. If your dad is active in the community, then it's going to rub off on you."

Sylvia Oldenziel's memories evoke the image of a very small girl sitting quietly in a pew: "Often I was at meetings where I was expected to be seen and not heard. I was expected to sit politely in a chair until someone offered me something. I feel that I developed a lot of character and patience through experiences like that."

According to Charles Vickerson: "Culturally, it gives you a great head start in university. I was able to understand William Blake and the whole area of Christian imagery. If you know your Bible and something about the history of Christianity, you have a great boost in the Liberal Arts program. University is a whiz, because so much of Western culture and the idea of philosophers and art are based on the church. It puts you in tune with the society in which we live. Lester Pearson, another P.K., was tremendously in tune with the psyche of the state. Ministers' children are often so in tune with what people want, that they can fit in anywhere. Alice Cooper is another P.K and – positive or negative – he sells records because he is in tune with society. These people are the movers and the shakers of society."

Long before the popular fascination with punk rock, Alice was strutting on stage in a defiant attempt to personify everything hated and feared by people in pulpits and pews. He appeared to be the incarnation of raw evil. Rebellious young people loved him. In tune with the rebellious element of society, he chose to be the high priest of defiance, feeding his followers with violence and sexual extravaganzas. One of his favorite tricks was to do a song from his album, "Killer," entitled "Dead Babies." Alice would walk on stage with a life-like doll; with a hatchet, he would chop it into pieces, and then gleefully throw the appendages into the audiences. Blood capsules, fastened to the doll's back, squirted what appeared to be blood, in every direction. Afterwards, Alice would stand on stage, holding the head of the doll like a decapitated enemy. With one final demonical thrust, he would impale the head on a microphone stand.

Another favorite audience grabber was his simulated suicide. Alice would climb on a gallows erected as part of the stage set. With the noose around his neck, he would wait for the platform to be tripped. As it suddenly opened beneath him, the lights would be cut; moments later, he would reappear in a top hat and white cape, apparently resurrected from the dead. This was generally followed by a partial striptease. On one occasion, the noose slipped for real and Alice almost hung himself. That wasn't the only accident. In New York city, a twelve-year-old boy, attempting to emulate Alice, tried the suicide stunt. Somehow it didn't turn out the way Alice did it, and the boy died, his neck broken by the noose.

What makes an Alice Cooper? Why would a boy raised not only in the church, but in the home of a minister, choose to be this type of a leader? According to Alice himself, "Rebellion is the basis for our group. Some of the kids who listen to us are really deranged, but they look up to us as heroes, because their parents hate us too much."[4]

By aggravating parents, Alice feeds the rebellious thirst of young people. In one sense, he has followed in the footsteps of his father; he, too, is the shepherd of a flock. He's just leading in a different direction.

Recently, Alice seems to be cleaning up his act and changing his image. Why? We can only speculate, but what about that verse in Proverbs that promises that if a child is trained up in the way of the Lord, when he is old he won't depart from it?

In sharp contrast to Alice Cooper, is Denny Duron. Although their chosen lifestyles differ markedly, Alice and Denny have certain similari-

---

[4] "Circus," February, 1972, p.61

ties in their backgrounds, the main one being that Denny's father, too, is a preacher. Denny, who played professional football for the Washington Redskins, was interviewed by Youth Profile magazine. In the interview, he emphasized the fact that his dad preached the Gospel on Sunday morning and then on Monday morning he lived it – a great key to a P.K. developing a strong relationship with God. Denny says: "I knew it was real, not only because the Book said so, but because my parents' lives said so." Denny feels his home life helped to prepare him for the problems of life as well as the good times. He has discovered his joy as a Christian is a "non-circumstantial" joy. "It is there," he says, "no matter what I face in my environment. I'm not victimized by the circumstances that prevail in my life."

SUMMARY

Continuing through the book, other benefits and disadvantages will be mentioned as well as these. But for now, here is a point form summary of those already brought forth.

It is interesting to see how many of the problems mentioned are given as benefits as well.

It is important to note that the number of items in each list is of no value in comparison, as one item in one list may far outweigh ten items in the other.

BENEFITS

1. being made aware of God
2. background of Scripture
3. opportunity to develop leadership abilities
4. opportunity to serve God
5. greater opportunity to work together as a family
6. greater opportunity to see God at work in divine intervention

7. pride in parents
8. exposure to many kinds of people
9. opportunity to become articulate and poised
10. appreciation of money and budgeting
11. many friends in many places
12. having a ready-made group of friends waiting for you wherever you move
13. advantages of being raised by well-educated, professional people
14. learning to be discreet
15. more attention from people than usual
16. involvement in the community
17. development of patience and character
18. wide cultural background to draw on
19. awareness of the mission fields and the larger world
20. being a part of making life better
21. opportunity to see a sermon in operation in life
22. opportunity to develop and practice personal skills in public
23. access to free housing

ISSUES

1. being put under more restrictions than usual
2. lack of material luxury
3. pressure to maintain an outward show of religion regardless of inner attitudes
4. pressure not to disgrace the preacher-father
5. feelings of isolation – no other P.K.s in the church group

6. feelings of not fitting in anywhere
7. inability to be accepted as an individual
8. frequent moving
9. ridicule
10. feelings of uneasiness and insecurity resulting from ridicule
11. being vulnerable and open to the criticism of many people
12. feelings of having to work hard at proving normalcy
13. pre-conceived ideas people have that P.K.s are angels
14. feelings of great importance in childhood and consequent realization that you have no individual importance apart from your father
15. pressure to fit into a mold of what a P.K. is expected to be
16. pressures to be examples to others
17. feelings of being constantly watched and judged
18. pressure to protect father's position
19. scheduling of time to permit family times together
20. feelings of inferiority, living in the shadow of a leader
21. hesitancy of peers to relax in a vicarage
22. the inability to be oneself
23. getting past father's theological ego
24. fear of not being accepted by parents if attitudes and beliefs differ from theirs
25. pressure to be just like parents
26. competition with congregation for father's attention and time.

The final problem dealing with the congregation is the focal point of the following chapter.

PART TWO – CHAPTER TWO

Congregations

THIS CHAPTER IS DIRECTED TO that great body of people loosely referred to as "the congregation." What an ominous sounding word! To many P.K.s, that word has a negative connotation.

Charles felt, "the congregation was like a tiger ready to pounce. It could hurt me. It inspired fear in me. Many times my dad seemed to be in fear that he couldn't do what he thought to be the right thing, because he thought the congregation might criticize him. What I saw from a very early age was a tremendous depersonalization of my father. He was afraid to speak out his true thoughts and feelings. One cannot be a whole person if he cannot be honest about his beliefs and feelings. He will become a non-person. I felt my father was belittled because he did not stand up to the tiger. I saw him as a weak person. Whenever I went out of the house, my mother would say, 'Now don't embarrass your father.' Disgrace before the congregation was the great issue."

To others, the congregation is a great support group, regarded with love and appreciation. For instance, in Karen's memory: "Congregations have really helped me. I can see the love of Jesus in them, and they give me a warm feeling. That makes me more able to reach out to God."

What a contrast between these two perceptions! True, it is evident in the first account that not all of the blame should have rested on the congregation. The parental approach and reaction to the situation was much less than healthy. However, it is very important for the members of any congregation to take a good look at themselves. Are they interfering more than necessary in the minister's private life? Are they hindering his relationship with his children? Are they contributing to the spiritual growth of the P.K.s? What could they do to help balance the scales?

Although fifty percent of the respondents were positive in their general attitudes toward congregations, twenty-five percent had mixed feelings toward them. The other twenty-five percent were decidedly negative in their response. Why? What is the dynamic that exists between a P.K. and the congregation? Most often, members and adherents of churches are not even aware that such a psychology exists. They simply carry on their merry little ways, totally oblivious of the effect they are having on someone else's life.

Most often, it is the lack of thoughtful action that has the greatest negative result, while just a tiny act of kindness or understanding can result in many years of warm memories for a P.K. What is that little preacher's kid with the big brown eyes really thinking when he hears you say, "Now Johnny, you sit up straight like the minister's son. He's not jumping all around, is he?" And what are you doing to his spiritual growth when he sees you acting pious in church and then hears you cursing when he happens to be playing at your house and you're having mechanical problems with your water pump. The minister has been out on church affairs for seven straight nights. Are you going to do anything to make sure that he has some time off to be with his family this week? Do you regard the time he spends home with his family as slack and lazy time; or as a necessity high on the list of priorities? Take a look at your attitudes. Are they healthy and understanding, or are they self-centred and uncaring?

There can be a strong element of sibling rivalry between a P.K. and members of the congregation. In a church, the minister is seen by some as a father figure. He is the person of authority in a situation not unlike that of an extended family. Ministers' children feel the backlash of these special relationships. It's a form of sibling rivalry.

When I was nineteen, a member of our congregation dropped in one day when I was at home and my parents were out. I remember acting very self-assured and feeling quite superior as I invited poor Helena in for coffee. As I remember her now, she was a well-meaning, humble person; wise in her plain ways, and a very conscientious Christian. But she happened to be a highly vocal and visible member of the church, with whom my parents spent a lot of time. They obviously approved of her behavior more than of mine and somehow I felt that she belonged more with them than I did. I resented her. I don't believe they had any inkling whatever of my feelings. Even I was unable to pinpoint, in my own mind, the reasons behind my resentment. Now I know I was simply jealous. As our conversation progressed, somehow we got on the subject of Hugh Hefner and my attitude toward Playboy magazine. Truthfully, I didn't care one way or the other about the magazine. I'd look at it occasionally if one happened to be available in someone's home, because it felt deliciously wicked and in those days it was exciting to feel wicked, but it was really of no importance to me. However, knowing Helena's attitude to be very conservative on such matters, I zeroed in on her with my 'hurt' button pushed. Christians were sensitive in the areas of decency, and here was a place I could take a shot at her, behind my imagined licence of popular opinion, cultural enlightenment, and artistic appreciation. In spite of the fact that the magazine was not overly important to me, I defended it wholeheartedly; attemping, in the exercise, to make poor Helena, God bless her, feel like an old-fashioned, unsophisticated fool. Helena represented the enemy. She was my competition for the attention of my parents. At the time, I didn't realize why I was acting as I was. I just felt compelled to act mean.

In the questionnaire, I asked, "Who comes first in importance with your parents; you or the congregation?" In tabulating the responses, I found that 58.4 percent felt they came first, while 20.8 percent felt the congregation came first. Another 20.8 percent felt they were equal with the congregation in importance to their parents.

Another question was, "Do you feel that congregations in general, have helped or hindered your relationship with your parents?" In response, 54.2 percent said that the congregations were a positive factor in their relationships, while 41.6 percent felt that the congregations had hindered the relationships; 4.2 percent had mixed feelings and said they felt the congregations had exerted both positive and negative influences.

It is interesting to look at the factors which determined those perceptions.

THE CONGREGATION AS A FACTOR IN THE RELATIONSHIP BETWEEN P.K.s AND THEIR PARENTS

"Congregations are always watching you. You grow up with the feeling that you're constantly being watched, and so you'd better be on good behavior. Many P.K.s rebel because of that. They don't want to be known as goodie-goodies. They want to be the same as their peers. Many go the opposite direction, just because of the pressures from the congregation."

The pressures to live exemplary lives were very real to most of the P.K.s. As with all other forms of pressure, release valves are necessary, or there will be problems.

"I believe that congregations really tended to mess up my relationship with my parents. My parents never wanted the congregations to spoil me, and that seemed to be a real concern. I sort of felt that my parents and the congregation were conspiring together against me. The congregation always put my parents on a pedestal, and my parents allowed that to happen. As a result, we were always separated from real people. We had to be exemplary as a family, and I was never to confront anyone with anything that made me really angry. You can probably hear even now some of the anger in my voice, because I believe in up-front, right-on relationships. But somehow, because I was the minister's kid, I couldn't get angry. I was always told I was welcome to say anything I wanted to say, in the home – but to save it until I got home. I really didn't realize until I was into my twenties, how very angry I really was at a very deep level, as a result of all of the suppression and expectations."

According to my research, it was in small town situations that the P.K.s felt the eye of scrutiny most strongly. One boy said he couldn't even relax at a hockey game without wondering who, from the congregation, was there watching him. It wasn't so much that he wanted to misbehave, as that he just wanted to feel unwatched. Resentment of the father's position can lead to resentment of the father himself. Where this is a problem, an effort should be made to get away from the familiar surroundings for times of pure relaxation. Everything possible should be done to provide a release valve for building pressures.

If parents dedicate their lives to God and build their whole lifestyle around His principles, that is the pattern their children will follow for the first few years of their lives. But as they get older and begin to notice things and weigh their observations in their own minds, they become more independent in their own choices and decisions. If parents extoll the virtues of the Christian life – and then the children see so-called Christians acting worse than some heathens – then, in the child's mind, the credibility of the parents can be diminished. In actual fact, the congregation should be expected to be the examples for the P.K.s, but it doesn't always work out that way!

Time is an important factor in any relationship. If you spend little time with your wife, there is a good possibility that your relationship with her will deteriorate. The same is true with children. A healthy relationship has to be nourished with time, attention and togetherness. Mrs. Walter E. Hobkirk, a minister's wife from Newark, N.J., was very concerned about the whole issue of pastoral relationships. She conducted a survey of 78 ministers' wives, in eight denominations, and discovered that 80 percent reported that their husbands found no regular time to spend with their families.

Why? Consider the demands of the congregation. They interrupt the pastor's dinner hour, calling to get other members' phone numbers; they expect him to attend church functions six nights a week and on and on ad infinitum. They expect all these things, with no thought of being supportive of their pastor in the preservation of his home life.

On the other hand, there are times when the unthinking pressures of the congregation can be a factor in the solidarity of the minister's family.

"It bothered me that dad was taken advantage of so much by the congregation. I used to get very annoyed at the people who took advantage of my dad spiritually, mentally, and emotionally. It really irritated me to see this happening. I loved my parents, but I didn't feel as good about them as I might have otherwise. The outside influences may, however, have drawn us closer within the family."

Although criticism is generally regarded as a destructive force, it was cited as a possible unifying factor in ministers' families.

"I grew closer to my parents when the congregation criticized me. I usually confided to my mom and dad about it, saying 'Do you know what they said about me?' That made us feel like a closed unit, supportive of each other."

One P.K. said he would drive miles to support his dad's church and carry the load as much as he could. But he touched on some unusual aspects of ministers' families relationships within the congregation.

"Preachers seldom can get close to people in the congregation. They always have to guard against the formation of cliques, and hurt feelings. There is more solidarity in the family because everyone in the family knows everyone in the church, and therefore there is always something to discuss."

In my own family, my parents were always very conscious of not spending too much time with any one family, socially. They were concerned about not becoming a part of any clique, or showing preferences for particular people, because they were aware of how easily others can feel hurt and left out.

What often happens in these circumstances, is that the family becomes a clique unto itself. It is a small, exclusive group of people, more greatly unified by their social isolation from others.

On a more positive note, another unifying factor exerted by congregations was summed up well by Elaine Mainse Stacey.

"The congregations really liked my parents, and consequently, it made me like and respect them more. If the congregation had disliked my parents, I would have probably thought that they were doing something wrong. The congregation's appreciation of my parents made me appreciate them more."

Children react to reactions. They are watching, watching, all the time. Often, P.K.s are more in tune with the true attitudes of the congregation toward their parents, than the parents are themselves. As people are talking among themselves, sometimes they fail to notice the little ears around the corner. Children are quick to pick up on voice intonations and facial expressions. Often, people will attempt to hide their real feelings from a minister because they try to impress him, just as some ministers are trying to impress them. However, children are often sensitive to the realities below the surface. Generally, they are influenced by these reactions. Jean Windatt has warm memories of the love of the congregation.

"I saw sincere people in the congregation, and their respect for my dad increased my respect for him. I was very proud to have so many people in our home, and I loved to pass out the goodies in the meetings! Whenever we left a church, there were always gifts for me too, and I was always taken up on the platform with my parents. I never felt left out."

What beautiful memories for a child to carry through life. This same feeling of warmth and love is echoed by Chris Kirby.

"Many people in the congregation were good friends with my parents, and the fellowship with them just sort of helped to build the relationship all around."

A congregation is built on individuals. Each person is an important part of the whole. Sometimes, a few people seem to set the tone for the entire congregation, whether it be warm and loving, or cold and impersonal. How very important it is for the warmth to be encouraged and nurtured, so that the love of Jesus can shine through. Just as a congregation can influence the relationship between a P.K. and his parents, it can have a profound effect on his spiritual growth.

THE CONGREGATION AS AN INFLUENCE ON THE SPIRITUAL GROWTH OF A P.K.

In the questionnaire, I asked, "Do you feel that congregations have helped or hindered your relationship with God?"

In response, 45.8 percent felt that congregations had been a positive factor in their relationships with God; while 50 percent felt they had hindered their spiritual development. 4.2 percent indicated that they had both helped and hindered.

A young married woman says, "Being involved with people who worshipped God put me into situations where I worshipped Him and prayed more to Him, too. Through all of the group times of prayer, my relationship with God grew."

There is tremendous value in nurturing each other in the faith. In the book of Hebrews, we are admonished to "Be concerned for each other, to stir a response in love and good works. Do not stay away from the meetings of the community, as some do, but encourage each other to go; the more so as you see the Day drawing near."[5]

The main function of a congregation is to encourage one another spiritually, as they wait for the return of Jesus. The Holy Spirit teaches each one individually, as each one opens himself to teaching. This knowledge is to be shared with the body of believers. According to Brenda Miles, the others in the congregation help you to understand the Bible. She says that everyone works together helping everyone else to understand. That is the way it should be. According to Diane Osborne, if you have strong people in the congregation, you develop more, because they help you.

To me, Dave Lawrenson's experience with a congregation was absolutely beautiful, and exemplifies the purity of faith that should distinguish a body of believers. Dave is the son of a Baptist minister who started the Gospel Light Mission in Toronto. He went through a difficult period of rebellion and was in jail more than he was out, in his teens and early twenties. The first time he went to jail, his dad faced his Deacon's Board and told them that he felt that he should resign as Pastor of the church because of his son's actions. "Oh no," they said. "We know God is working something out. We know He is doing something in that boy's life. We won't accept your resignation."

And so, his mom and dad held on, and that congregation held on and prayed for him. At the same time, the congregation where his sister was attending church also prayed and prayed for him. All this prayer and belief in God's power to change people was happening when things were looking the blackest. Dave had the worst record of any man who had ever been in the Guelph Reformatory at that time. But God works in mysterious ways. Because Dave did so much ripping and tearing, he was in detention most of the time. In detention, the only book allowed is the Bible. He read it six times, from cover to cover, while serving detentions in jail.

---

[5] Hebrews 10:24, 25 The Jerusalem Bible

Now Dave is a happily married man with two children and his own business. In his free time, he travels around playing the guitar and singing songs for Jesus. He is a deacon in a Baptist church and has experienced the life changing baptism in the Holy Spirit. He attributes his astonishing conversion to the prayers and support of God's people. When they could have condemned him and given up on him as a hopeless case, they loved him and believed God for his salvation.

Prayer changes things. Brian Ruud, the now-famous evangelist wrote this letter to his mom and preacher-dad from prison:

"Dear Mom and Dad:

First of all, please sit down, because you won't be able to take my news standing up.

I asked for a Bible while I was in the Hole and praise the Lord, Jesus came to me.

God is closer to me than the ground. He is in my heart for keeps, and you'd better believe it. Hallelujah! I've read all the Gospels, and they're beautiful. I've learned all the names of the books of the Bible by heart and memorized a lot of verses. I don't know which verses to memorize, so when you write, send me some suggestions.

Dad, I didn't know life could be so great, even in jail. God has given me a dream of praying for a great multitude, and I know it will come true. Oh, Dad, I could say so much more, but I'm not allowed to write on the back of this piece of paper.

I'm leaving the charges against me up to God, even if I get thirty years, I'll serve God in jail. All I can say is, someday you and I are going to walk those golden streets together hand in hand with the Lord. You were right all along. Pray for me, and then you'll know what I'm writing is true.

Lots of love, Your son,

Brian.

P. S. They're calling me "Reverend" in here. Write soon, Dad and let everybody read this letter. I want everybody to know. Hallelujah! Please send me a new Bible."[6]

---
[6] *Son of a Preacher Man* by Brian Ruud with Walter Wagner, Brian Ruud International, 1972, p. 141.

That letter was written by a person who had been deep in crime, a person who had appeared to be a lost cause. But his parents hung on to him in prayer, and the congregation supported them.

Too often, however, congregations are composed of individuals who are too concerned with themselves and their own problems, to have anything left over to give. They are the ones who congregate together on Sunday, but leave nothing of themselves behind for the nourishment of others. Over and over in discussing the congregations, the P.K.s brought up the lack of real Christian understanding in the churches. The reality is that many people are at church looking for something and, until they find it, they have nothing to give to other people.

Sylvia Oldenziel says, "I feel that there are many sincere people in the church. Many of them are perhaps a little misguided about their reasons for being there. They are looking for something, and even though they perhaps haven't found it yet, deep down they know that that is where the answers are. Others go out of sheer habit."

Tanya Marshall says, "In some senses they hindered my relationship with the Lord, because God didn't seem to be particularly real to them. There really weren't many exciting things happening in the church, and I guess I always wondered how much farther than just church their Christianity extended. I think that if I had seen some dynamic, courageous Christians, it would have helped me tremendously to relate to God. I didn't feel that I related to God in the fellowship of the congregation at all. I always felt that it was a lone wolf sort of thing."

Tanya is now a dynamic Christian girl herself, and she longs for the people of the churches to enter into an exciting, living relationship with Jesus. David Harris claims he went to church for eighteen years, and was raised in a minister's home, but never once heard the Gospel. He said most of the people in the congregation didn't know the Lord. After he left his dad's church and found a church where the Gospel was preached, he became saved and associated with people who truly knew the Lord. They helped him tremendously in his spiritual growth.

There is a missing element in many churches which cripples the people as effective witnesses. Bob Wells puts it this way:

Printed with personal permission from Brian Ruud.

"A lot of people in congregations are pretty stagnant Christians. They know the Lord as Saviour. Period. They leave it there."

At this point, many Christians get so involved in the organization of the church that they fail to grow spiritually. They get their eyes on the groups and their duties rather than keeping them on Jesus.

A school principal who has not yet returned to the Lord says: "The social structure turned me off. I tend to shy away from organized groupings. I guess I was over-systematized as a child. I have rebelled against that. I didn't want to be a gregarious person 24 hours of the day. I wanted time to be by myself, and that is partly why I went away from the church. In a lot of groups, you have to put on a bit of a phony front in order to belong. I just want to be myself. There doesn't seem to be any spontaneity in the church. You could always predict what the people would wear and where they were going to sit. A congregation does not allow you to express yourself in any way in a service."

The word "hypocrite" was mentioned over and over again by the P.K.s. But without the help of the Holy Spirit dwelling within, how could a churchgoer be expected to appear to be anything more than a hypocrite? Humans are naturally sinful people. The only way to change that is through a supernatural intervention – namely a spiritual rebirth.

A great problem according to one respondent is that, "You look at people who are hypocrites who are supposed to be the church, and it can't help but raise a lot of questions. You can see people, but you can't see God."

Another girl who prefers to remain anonymous, says: "When I got out into the world, what really surprised me was that a lot of the people were more loving and kinder than the people were in the churches. If you don't have a personal relationship with Jesus, then you don't know what love really is."

This girl contends that while she was growing up in the church she never saw the reality of Jesus as attributed to Him, and that she was never given any instruction, or opportunity to observe, the born-again experience. She never even knew what a born-again Christian was!

In my own experience as a teenager in the church, I felt uncomfortable with many of the people in the church, probably because they were uncomfortable with themselves. They knew how they were supposed to act, and they tried to act that way, but it came off as unnatural, stiff, and contrived. Many of them simply had not yet experienced the release of the Holy Spirit. Until people are at peace with themselves spiritually, they cannot contribute positively in a leadership capacity, to the spiritual growth of others.

There are real complexities involved here for the churchgoer who has not experienced this release. According to Charles Vickerson, a P.K. who is now a minister himself,

"A lot of people in the congregation are in fear because they don't know the real meaning of Christianity. They cannot be honest and are living a lie. They are afraid that the minister won't accept them if they are honest about their drinking, depression, affairs, et cetera."

Unfortunately, without being honest with the minister about their problems, it is difficult for people to receive help with specific problems. Pride is one of the greatest, if not the greatest, barriers to spiritual release. Before it is loosed, it seems so important to maintain it; after it is loosed it is seen as being truly worthless. It is impossible to relax until one lets go of pride.

I asked the respondents what advice they would have to give to congregations in regard to their treatment of P.K.s. There was a lot of repetition in the replies, but it is important.

P.K.s' ADVICE TO CONGREGATIONS:

Joan says:

"Look into what it means to be a born-again Christian. Start to search and search and search. Think more about your personal relationship with God, and not about what the person next to you is thinking."

From a person who went through some negative experiences in his attitudes towards congregations, but who has emerged with a deeper understanding, comes this advice:

"Be the body of Christ, and accept that each part of the body is a little different. Don't be critical. Take the approach that Jesus would take. Be caring. Emphasize the personal Jesus and show that there are no standards in the Christian church apart from the standards of Jesus."

Tanya Marshall is explicit in echoing the desires of other P.K.s to be treated as individuals. She says:

"Don't take anything for granted. Treat us as individuals, not as "part of the package." You didn't hire us. You called and hired a minister. We come along, but not as part of the package. We are just children. You should be more concerned with giving spiritual benefit to us than with asking it of us. Get with it. Recognize your own responsibility. Don't lay everything on your minister. Please – be a friend to him. Remember that he and his family are people. Treat them as such. Be concerned about them. Be concerned about who is the preacher's pastor. We all have a responsibility to each other, and don't you ever think it's not lonely up there. If you put your minister on a pedestal, and he allows you to do that, you're in trouble. Don't criticize him. Pray. Pray for your minister's family. Pray for his kids, and if you have something negative to say, just keep your tongue still if it's not in prayer."

Jennifer Holmes believes the individual members of congregations should follow the example set by Christ. They should question the doctrines and dogma advocated by their own denominations and ask themselves whether they are merely following the dictates of their particular denominations, or whether they really are being spiritually fed by their church.

Chris Kirby feels that it is tremendously important for congregations to encourage the P.K.s, and pray with them the same as they do with any other child in the congregation. P.K.s need to know that the congregation is standing with them, and is supporting them.

Karen Gamble says: "Love the kids. Look at them through the Lord's eyes, and overlook some of the silly things they do. Love them and accept them the way they are, instead of saying, 'You're a P.K. and you shouldn't act that way.' Don't expect them to be an example to anyone."

According to Paul Timpany, the first thing congregations should do, is acknowledge the fact that P.K.s are just the same as any other kids. The second thing is to realize that they need to be ministered to, just as much as any other child. P.K.s are just learning too, and they don't have all the answers.

Here again the respondents were repetitive in stressing the importance of time. They request that the congregations be more considerate of the minister's time, particularly at mealtime. While it is true that irregular hours must be accepted as part of the minister's position, yet most felt that there was much needless interruption of his home life.

The need for honesty in congregational relationships is an important issue. Sylvia says: "When the minister visits, most people put on a front, and they don't need to do that."

In supporting the need for P.K.s to be treated just like everyone else, Laurie Brady adds, "Realize that P.K.s don't usually have as much time with their parents as most kids do. Although they may appear to have more potential for exposure to the Scriptures, just the opposite may be true because of the great amount of time their parents spend outside the home."

David Harris sums up the essence of what the P.K.s want to convey to congregations. He says: "Most congregations are either 70 percent sincere, or 70 percent hypocritical. They should treat the kids like anybody else, not as though they're different. As soon as you're recognized as a P.K., it causes problems. Even if people don't expect special things of them, P.K.s still feel they do. You think they expect you never to do anything wrong. When people get to know preachers, they find out they're not perfect, and it's the same with P.K.s. Just ignore the fact that they're P.K.s."

Sometimes P.K.s feel that their individuality is lost because it is assumed they are a part of their dad and therefore should hold his views. Any departure from the minister's opinions is regarded as wayward in the child, and sticks out like a sore thumb in the community. P.K.s are real people. They are originals, not clones.

PART TWO – CHAPTER THREE

Developing a Self-Concept Beside the Pulpit

JESUS SAID, "LOVE YOUR NEIGHBOR as you love yourself."[7]

In order to have a healthy, overflowing love for other people, it is important to love ourselves. This necessary self-love is not an egotistical sort of vanity, but rather a respect for oneself and an acceptance of God's love for us. God created us for His glory, and He wants to express His love through us. In order to do this, we need a good self-concept. We need to be aware of our flaws, and yet love ourselves much as a wise parent loves his child – with understanding, with tolerance, with appreciation for our strengths, and with a goal to see the weaknesses corrected.

If the self-concept is faulty, it will make a big difference in the person's self-confidence, in his treatment of others, in his ability to love others, in his reactions to life situations, and in his methods of coping with life. The concept of self begins and grows in the same way any concept does – through experience. People try themselves out, hear what other say about them, see themselves in mirrors and contemplate how other people react to them. They compare themselves with others, note their successes and failures, and consider their similarities and differences in experiences and activities. Unfortunately, the conclusions we reach as a result of our observations may be inexact, very limited, or even full of error. Ideally, a person should have a clear and accurate picture of himself. However, the picture will be unavoidably out of focus if the responses to himself which he observes, are distorted, unfair or unrealistic.

Thus it is that P.K.s often have trouble feeling comfortable about

---
[7] Matthew 19:19, The Bible, G.N.V..

themselves. The input they observe is different from that which they see in other people. They often don't know quite what to make of themselves, because their cues for responses differ from those of their peers. They often have no one to emulate in their responses because they are generally isolated from other P.K.s. As a result, many P.K.s expend a tremendous amount of energy in trying to prove themselves normal, often just as much to themselves as to other people.

It was interesting to note in my research that 84.5 percent felt that people in general reacted positively to their dads' professions, and another 84.5 percent felt well liked by their peers. However, there did not appear to be much connection between the two. Some who felt people reacted negatively to their dads' occupations felt that they themselves were well liked by their peers, and vice versa.

The high incidence of perceived peer approval, however, was found in maturity. Generally, it followed a difficult time of unusually high expectations from other people. Many P.K.s actually met the expectations later in life. They became high achievers. Along with occupational and personality success, they most often found peer approval. In expending great effort to be accepted by people, they often developed conscientiousness in their drives to succeed in other areas of their lives. During the developmental years, the high expectations placed on them were perceived in almost every case as a disadvantage, and a very real problem. However, in maturity, it appeared to be a strengthening factor. Let's take a look at how the respondents felt.

GREAT EXPECTATIONS

Many people looking at a new-born baby of a minister assume this child will be perfect. He or she will be raised in a perfect home on perfect principles, and will be the perfect example for other children. However that tiny, soft little pink or blue bundle has as much potential for sin in him as the most depraved, trigger-happy murderer in the world. Just because a minister is walking closely with the Lord, doesn't mean that his offspring has any magic sky hook into Heaven. Unless a child has Christ living in him, and has given his life over to the Lord, it is impossible for him to act in accordance with the standards set.

Paul said, "It is not I who live, but Christ who lives in me."[8] In spite of this, many people expect P.K.s to meet standards of righteousness through their own efforts. This is a total impossibility because of their naturally sinful natures. The expectations are unfair. The P.K.s need loving nurturing and guidance in God's ways from their parents and the members of the congregation. They need to have examples rather than to be examples. After all, the members have chosen to be a part of the church by their own free wills; while the P.K.s have not chosen, but are there by design.

In Tanya's home, "There was a great emphasis on the appearance of things. What would people think? How would it look, etc. I do feel, however, that as Christians, we should be examples to others."

As Christians, yes, we are Christ's ambassadors here on earth; we are the representatives of His Kingdom. But could we expect a Chinese child to represent Russia as an example of a Russian just because he happened to be living with a Russian family? Only a native born Russian can be expected to be a true example of a Russian; only a born-again person can be expected to be a true example of a Christian.

Wendell's behavior in his day to day activities was expected to be an example to others. He wanted to live his own life and did not feel comfortable about the pedestal on which people put him.

Jennifer Holmes knew from her earliest memories she was expected to behave differently from other children.

Chris Kirby experienced the same type of pressure: "Sometimes it bugged me. There were things that I just didn't want to do, and I didn't care if I was supposed to be an example or not. When I was younger, I just had to give in and do it, but I guess it didn't really hurt me."

Now, however, Chris says she will not allow herself to be pushed into a mold. She does things because she feels that she wants to, and not solely as an example for someone else.

There is often more at stake for a P.K. than his own comfort in this realm of pressure to be an example. He may feel that he is responsible, in some measure, for his dad's success or failure in the ministry.

---

[8] Galatians 2:20

Laurie says his dad was always very concerned about the impression they might give as a family, and feels that, "He was always more sensitive about that than he should have been. He was always concerned about hurting someone's feelings or giving the wrong impression. I really led a double life. I was one person at school, and another person at church."

Bob, too, felt the pressure to maintain family standards for the benefit of the pastor-watchers: "You always feel you'll be an embarrassment to your dad if you do something wrong – not that Christ wouldn't want you to do it, but that you'll be an embarrassment."

Charles, on the other hand, not only felt pressure to be an example to others, but also a conviction that his dad's job almost rested on his behavior: "I constantly was made to feel guilty about my actions, and fearful of the watching eyes of the congregation. I had an image of the congregation as a great huge tiger ready to pounce and do me harm. Now I still find it difficult to accept criticism."

Karen Gamble, "...knew that the other kids watched us. Our parents never put it into words that we were to be examples; it was just generally accepted. Now I find myself watching our pastor's daughter in the same way that people used to watch me, and I kick myself when I do it. Nothing made me more angry than hearing someone say, 'Well, Karen does it, so I can do it too.' The core reason why P.K.s rebel is that they have too tough a standard to live up to. They have to try so hard to prove to everyone that they are just ordinary people. Often they end up going way overboard the other way."

Jean Windatt's experience bears out this observation: "I resented having to be an example in my teenage years. One time, in rebellion, I went and rang the church bell for a few nights. It was just my way of causing excitement and attention. No one would ever have guessed that it was the minister's daughter. I didn't want to have to live up to being the perfect minister's daughter. I used to go out with one boy at seven and then out the back door with another one at nine! I was always trying to prove I was normal. In that effort, I really went overboard and did strange things."

A young mother who prefers to remain anonymous, and who has not yet come into a personal relationship with the Lord, feels that the constant pressure to be an example is one of the greatest problems of a P.K. She says that if ministers' kids get off track, that is often the reason for it, because they end up trying so hard not to be an example in order to get along with their peers.

Sometimes the kids strain so hard against the pressures to conform that their parents finally realize that it is useless to expect them to be a positive example. When this happened in Tim's family, he says: "They really didn't expect me to be an example, but they were pretty disappointed when I would come home drunk, and collapse in the hallway."

Rebellion. The wildest kids in town. As I tallied up the responses, I discovered that 66.6 percent claimed to have gone through, or were presently expressing, rebellion. Why? Truly, the pressure to be examples was cited as a major factor, but there are other factors at work as well which appear to be common characteristics of ministers' children.

WHY P.K.s REBEL

According to Tim Stafford in his article, "Reflections of a Preacher's Kid,"[9] preachers' kids can't win. "If we are good, it is not a virtue. Whatever we do right, we have been trained or forced to do; whatever we believe, we were taught to believe. I remember trying to convince an incredulous friend that I went to church because I liked to, not because my father would beat me if I didn't. The only way to get any credit for individuality, in fact, is to be bad, and even that is tainted. Everybody knows that preachers' kids don't have to work at sin. They come by it naturally. A child raised in a pastor's home is likely to know the gospel and to be aware of his need for a Saviour. He rarely needs to have the lesson banged home. However, since nearly every teenage kid would do anything to avoid being an exact replica of his parents, pressuring him may make the decision much more difficult for him: to say no is the only way he can prove that he is an individual."

Tim Stafford did not go through an overt period of rebellion against his dad's beliefs and lifestyle, but he was given a spiritual freedom to make

---

[9] "Reflections of a Preacher's Kid," by Tim Stafford, *Leadership Journal,* Winter 1980, Vol.1, No.1, published by *Christianity Today.*

God his God and to find his own relationship with Him. He claims never to have been expected to be any better than anyone else's kids, and never to have been threatened with what the neighbors would think.

Elaine Mainse Stacey did not go through a period of rebellion either. She feels that often ministers and their wives get so involved with the church that they don't have time or energy for their children. She says her parents always made up the time with their children, playing football, shopping with them and so on.

Denny Duron, when interviewed for Youth Profile[10] magazine, also denied having to endure a period of rebellion. He confesses short periods of resentment, but says, "Those were the times I was out of touch. It was just a matter of my relationship with the Lord not being right."

His parents always seemed to have a way of putting his rebellion into proper perspective: "They let me know that the rebellion was a spiritual problem, not a social problem, or a family problem. When I began to see it as a spiritual problem, I began to see it as my responsibility to God to make it right. My parents and I are just the best of friends, because we have our own relationship with the Lord, and those relationships are our own responsibility. When they're right, they just naturally draw us together."

Unfortunately, not all of the stories are as positive. Jean was a pampered, special child when she was a little girl; the darling of the church, held high on a pedestal. As she grew older, however, she felt the attention waning. In her struggle to maintain the attention to which she had become accustomed, she rebelled and became a troublemaker. She discovered that good behavior was simply expected of her, and that it brought her no attention. Only by misbehaving was she able to stand out in the crowd. How important it is to show appreciation for positive behavior, and not just to take the good things for granted.

Ministers' children generally receive a tremendous amount of attention when they are young. They are made to feel that they are very important people. As they get older, people pay less and less attention to them and they begin to realize that they have no importance apart from their fathers. This is very difficult to accept for many P.K.s. They have become

---

[10] *Youth Profile Magazine*, Vol. 5, No.3, July-August, 1978.

accustomed to the limelight and they feel frustrated and insecure without it. There is often a sense of having to fight to get the attention back. It is as though they are drowning in a sea of unimportance and they have to constantly struggle to keep their heads above water where they can breathe in the life-supporting feeling of self-worth.

That is one reason why P.K.s are often high achievers – whether positively or negatively. They are fighting to regain the recognition which was once so freely given to them.

At school, Laurie found himself trying to out-swear, out-drink, and generally out-do everybody else. He says: "I was immature, and it was my way of compensating for all of the kidding I got for being the son of a minister. I felt that there was more social acceptance if I could show that I was as tough as they were. I see now that I overdid this, but that was all part of the immaturity. This stage lasted for five or six years, from about age twelve to seventeen. When I was seventeen, I quit school, left home, and played professional baseball for a year. That smartened me up fast, and I discovered that the world is not a bed of roses. Being on my own was different than I had anticipated. I used to say, 'Boy, if I ever get away from home, I'll never go near another church.' In actual fact that was one of the first places I headed. I guess the scriptural seeds that had been planted began to work in. Through all of my time of rebellion, I always at least believed that there was a God."

In the process of trying very hard to prove to everyone that they are normal, P.K.s often go too far and end up worse than everybody else. Instead of being accepted by their peers, they end up being rejected as rebels.

B.J. is twenty-one-years-old. This is the story of his rebellion: "While I was growing up, I was forced to go to church every Sunday. When I was seventeen, I just stopped going, and never went back into a church again until I was saved when I was nineteen. As a teenager growing up, if I didn't sing a hymn in church, I was punished. To me, that seemed really stupid, because I didn't mean the words. To force me to sing something that I didn't mean seemed hypocritical to me. I really resented that. When I was about sixteen, I started to go out and get drunk instead of going to school. The first time I got drunk, I got alcohol poisoning and ended up in the hospital. My parents were pretty surprised. I wanted to be accepted by people and I wanted happiness. I didn't have either of those, so I thought I'd try doing what everybody said was cool. When I was seventeen, I started smoking marijuana. By the time I was eighteen, I was in college and I tried dealing. However, I only got through a couple of pounds, and I got so scared and paranoid that I was looking for cops behind every rock and tree. Through all of my time of rebellion, however, I still respected Christ and the truth that He stood for. I never actually lost belief in God. I believed that He was there all the time. What I really lost faith in was religion – in the organization of Christianity. It was the organization that put me off; not God Himself. When you see the human aspects, you see imperfections and that is all I was looking at. My dad and I had a very bad relationship. I had a lot of bitterness inside. Naturally, I would have liked to have had a good relationship with my dad, but it was like there were two forces within me battling. I guess I always knew that my folks loved me, but when my views differed from theirs, I didn't feel that they respected me, and I wanted to be respected. My dad disagreed with my lifestyle, and he tried to straighten me out with his reasoning which I already understood. But I just really didn't care about religion. Facts and figures he presented to me really didn't scare me."

B.J.'s story has a beautiful ending, but I'll tell you about that a little later on. It is interesting to notice the parallels between B.J. and Laurie. Despite all outward appearances, neither of them ever actually lost their faith in God. This was a common reality in the majority of the rebellions.

Another commonality was the desire to be respected as a thinking individual, particularly when views and beliefs differed from those of the parents.

Tanya Marshall was not alone in feeling that if her views differed from the desired patterns, then she herself, and not just her views, was rejected. She remembers: "I really had to stand on my own two feet as a P.K. and as a Christian. Either I had to completely rebel against the P.K. thing or I had to explain the Christian thing somehow. I often felt that I was called upon to be sort of brave and pioneering at school. When I got away from home, I became very dissatisfied with what I saw of the ordinary church. Looking back now, I never remember my father saying that I was a beautiful child, or unusual in any way. In retrospect, I was very unusual in several ways, not the least of these being the situation I was in. I always felt that he just took it for granted that I was intelligent and a good kid, and that I would never hurt them. I was always assured that they would love me no matter what. But when the real crunch came and I got into one of the no-matter-what situations, my father was extremely angry with me. He does not accept failure in terms of sin, nor failure in terms of his expectations. But that is because he does not accept it of himself, at all. I wanted to be loved. I had received a great deal of love from my mother who was a very warm person. But I got out into a world where there was none of this warm overt loving of me. I really wished that I had had brothers so that I could have gotten used to men. To tell you the truth, I thought Christian men were pretty gutless, at least the ones in the church that I had been exposed to. I think that had a lot to do with the rebellion. I just figured I'd go my own way, and too bad if my parents couldn't handle it. Let's see if they really did love me no matter what. I didn't care two hoots about the church. When I left the church, I was so hurt by the kind of gossip that went on during my rebellion. I was just devastated by the way the church people started rumors. I really heavily blame the church for my rebellion."

The dictionary defines "rebellion" as, "a defiance of, or opposition to any control." This defiance can take many forms. In Dave Lawrenson's experience, it led him deeply into crime, and resulted in many years of detention in reformatories and penitentiaries.

When Dave was a child, he was well grounded in the Word of God, but he says: "Somewhere along the line, Satan beguiled me. He was subtle, and he drew me away from the simplicity that was in Jesus. I began to make it complicated for myself and thereby began to complicate my life. The Word of God is not complicated. I really began to get into trouble when I was seven or eight-years-old. The reason was that my mom and dad were so involved in church work that they had no time for me. I was the type of kid who really needed a lot of attention. I was a real outgoing, active little guy. We were poor, and my dad was working at two jobs and pastoring a church at the same time. He has since said that the fact that he never had time for me was the greatest cause of all of the problems that I have had. However, I believe that no matter what, if a child is exposed to the Word of God as he grows up, it will always stand him in good stead. When I was 15, I left home. I had had enough. I was fed up, and I figured that my old man knew about as close to nothing as anyone could. This guy was square. We couldn't skate on Sunday; we couldn't sing anything but gospel music on Sunday. It wasn't long before I landed in the Guelph Reformatory. Even in there I was rebellious, and spent months in detention scrubbing stone floors. I just rebelled against everything that was said and done. Satan just had such a hold on my life. I was determined that I was going to prove my dad wrong. I was going to prove to that religious fanatic that Christianity was not the only way. There were lots of ways a guy could get what he wanted out of life. I got to the point where I didn't mind doing time. I figured that it wasn't all that bad. These days, there's nothing you can't get in jail. When I was in jail, I had more money from gambling than I usually had on the outside. I had all kinds of booze and drugs. Anything I wanted was there. I got to the point where I thought there was no way I was going to straighten out, and I thought I might as well just carry on and have a good time. Once in a courtroom, the judge said to my mother, 'Forget him. Give it up. This boy will be in and out of jail for the rest of his life.' At that time, I had just come down off a wave of crime that resulted in over fifty charges, ranging from break and enter, to car theft and armed robbery. My mother just stood there and looked at the judge, and said, 'I'm going to tell you something, mister. That boy is going to be preaching the Gospel someday. I'm not going to give up. I won't accept this. I don't have to. The Word of God says that I have authority over what my children do, and where they go; and I accept that authority. That boy will learn to serve and praise God, and I'm going to live to see it!' Now she just thrills to see me get up to worship and praise the Lord. In my case, it took 28 years, seven of those in prison, and involvement in drugs and crime and booze, but the Word of God held true. 'Train up a child in the way he should go, and when he is old, he won't depart from it.'[11] My dad often said that every single word in the Bible works, if you apply it. My parents made a lot of mistakes with me, and they realize that. When I was a little boy, I don't ever remember sitting on my dad's lap. They were always too busy for me. But they hung on to God for me when they realized what had happened, and that brought me through."

[11] Proverbs 22:6

When James A. Johnston, who was for many years the Warden of Alcatraz Prison, was asked to comment on the crime rate in the United States, he said: "The crime problem is the boy problem, and the finest prisons in the world are only monuments to neglected youth."

Dave's rebellion was externalized. It was abundantly obvious to all observers that Dave was defiant, and not about to accept the Christian principles for living. With some other people, the bitterness is just as acute, but is expressed internally, rather than out in the open. So it was with Janice Crump Remple.

"My rebellion was a very personal, internal rebellion, because I was very conscious of my dad's role, and I did not want him to be hurt because of my behavior. My sister's rebellion was much more open and honest. I was always very concerned about how things would reflect on my dad. My rebellion started in my early teens, and lasted all through my teens, but it was so much inside of me. I didn't go around breaking all the rules or anything, but I had a lot of frustrations and anger inside. I was married when I was 19, and that could have been a rebellion in itself, but I don't think so. Probably the major cause of my rebellion was my own insecurity. At one time when my dad was especially busy getting a particular program started, I went through a particularly difficult time. I was 11 or 12-years-old. I really felt left out and unimportant through that whole thing. I was sort of around, and I existed, but my parents were far too busy to notice what I was doing. I just sort of ran wild and did whatever I wanted. I spent a lot of time with a girlfriend who lived nearby. We practically lived in her room. She was having problems too. Her parents were involved in the project as well. The two of us really rebelled and did all sorts of dumb things. I found it really hard to accept that my parents were so busy that they cared about all of these people ahead of me. That continued until I was old enough to become involved in the project myself, and could see the value of it as a ministry. But all that time, I resented very much being given joe jobs to do. These things were things that no one else was going to do, so they gave them to the little kids. The resentment lasted until I felt that I was truly contributing."

Bob felt much the same way as Janice. He, too, wanted to protect his father and did not want to bring shame on his family. He says:

"I grew away from the Lord in adolescence because I didn't want to be pegged as a Pentecostal preacher's son. I wasn't allowed to go to shows or dances, and I felt that I was missing out on so much, so I thought that I'd take part. I tried to do most of my rebelling in a sneaky way, because I didn't want to bring shame on my parents. This continued until I was 17 in Grade 11, when I faced a crisis. I had a car, thanks to a part-time job, and my friends and I used to go across the river to the U.S. a lot to get liquor. At that time, the drinking age here was twenty-one but it was eighteen in the States. One time on the way home, the police caught me, and charged me. The hardest thing I've ever had to do in my life was to get a ride home, and sit down with my dad and explain what happened. We prayed together. I knew it was a shock to him, but I also knew that he was a young fellow once, and he took it in his stride. He didn't shame me. I think that that was the turning point in our relationship. From then on, I knew that he knew I was growing up. It was a turning point for me too. At that point, I started to feel like a man. I had to go to court after that, and dad went with me. Eventually, the charges were dropped. That was the first thing I had done on my own, under the shadow of no one. That was when I started to feel responsible for myself, and I rededicated my life to the Lord when I was 18."

A schoolteacher who has had enough time away from the church to be able to weigh things in a fairly balanced manner, has not yet returned to the ways of the Lord. But he is beginning to take stock of his situation, and is finding it wanting. He says:

"As I began to mature, I became critical of my dad, and became aware of others who were critical. That increased my insecurity and my uneasiness, because I always felt open to criticism. When I was about twelve, I began to get more critical of everything myself. As I have matured, some of my attitudes have had a reversal. There are some areas where my thinking has come more in line with my dad's. I think if you don't go through a stage in your development where you question everything, you will just end up being a follower all of your life. I did not openly rebel against my parents. I went to church regularly and was involved in quite a few church activities. It wasn't until I got my own apartment that I openly started going my own way. I wasn't openly rebellious, but I've always felt that my parents are disappointed that I haven't become involved in the church. At this point, I am beginning to have guilt feelings because I know that I benefitted from being raised in the church, and right now, my wife and I have a little two-year-old guy, who will not have the same benefits as I had, unless we change our ways pretty quick. I am finding that the things that used to attract me, that were no-nos in my home growing up, do not hold the same attraction for me that I once thought they would."

As a teenager, David Mainse, well-known host of the daily Christian T.V. talk-show, *100 Huntley Street,* went through a time of uncertainty before he truly dedicated his life to the Lord. In his book, *100 Huntley Street,* he tells about the changes that took place within him:

"At the same time that I was in the height of my rebellion, I was being forced to take stock of some pretty far-reaching alternatives. I had a part-time job at a service station, as a pump jockey and general handyman. The men who hung around that place used the foulest language I had ever heard; drinking and smoking, and maligning all women with filthy humour. I could not help but compare that lifestyle with my parents, and I knew I didn't want to come into adulthood and live that way. Yet, on the other hand, I wasn't ready to make any kind of no-strings- attached commitment to Christ either. And so there I was, turning over a slow fire."

Adolescence is a time of changes. It is a time of testing and experimenting; it is a time when kids are crying out for recognition and attention, and yet consciously give misleading clues about their real feelings to throw their parents off the track. Often they feel that their parents just aren't "with it," that they don't understand the importance of keeping up with the crowd. And so sometimes the kids become two people inside. The parents know only one side of the child, and since they often seem satisfied with that, the kids conclude that it's easy to fool their parents.

Listen, watch, talk. Love, love, love.

In my own rebellion, I unthinkingly left myself wide open for all sorts of disasters to befall me, but I had praying parents. I used to drive down the highway at 110 m.p.h. and laugh at caution; but I was protected from killing myself and others. I could have become pregnant before marriage. I could have become an alcoholic. There were so many evils that could have befallen me; but Jesus allowed only those things which I was able to bear. He protected me from things beyond my endurance.

Through the rebellion, however, I find that He has given me greater understanding and love for those people who are enduring the problems I experienced.

Lloyd Ogilvie once said, "Nothing can happen through us that hasn't happened to us."

PART TWO – CHAPTER FOUR

Reverend Daddy

SEVERAL OF THE QUESTIONS IN MY SURVEY confronted the issue of the duality of the role of pastor in the life of the children of those in ministry. I asked, "From your perspective, what is a minister?" Some respondents were shallow in their understanding of their fathers' positions. Others showed a depth of understanding for what their fathers had been called to do. Generally, this understanding seemed to be dependant on the pastor's ability to communicate God to his children.

In random order, the respondents answered variously that he must be:

- a man of God
- involved in the community and visitation
- able to help people with their spiritual, physical, emotional and family problems
- able to control his temper
- a shepherd who cares for and oversees God's people
- responsible first to God, second to his family, thirdly to the congregation, and then to the community at large
- able to realize that he's not perfect and sometimes he can learn from members of his congregation
- prepared to practice what he preaches if he wants to get the message across
- responsible for teaching the truths of the Bible and guiding people as they study the Bible themselves

- a unifying force in the community
- able to train people to be disciples of Christ, equipped to lead others to the Lord
- full of the knowledge of God and grounded in God's Word from cover to cover
- praying without ceasing for God's people
- prepared to be there when his people are in need
- empowered to do all of his ministry by the Holy Spirit
- prepared to discipline wayward members
- prepared to expend tremendous energy and effort, and in the case of a pioneering work, physical labour
- able to trust God as his strength and not get depressed
- able to see and deal with individual needs, not just the needs of the whole congregation as a unit
- able to organize groups; not necessarily the wheel that keeps things going, but at least the wheel that gets things started
- the chief administrator of the church
- able to prepare messages
- prepared to conduct wedding ceremonies, baptismal services, funerals, etc.
- prepared to attend conventions, retreats, etc.
- able to accept the fact that each minister is unique and human and functions more effectively in certain areas than in others.

There is no doubt about it, the responsibilities are great. No person could possibly fill all of those expectations adequately. The last point in the list is very important. God does not give anyone a load that is too heavy to bear. However, sometimes, ministers try to carry greater burdens than God has given them. They try to do the work required of the whole body of believers. Seventy-three percent of the respondents felt that their dads measured up to their standards for a good minister.

Tanya is one of those who does not feel that her dad is a good minister. In discussing the problems, she said: "He always preaches sermons to convert people, and I think we should have worshipped God and praised Him and thanked Him more. I think that that was really missing in our church. Another problem is that my dad gets so depressed. Like a doctor who specializes in cancer patients, a minister jolly well shouldn't go into the work unless he knows that he's going to be given the grace to cope with the failures. I think that if a minister can't handle the situation, if it depresses him and drags his own spiritual life down, then he'd better find a remedy or another kind of a job. My opinion right now is that my father really needs to know the empowering of the Holy Spirit. I think he needs to know that he's loved and he needs to know his worth before God. He needs to know that what he is doing is what God is asking him to do, and everything else will fall into place."

Why doesn't Tanya tell him that? Why not just sit down and show him her love and concern, and discuss with him what she sees as the necessary solution? What? Tell her father – the minister – that she thinks he has spiritual needs? He is supposed to be the authority on spirituality. The thought of confronting the theological egos of so many ministers, is unthinkable to the majority of P.K.s. Kids feel as though it would be like criticizing God to criticize a minister.

If, on the other hand, a minister is strong enough to allow his family to criticize his sermons and his methods of ministering, it can be rewarding on so many levels. It makes him more approachable in their eyes, and shows that he has not placed himself on a pedestal beyond their reach. Another sure plus is that it will help to keep him humble!

If a minister decides to open himself to the critiquing of his family, he must be prepared to really listen to them. It cannot be token listening, or the family will clam up again. Ministers have a way of appearing to listen for a while, and then jumping in and coming forth with 'the truth.' The other person is often afraid to disagree, because that will be the end of it.

According to Jarrell Garsee,[12] the average minister spends 60 hours

---

[12] *What You Always Wanted to Know About Your Pastor-Husband*, by Garsee, Hamilton, Paul and Wiseman, Copyright 1978, Beacon Hill Press of Kansas City

per week in his ministry. Obviously, something has to slip or be left out entirely. True, Jesus must come first in the minister's life, but does He really require a minister to devote so much time to the church that he neglects his own family? Doesn't he want him to be able to father the family with which He has entrusted him?

I believe the roots of some of these problems are often purely psychological rather than spiritual. People tend to put pastors on pedestals, and too often, the pastors themselves love the view from up there. They try to appear to be above the problems of mere humans. It may work for a while with the outside world, but how long can a man hide his humanity from his family? A minister with strong ego needs may begin to feel that his family doesn't appreciate his greatness, and so spending time with other people sometimes becomes an escape from reality into an egotistical "glory trip."

Tim Stafford, in "Reflections of a Preacher's Kid,"[13] says that in his opinion, the ministry draws certain types of people and shapes them in particular ways. Generally, they are "competitive, intelligent, idealistic, lonely, and in need of reassurance. They are public people who both love and hate the limelight."

Subconsciously, churches regard their pastors as 'stars.' They are highly visible people who 'perform' before an audience. Generally, it is only the children of actors, politicians, and preachers who regularly watch their fathers perform. Other fathers disappear to perform. It's difficult to feel that someone who belongs to the public is your own. Often he becomes more a symbol than a person. You're never quite sure what is real and what isn't. In the child's eyes, the minister may appear hypocritical, unable to make his public and his private lives match.

I asked the P.K.s whether or not they felt that their fathers had two faces, one public and one private. Thirty-seven percent replied yes, that their fathers had a private face that differed from his public face. The main thing that was different about the private face was simply that it was more relaxed than the public face. Anita's response to this question was humorous:

---

[13] Leadership Journal, "Reflections of a Preacher's Kid," by Tim Stafford, a publication of *Christianity Today*, Inc., Winter 1980, Vol. 1, No. 1

"Well, I guess you'd have to say he had a public face and a private face. We have a kind of joke at home. Dad was a man who wanted to get along with the very conservative factions as well as the more liberal ones. But my dad always enjoyed a pipe or a cigarette or some sort of a smoke now and then, having been brought up on the farm and then having gone through the war. Well the dear old Methodist ladies would not have liked that! So, my dad would not smoke in his study or in front of them, and even at home he didn't want the smell of smoke to be in the house in case any of them came in. So – he had a little room just off our bathroom where he always used to go after dinner for a smoke. He would sit in there on an old bed with an old mattress. One night my brother and I were at home alone. My mother was at knitting circle and my father was at Lion's Club. We were at home doing our homework. Well, we began to smell smoke, so my brother went and checked the furnace, and everything there seemed to be alright. It wasn't until we went to bed, when I was in the bathroom, that I noticed smoke coming out from under the bathroom door. So, we ran to the next door neighbor's house. He, of course, wanted to call the fire department, but I said 'Oh no, you can't do that' because I knew that the whole congregation would find out that my father smoked! Well that was one of the heaviest pressures ever put on me. The neighbor said 'I have to,' and so he did. Of course the whole town and the congregation came out to the fire, trampling all over my father's geraniums. In the commotion you could hear them all muttering, 'It must be the young'un what done it,' because of course only my brother and I were at home. And to this day, they probably all believe that; except for my youngest brother's best friend, who when playing a saxophone solo at church said, I'd like to dedicate this number to our minister," and proceeded to play, 'Smoke Gets In Your Eyes.'"

Often kids can't cope with the differences between the public face and the private face. They are quite often the ones who rebel most aggressively. In the rebellion, they are not necessarily trying to punish anyone but themselves for the guilt they feel in the web of hypocrisy.

Those who don't rebel are usually the ones who have, through wise management, coped with the demands of public life and understood the worth of the secrets that must not be trampled by public knowledge. This ability to cope with the pressures does not just suddenly happen. It must be nurtured and taught with lots of comfortable communication. Forty-six percent of the respondents felt they were able to discuss things easily with their fathers. Forty-two percent claimed to be unable to communicate with them, while 12 percent said there was a certain amount of real communication possible.

In the hope that the dads who are unable to stimulate communication with their kids would like to know how other dads succeed in this area, I asked the respondents how their dads helped to make communication easy.

EASING COMMUNICATION BETWEEN P.K.s AND PREACHERS

Anita had a warm relationship with her father until his death two years ago. She herself has not yet experienced a dynamic relationship with God, but her dad left her with a wealth of warm memories. She recalls:

"He always put his family before the congregation. He was a strong supporter of us in all of our school sports and things. He always tried to be there for at least part of a game. When my mother was ill, he spent a great deal of time visiting her; and although some of the congregation was critical, thinking it was cutting in on their time, he didn't care because his family came first. He was not a narrow person, and he took part in community activities as well as church life. I was really attracted to his intellectual ability. He was a man of honesty, and hated dishonesty. He confronted problems head-on without getting excited. He would just think about a problem for awhile, and then say: 'Okay, this is what we are going to do.' And that's what we did."

When David Harris was living at home, he was dissatisfied with what he saw in his dad's church. He was confused, because his dad's life didn't demonstrate any difference between a Christian and a non-Christian. He did not see his dad having a living, vibrant, working relationship with God. At home, they never said grace, never had family devotions nor any of the things which one associates with a minister's home. His dad used to swear a bit, and generally, the things he did were the same sort of things that everybody else did. David concluded that God was just something that you either did or did not believe in, but it had nothing to do with everyday life. Finally, David realized that his dad had an inadequate spiritual situation and he became hungry for more depth. When he eventually rebelled against his dad's church, David says:

"Dad actually suggested other places I could go for help – to churches other than his. He was a little disappointed that I was leaving his church, but he was pleased that I was seeking spirituality. I appreciated the fact that he set aside his pride for my growth. One day I would say, 'there can't be any God,' and the next day I would contradict myself. He just left me to it. The teenage years are such a time of change; I could say and believe almost anything one day, and be totally different the next day. However, he was pleased to see that I was going on with the Lord, possibly more enthusiastically than he was."

David's situation was unusual in several ways, but to me, the beauty of it was the fact that his dad yielded to David's growth without any apparent thought for his own theological pride. When he did that, it left the doors open for communication. He saw that the essential core of what David was doing was good, and he didn't clutter the issue with self and ego. Often a situation such as this would have been perceived as threatening to a minister's status and image in his own congregation.

Listening is the key to effective communication; giving one's total concentration to the expression of another person. It is difficult for a busy person to slow down long enough to truly absorb the things his child may be trying to tell him.

Elaine Mainse Stacey stressed the importance of her dad's capacity for listening fully to her. She says: "If I have something to say, he always listens to me completely, and then he says whatever he thinks. He always lets me say whatever it is first, without ever butting in. He's a very good listener, and very fair. I always felt that I got a fair shake. He is very honest and never hides his feelings. We see him laugh and cry, and he doesn't try to hide things from us kids. He's very affectionate with us, and every night, he prayed over each of us a little. That individual time always gave us a chance to discuss any problems we had with him."

The saying goes that if you want to get something done, you should ask a busy person to do it. Not many ministers could be busier than David Mainse, and yet he always found the time to spend with his kids. They felt important to him. Has his ministry suffered as a result? On the contrary. God has blessed his ministry to the point where he probably reaches more people for the Lord than any other pastor in Canada.

Bob Wells enjoys a close relationship with his dad. He considers his dad to be his best friend, and would drive miles to give him a hand with anything necessary. Why?

"I have to really commend my dad. He used to spend a lot of time with us, and he did all he could for us. In spite of our very tight finances, he always made sure that we always had our own sports equipment, and he always made a rink for us in the backyard, and so on. He was a very hard worker and was a good example to me. Now we are best friends. Whenever I needed him for anything he was always there. Dad and mom had a very close relationship, but it was always known that dad was the head of the home. They never argued or fought in front of us. Dad and I used to always talk about sports, but now I'm finding that I really like to discuss spiritual things with him."

Karen Gamble appears to be a particularly secure person. She was raised in a cocoon of love and radiates a peace that is not generally characteristic of her teenage peers. In speaking of the communication that exists between her and her dad, Karen says:

"My dad has always been very well-respected in his profession. He is very open and I love and respect him for that. He is flexible. We do a lot of things together like bowling, shopping, skating, and camping. That is so important. If a preacher is too involved in his church, and forgets about his family, then his family is going to forget about him. His love for the Lord is the major thing that makes our relationship good. In every relationship, if both parties are drawing close to the Lord, they will automatically draw closer to each other. Dad doesn't always claim that he has the answer. He just knows that if he's there to listen to me, then we can take it to the Lord together in prayer; and that's what's important. I always knew that whenever I took a problem to dad, he would just sit there and listen to me, and then say, 'Well, I don't have the answer, but we can take it to the Lord.' I always knew that he would say that, but, I always still took my problems to him."

Chris Kirby also stressed the importance of spending time together as a family, doing things other than church related activities. Fifty-eight percent of the respondents felt that their dads spent time with them doing other things. Thirty-three point three percent said their dads were too busy. Sixteen point six percent said that there was some time spent together in such a fashion, but not much. Sixty-two point five percent felt that they would like to spend more time with their dads. Chris says:

"We do a lot of things together as a family. It's important to participate together in things other than church activities, because if you don't, there will be a gap there, and there won't be much chance of a father-daughter relationship. He makes me feel important to him by spending time with me. We've always had a good relationship. A lot depends on the child's attitude too. If you're both right with the Lord, then obviously the relationship is going to be good. It won't be if you're both pulling in opposite directions. Our relationship has a lot of trust, and we're comfortable with each other."

In order to be able to communicate effectively with their children, pastors have to be able to communicate honestly with themselves. They need to be in touch with their own feelings and needs. In striving to meet the demands of congregations, pastors often repress their own needs which are interdependent on the needs of their families. It is so comfortable to be able to recognize and honestly communicate personal needs. Pastors are often afraid to let people see who they really are, for fear of having to admit weaknesses and flaws to themselves and others. When they do take the first, faltering steps of admitting to personal needs, they are generally surprised by the relief, warmth and acceptance which meets them. The rejection they feared was nothing more than a lie of the devil.

Tim Stafford[14] says: "When I was growing up, my father was not, as they say, 'in touch with his feelings.' But I think that he was enough in touch that we all had a sense of pity mixed in with our pride; we knew

---

[14] Leadership Journal, "Reflections of a Preacher's Kid," by Tim Stafford, a Publication of Christianity Today, Inc., Winter 1980, Vol. 1, No. 1

his job was not easy for him, though I doubt he ever exactly told us so. Then, when we were all nearly grown, he went through a series of crises. He learned how to express how he felt to us. It was a wonderful release, for me as well as for him. I began to be able to freely enjoy his abilities without worrying so much about his weaknesses. I understood better that he was only human, a fellow man. It opened the way for a peer closeness with my father, which is, I think, the joy of very few sons. I don't suggest compulsive candidness. But I do suggest that there is a time and a place for confessing doubt, even to your own family, and I am afraid that there are many pastors who have never confessed it to anyone. The only way my father, as a public person, can also be specially mine, is if he shares the true feelings of being a public person with me."

The P.K.s had a lot of suggestions on how the relationship between themselves and their fathers could be improved. These improvements involved changes in attitudes and behavior on both sides. They expressed a desire that their dads should:

- worry less about what other people are going to think
- not be such respecters of persons. People are equal in the eyes of the Lord, and all that counts is how much each one lets God use him
- give more good solid Bible teaching at home, in spite of the fact that a preacher is somewhat like a plumber who doesn't want to have to go home and fix drains
- come closer to the Lord
- be more open to listening and discussing spiritual matters with their children instead of just dictating their thoughts
- stop being so stubborn
- keep up with the times
- not argue about stupid things; control their tempers
- show more love and care for their kids
- show a genuine interest in the concerns and activities of the family

- utilize their talents as fully as possible
- be more honest about their feelings and attitudes
- give the kids a feeling of worth instead of inadequacy
- be more tolerant of individual differences
- be more open to the fact that they are not always right and that that is okay
- not always have to have the last word
- foster an atmosphere where the kids feel free to be open and honest
- show a whole lot more affection
- stop making the kids feel guilty all the time
- discipline the kids if they behave improperly, and let them feel the release of the guilt in the disciplinary action
- pay more attention to the kids when they do spend time with them. Don't be so preoccupied all the time.

The respondents also recognized many areas where they, themselves, should change in order to alleviate the situation. They felt they should:

- put more trust in their dads
- strive to overcome their fears of their dads
- try to show more love
- stop focusing on the disappointments and fears
- learn to be more patient
- try to control their tempers
- express how they feel on the inside, and be more open and honest
- make more of an effort to establish a close relationship
- develop a closer relationship with the Lord

- see that everyone has problems, and that if the problems aren't dealt with, then they're going to affect other people
- be open to healing of hurts and bitterness
- be forgiving
- learn to accept the unexpected
- try to understand their dads' positions more
- not wait until the last minute to tell their dads about something they want him to do with them
- be more enthusiastic about their dad's attempts at family togetherness
- try to be more interested in the things that interest their dads
- accept the fact that ministers are not supposed to be perfect
- be more tolerant of their dad's weaknesses
- develop more boldness in expressing their views and daring to be seen as individuals
- be more respectful and honouring toward their parents.

Dad and I were always afraid of hurting each other. We still are sometimes. We've still got a long way to go. But each time we dare to be honest, we discover that it gets easier and easier, and that we actually hurt each other more by trying to hide things than we do by being honest. I am finding that my dad is less fragile than I thought he was. He is able to take things on the chin. The heart attacks I feared just don't happen. Each time I speak out, I find that my strength grows. I feel stronger and more worthwhile. It's nice. If we have a confrontation, sometimes I still cry, or maybe he gets red in the face and loses his temper a little, but Jesus heals us. Problems get aired and resolved, rather than left to fester in despair and resignation. I see now, that troubled rapids flow into peaceful lakes, while perpetually calm waters are generally polluted and stagnant underneath. I would rather brave the rapids with hope of a fresh clean peace, than to rot in a pool of polluted resignation.

And yet in our assertiveness, let us remember Christ's admonition to be submissive to each other. This does not mean being in a constant state of fawning subjection; rather it means being strengthened in Christ through empathy one with another. We must be assertive in love, and never with the desire to be hurtful.

The most important key to successful communication in a situation of confrontation is prayer. Pray before you say one word. Give the situation over to God. Then, as you are talking, be aware of a right-angled relationship. You are at the point where the horizontal meets the vertical, reaching out horizontally to people and vertically to God. Let God pour His strength and wisdom through you, and it will flow out to others.

Children are watching, watching, their parents all the time. Often, the reason they pay no attention to their parents' verbal instructions is that the actions of the parents speak louder than their words. They overpower and eradicate the value of what they're trying to say. If you are a Christian parent, how would your child evaluate your spiritual situation? Would he say that you appear to have a good relationship with God? Seventy point eight percent of the respondents replied positively, claiming their dads seemed to have a good relationship with God. Eleven percent responded negatively, while 9.1 percent said that sometimes they thought that he was close to the Lord. It is very interesting to read some of the responses to this question.

HOW THE P.K.s SEE THEIR DADS' RELATIONSHIPS WITH GOD

Anita has not yet discovered the joy of a personal walk with Jesus. She goes to church most Sundays with her two little children, but she does not seem to have the happy peace that Jesus brings. In recalling what she saw of her dad's relationship with Jesus, she says:

"I think he had a good relationship with Him, but he didn't go overboard. He was not an evangelical type. His degree was in philosophy first, and to go from philosophy into religion is really something. So there had to be something pretty deep there, but it was more on the thinking rational level, than emotional. He accepted what came along, and had a real temper at times which resulted in fiery sermons if things did not go well."

Obviously, Anita's dad's relationship with God had a great influence on her own relationship with Him. Her dad was a model of spirituality for her, and her own spirituality now is intellectualized, but lacking in the overflow of reality for everyday life. She recognizes the validity of spiritual truths, but it has not been brought to life within her. She did not see the example of what Christ has to offer her in an abundant life right here on earth. Her dad did not impart to her a knowledge of the absolute veracity of the Scriptures. He was not too sure himself whether or not there was an afterlife. If a minister's faith in God's Word is wishy-washy, it is pretty difficult for him to impart strong spiritual growth to his children.

Terry is sixteen-years-old. I have used an assumed name for him, for several reasons. He is a confused boy who is resentful of his imposed role as a P.K. People no longer expect Terry to be a "goody-goody" because he has strained against the bonds of positive expectations, and broken free to the extent that people now expect him to be rebellious. He takes a certain expressed pride in his independence, but in reality, appears rather lost. He does not think he has seen the power of God at work in his home. His mom is busy teaching school and does not appear to be particularly interested in spiritual things. His dad views the church as somewhat akin to a service club, performing a function in the community not too far removed from the idea of the Lions' Club or the Kinsman's Club.

Terry says: "Yeah, I think he probably has a good relationship with God. That's why he said we moved. I don't know whether to believe him or not, but he said God told him it was time to move on. I don't really know whether He did or not. That's the way he feels so I guess he does. I think he enjoys his relationship with God. He gets tense every once in a while about it, and lets off his steam on me or something, but I think he likes it okay. I don't think he really believes in all the miracles and things. I've heard him talking about it sometimes, and he says it's a lot of bull roar. I guess if he doesn't believe in it, I don't either."

This young man looks to his father as an example and trusts the opinions of this man, who is highly regarded in the community. When the minister's theology is weak, it's difficult to expect more from the child. What a contrast when we hear Dave Lawrenson say: "My dad often said, 'You may be a dispensationalist, or think that this or that is or isn't for today, and I won't argue with that. But I'll tell you this one thing; every single word in the Bible will work if you apply it, whether it's in the Old or the New Testament."

Dave's dad did just that. He put the promises in the Bible to work when he had difficulties, and the effects of that had a profound influence on Dave's life. God totally rearranged Dave as a result of faith and prayer at work.

Lenore (an assumed name) says she didn't realize until she was about twenty-years-old that her dad was very committed to God. She says she guesses he is one of God's chosen ones, and that it just shows up in little ways.

I say that that's not good enough. There are many ministers who are living wishy-washy spiritual lives. If a man dares to assume the responsibility of leading a church, he needs to be a strong man of God, filled with the power of the Holy Spirit. It is ludicrous to think of commitment just showing up in "little ways." I believe that would deeply grieve the Holy Spirit of God, and that those men will have a lot to answer for when they stand before God at the end of time. I believe that one of Satan's most powerful weapons in North America is a whole troupe of impotent preachers who befoul the pulpits with their unbelief and spiritual insecurity. If you are a preacher in this situation, I would strongly suggest that you inform your congregation that you are taking a leave of absence for a month; rent a cottage in the woods, take your Bible and very little food with you, and prepare yourself for a time of getting in touch with God. Spend your time in prayer, fasting, and feeding on the Word of God. Expect a miracle. God is hungering for you to be complete in Him. But He will not force you, He will only wait, gently longing for you.

B.J. had no respect for his dad until two years ago. There were other factors involved as well as his dad's spiritual situation, but that was the root of many of the problems. There has been a great change in their home.

B.J. says, "About five years ago, Dad received the baptism in the Holy Spirit, and he has changed a lot since then. He's more dedicated to the Lord. He's a lot easier to live with now. Before that, he did not live an appealing kind of Christianity. I didn't see anything I wanted from his kind of life. While I was growing up, I knew he was really religious, and he was always preaching religion to me, but he didn't seem to have any peace then. He got angry and yelled at me a lot. I was a very sensitive person and took things very personally."

Tanya knows the Holy Spirit could change things in her home too. She longs for her dad to experience a deeper relationship with God. Her comments reflect the feelings of many P.K.s. "I do feel that my dad does have a deep personal relationship with God, but he does not appear to enjoy it. I think it is a terrible burden on him to be so good. It is such a duty thing. I wish the Holy Spirit would give him power to have joy in his relationship. It's not how good we are; it's not about our merit at all. It's all about the graciousness of God. My dad is very tense and very depressed much of the time."

Many ministers are right on in their theology, and may even be tremendous theological scholars; but, too often, there is a missing element.

David Harris says: "My aunt told me that my dad does know the Lord, and that he's been saved for years; but it's just all inside, and he doesn't let it out. He's not on fire for the Lord. Whenever I asked him questions about the Lord, he was able to answer."

Bob Wells has a different sort of memories. "My dad is very spiritually awake. He begins every day on his knees with the Lord."

My guess is that Bob does the same thing now. He, too, is very spiritually awake and has a deep hunger for more and more of God. He is gentle and strong, quiet and assertive, peaceful and exuberant, young but obviously wise.

Laurie, too, had a strong spiritual role model. He remembers: "Dad lived a full Christian life. He lived and practiced what he taught. I felt as though he was a walking saint. You could just tell he was God's man. It wasn't so much what he said as the way he lived it and showed it."

It's not too hard to train a child to perform religiously. All you have to do is make sure he goes to all of the expected meetings and observes the niceties of the church organization.

Fostering faith in a child is something else. Hell will be full of religious people. Religion won't keep anyone out of the clutches of the devil. It is just a smokescreen that hides his mastery and lulls people into a false sense of security. It is only a deep and abiding faith in Jesus and a total commitment to God, that will ensure escape from the devil's traps and the wrath of God. In the Book of Proverbs, parents are admonished to "Train them up in the way they should go."[15] I believe this admonition requires careful study, and involves far more than superficial obedience to established rules.

In order to grow in strength in the Lord, both parents and children need the help of the Holy Spirit within them. It was not enough for Jesus to possess a holy nature; He, too, needed the Holy Spirit. Unfortunately, if God were to take His Holy Spirit out of this world, many churches and pastors would continue on as before without knowing the difference. When God's Spirit starts to work in a church, it's not uncommon for people to resist Him because they are not familiar with His presence and His ways. In His first sermon, Jesus proclaimed, "The Spirit of the Lord is on Me."[16] What would happen throughout this whole world if every minister of God could say the same thing with assurance!

---

[15] Proverbs 22:6
[16] Luke 4:18

PART TWO – CHAPTER FIVE

A Minister's Wife for a Mother

MOTHERS IN THE MANSE ARE SPECIAL PEOPLE. They are called on to be all things to all people. If high expectations are placed on P.K.s, the expectations placed on pastors' wives are monumental. Much has been written on this topic. It is very heartening to see that generally, the attitude toward ministers' wives is softening. People are beginning to understand that pastors' wives need special love and understanding, rather than increased demands.

While congregations are becoming generally more realistic in their expectations, it is not always so with the minister's wife herself. Often she takes on herself burdens and responsibilities that are not meant for her at all. She often struggles with unreal expectations of herself, and sets unfairly high standards for her own performance. She is married to a man who is generally assumed to be a high achiever and, in spite of the fact that she may be a talented person herself, she may feel she has to continually prove her own self-worth; her right to be married to a person who has to maintain a high profile in the community. She is married to a man who is regarded as a "man of God," and she may feel pressure to prove herself a "woman of God" in order to justify herself in her position.

How do the children feel? How do they see their mothers? What expectations do they have of ministers' wives? Where do the kids fit in? Where do they rank on the list of priorities? In what ways would they like to see their mothers change? How do they view their mothers' spirituality?

I asked the respondents what they felt were the true responsibilities of a minister's wife.

THE PROPER ROLE OF A MINISTER'S WIFE ACCORDING TO THE P.K.s.

Generally, the respondents felt that the primary responsibility of a minister's wife should be to her family, and that after that, it's between her and God what she should do.

Anita, a P.K., experienced great difficulty in her home as a result of the conflict between the roles of minister's wife and mother. She says: "Just because a woman is married to a minister doesn't mean she should have to help run the church as much as people expect. The church is a congregation, and the people in the community should be doing the major part of the work. Just because she married a minister doesn't automatically mean she has a career, although many people expect that, and she often feels the pressure to take charge of things. My dad often says that is why my mother had a nervous breakdown. The congregation expected so much of her, and she didn't learn to say 'no' until it was too late. But that comes with maturity, and at that time she had four little kids to look after, and was still being asked to do all kinds of things in the church, and she just cracked under the pressure. People in the community should accept more responsibility in the church, and not put such a heavy load on the minister's wife. She should be able to live her own life, and her chief responsibility should be to minister to her own family. Mom used to tell a funny story about when my dad proposed to her. She replied that she didn't want to be a minister's wife. He said, 'I didn't ask you to be a minister's wife: I asked you to be my wife!' She said that she always thought that he was pretty smart after that."

Paul Timpany agrees with Anita. He says: "She should take no more responsibility in the church than any other woman. Some churches feel that they hire the minister and get the minister's wife for nothing. That is not right. She must be first a wife and mother. The church responsibilities follow that."

Janice Remple suggests that if the church expects a wife to take a strong role with her husband, then she should be salaried for it. She feels that a minister's wife should be allowed to be herself. She says: "If she is a speaker, then let her speak, but don't force her into anything."

In the Book of Romans, in Chapter Twelve, Paul speaks of the many parts of the body of believers. He teaches that each part of the body has a different function, and that we are all to use our different gifts in accordance with the grace that God has given us. "If our gift is to speak God's message, we should do it according to the faith that we have; if it is to serve, we should serve; if it is to teach, we should teach; if it is to encourage others, we should do so. Whoever shares with others should do it generously; whoever has authority should work hard; whoever shows kindness to others should do it cheerfully."

Nowhere do I read that a minister's wife is supposed to be wife, mother, lover, counsellor, cook, president of at least three groups, choir member, pianist, hospital volunteer, Bible study leader, Sunday School teacher, Bible School leader, scrubwoman, beauty queen, church secretary, and special speaker, equipped with a telephone growing out of her ear, and correction fluid coursing through her veins to assist her in criticizing her husband's sermons!

That might sound far-fetched, but many ministers' wives feel they must carry the whole load themselves. Regularly, they demand more of themselves than does anyone else. Tanya says: "She should just be a good mother, wife and Christian. My mother's standards for a minister's wife petrify me, and I hope that I don't ever have to marry a minister! I don't know how I would ever break out of the role that my mother has created. It's an impossibly high scale!"

According to Sylvia: "The Bishop who married my mom and dad in Manitoba told my mom that her job was to stay at home, and make sure that her husband, the minister, was well taken care of, and that she was to bring up her family in the home. She wasn't to be out playing the organ, running the Sunday School, and A.C.W. and so on. Her first responsibility was to her family. And that is how my mom lived."

Perhaps the greatest responsibility a minister's wife has, in terms of church service, is to support her husband with concentrated prayer and encouragement. David Harris says: "A minister carries a very heavy load. For instance, when someone dies, he may think, 'Did I tell the family the right thing?' These are times when his wife really has to support him. Her husband is involved daily in discussions and dealings with life and death. These are so much more burdensome than the everyday things with which most people work."

Ministers are human too, and they feel the sorrows of the people who are in mourning or deep distress. Sometimes, when a minister has taken too much upon himself, the sheer weight of the pressures gets him down. The frustrations are great.

Karen Gamble says: "The greatest thing a minister's wife can do is to get behind her husband and support him when he gets down low. She needs to be there to pick him up and make him feel that he is a man. She must support him in the church. Often a church judges a minister by his wife. She must maintain a high standard of behavior. Even though she would often just prefer to stay home, she is expected to be at many of the church functions."

Bob Wells agrees that one of the major responsibilities of a minister's wife is to support her husband; but he adds: "I feel that she should take a part in the church, but she shouldn't dominate. She should be a leader, but she needs to be somebody that the minister can't be. I feel she has to be more of a counsellor; more of a personal, loving, den mother type. Often she has to be father and mother at home, because the church takes so much of the minister's time, and by the time he gets home, he's too whacked out to do much of anything. Every minister's wife has to be made out of some kind of special stuff."

Wendell Fisher brought up a very important aspect of the role of a minister's wife, that being one of a liaison, a catalyst between a minister and the congregation, and also between different parts of the congregation. This is a very important aspect, one that extends into the family as well as into the church and community. She is often the liaison and the catalyst between the minister and their children.

In order to be an effective liaison worker, one must know both sides well. This involves spending time with each side, loving and listening. That is why Jean Windatt feels that it is important that a minister's wife should not be in the choir. She feels she should be sitting down with the congregation where she can mingle and talk freely with people, and let

God's love flow directly through her to touch them in caring conversation. She should be that part of the pastor that is a part of the people in the congregation. One of the greatest prerequisites of a minister's wife is that she should be absolutely trustworthy in terms of confidentiality.

Eighty-nine point five percent of the respondents felt that their mothers made good minister's wives, and 84 percent felt their mothers spent enough time with them.

Among those who responded negatively, a major complaint was that their mothers were so wrapped up in church work that they didn't have time for the children. This generally resulted in family difficulties, rebellion, and spiritual retardation in the children.

One fellow (who prefers to remain anonymous) says that his mom had such a serious attitude toward everything that it made him want to break free and kick up his heels. He says: "My mother was a trained church worker. She was so involved that life was the same throughout the church and home. If my mother ever made something really good to eat, then I always knew that there was a church supper coming up. She was very involved in the church, and also at the conference level in the presbyterial where she took leadership roles. She had a great many speaking engagements for women's groups and church services. Her devotion to her duties was really heavy on her time. I felt that my parents were so focused on church work that they were lacking any impact on the rest of the community. I felt they should have been curling or something, so that they could have loosened up socially, and made contacts that they never would have made behind church doors. Their lives were just too one-sided. The spectrum should have been widened."

Another fellow who prefers to remain confidential says: "The Lord is really dealing with my mom. She tried to be a good minister's wife, but she could have really helped him with fewer complaints. She is a Spirit-filled Christian but she always seemed to be the other voice saying, 'Are you sure? Can we do that?' She didn't give my dad the pure trusting support he needed in order to proceed with confidence. My mom and I never really got on because I just sort of had to pick up the loose ends of her attention. She often seemed to resent the fact that she didn't have what others had materially."

Eighty-eight percent of the respondents felt that their mothers put them before church responsibilities, and only 32 percent felt that there was a conflict between the role of mother and that of minister's wife. But I feel that in spite of the fact that a minority of the P.K.s expressed problems with their mothers, it is necessary to look at the suggestions they had for ways their mothers could improve. Only 68 percent of them felt that they could take their problems to their moms. What about the other 32 percent? What were they doing with their problems? How could their moms have made things healthier for them? Let's take a look at the situation through the eyes of the P.K.s.

HOW THE P.K.s FEEL ABOUT THEIR MOTHERS

Brenda says: "Sometimes it's easier to confide in other people than in your mother. Sometimes they get so busy with the house and their other things that you don't really feel noticed. Maybe they show that they care, but they don't show that they can be trusted with your problems. Sometimes they forget that kids have problems too."

Jennifer Holmes has tremendous admiration for her mother, but she feels that she lives on such a high plane that Jennifer is afraid to confide her failures and problems to her mom. She doesn't think that her mom could handle it, and she doesn't want to hurt her. She says: "My mother tries to use all of her talents for the Lord. I wish that she could relax a little more and be less fearful in both roles. I cannot discuss my problems with her because I do not want to upset her. My mother's faith sustains her, but I would like to see more evidence of joy."

Tanya says: "My mother created an incredible role for herself. She was another minister! I mean my mother was something else. She was involved one hundred thousand percent, and I didn't like it! It was much too hard on her. She was tremendously involved in my life as well, but in subtle ways, her church involvement interfered with her relationship with me. She always felt like she had to appear perfect. She should take her role as minister's wife less seriously. She should not expect so much of herself. Her role model for me was too perfect. I could never live up to the standards she set in her example to me. I shared everything – every single thing with my mother all through my teenage years. Poor thing, every day she heard every single thing that I did all day. Then came my time of rebellion, when I would share nothing with her because she just whined and put a guilt trip on me, saying, 'Oh darling, now we don't want you to get hurt. ' She protected me so much that it drove me crazy. Now I don't want to tell her what it's like at my work, because she'd go nuts. She's already having enough problems with how busy I am, and all of the hurting that goes with my job."

Tanya's mom was a 'super-mom' and put a tremendous pressure on herself to do everything perfectly. Nothing appeared to be neglected. But who can relate to that? People do not expect anyone to be able to do every single thing well.

Jean Windatt's mom did not feel she was gifted in the area of speaking to groups and so: "Whenever we went to a new church, the first thing she always did was get up and tell the people that she could not speak to groups. She never led any meetings."

Sylvia's mom too, recognized her limitations. She was a shy woman, who found it very difficult to go into a room full of people. She forced herself to do it, but her major concentration was on her family. Sylvia's one wish was that her mother had discussed child-rearing and problems of teenagers more with other mothers so that she might not have been so Victorian in her mothering of Sylvia.

Elaine Mainse Stacey stresses the importance of appearances. She says: "My mom always looked good, and I think it helped our relationship. It's important for mothers not to be old-fashioned, but to keep up on the new styles, so that she can have a better relationship with her daughter. A girl wants to be proud of her mother when she goes to the school, and so on. Also, I feel that we have a responsibility to be attractive so that people will be attracted to us, and then to the Lord. Another thing I really liked was that my mom was always there when we left for school, and when we got home. She did her things in between. Once when I was in kindergarten, I got home and called, 'Mom, Mom," and there was no answer. I didn't know where she was, and I just cried and cried. Pretty soon, I heard, 'Elaine, Elaine, where are you?' and it was mom. She had been out in the backyard hanging out clothes, and I hadn't thought to look out there. I don't think people understand how important it is to a child's security and growth, to have the mother there when they need her. I will never forget that."

Joan was not so fortunate. She recalls: "Her church responsibilities interfered with our relationship very definitely. She always had to go to a meeting. She was always so busy. She used to compare the kids and say, 'Look at what Barbara can do.' This made me feel very inadequate and I rebelled. She didn't listen to us. Generally, she is very unselfish and was considered a very good minister's wife by everyone in the church. As far as everyone else was concerned, she was the salt of the earth. She was a very good entertainer."

If the children see their mothers acting one way at home and another way when they are out, it confuses them and can instill feelings of bitterness and resentment.

Charles recalls: "She says that she believes in God, but she swears and curses God. She is very involved in labour unions and is very negative toward the church. She receives a pension from the church, but is negative toward them. She was always fighting with my father and I always felt she was a double-crosser. I felt that the whole thing was just a big front with my mother. She was so big on me not disgracing my father in public, but she was of no help to him. She is a tremendously angry and domineering woman. I never could have a discussion with her because she was always criticizing me."

Being a minister's wife does not automatically make anyone a Christian. A minister's wife has to have a spiritual rebirth just the same as anyone else if she is to be a child of God. Few women marry ministers unless they are Christians, but it does happen, and the problems that arise from such a union are heartbreaking. They often result in separation. The children become very confused, and frustration and depression are certain to plague both marriage partners.

Eighty-five point two percent of the respondents felt that their moms appeared to have a good relationship with the Lord, and yet 29.2 percent claimed that their mothers were tense a great deal of the time. I believe that if ministers' wives who are tense could relax more in the Lord and allow his Holy Spirit to take their worries and strengthen their spirits, they could find great relief. The Psalmist says, "The joy of the Lord is my strength."[17] If we choose to accept joy and refuse worries, the Holy Spirit will give a great spiritual boost.

Many of the respondents showed real concern and understanding for their mothers. They were conscious of the tedious line their mothers were expected to walk.

Sara Cotterell says: "Often ministers feel very conscious of the opinion of people in regard to possessions. Usually, ministers don't have much, and what they do have is paid for out of the pockets of the people in the church. The people give the money for the Lord's work, and so usually, ministers and their families feel really self-conscious, and sort of guilty, if they get anything nice or new. It shouldn't be that way. Once my dad gave my mom a fur coat for Christmas and she loved it, but she felt so guilty wearing it that all of the pleasure of having it was taken from her. She never really felt comfortable in that coat until it was old and a little bit shabby. That is wrong. Ministers are paid a salary, and what they do with it should not concern other people."

Anita says, "You never appreciate your mother until you are one yourself. I could have been much more critical of my mother before I had my kids. She was really good, because she got involved in our activities, like 4-H Club, where she was a leader while we were in it. She supply taught in school while we were growing up, so she gave us a good example of career aspects as well as being at home as a mother. She didn't narrow herself entirely to church functions, but she didn't neglect the church either."

With peace, Karen says: "I knew my mom was human, so I couldn't see how I could raise a child any better than she did."

In most homes, it is the mother who sets the tone of the home. If she is joyful and confident, there will be a positive reflection on the children. If she is tense, nervous and serious most of the time, there will be a negative reaction from the rest of the family. If she feels buried under a

---
[17] Psalm 5:11

mountain of responsibilities which she feels has been imposed upon her, she will be resentful and uptight.

To ministers' wives, I say flow with the Lord. Let His peace be upon you. Don't accept any position until you have prayed about it in earnest and considered it in light of all of your other responsibilities. Would you truly enjoy doing it? Would you feel burdened by it? Ask your family what their thoughts are on the situation. Involve them in your decision. Ask them to pray about it with you. Let them know how important their prayers are to you. I don't believe the Lord is asking you to do more than you feel that you can honestly handle. I believe He means for us to be earnest workers, but workers who accept the limitations He gives us in terms of time, strength, and gifts. If you do not do this, I believe that you are doing the Lord a disservice rather than a service. He wants to shine through you in His radiant glory, that others may see Him through you. He can't do that if you mask His temple with worry and bustle and tension.

Relax in the Lord. If you do not feel led to do a particular job that needs urgent attention, then pray, pray, pray for a worker. It is God's work. If He wants the job done, then He has someone picked out to do it. If you jump in and take over just because you don't see the person He has chosen, you may be robbing someone else of the ministry that God had for them.

Concentrate on God. Make Him your source and your strength. Reach up, and then out to your husband and your little ones. Let them know how important they are to you. Let them know how you need their loving prayerful support. Let them know what your limitations are in a confident and joyful manner.

Have fun with your family. Radiate the joy that Jesus brings to you. Put the telephone down. Go for a walk with your kids. Pretend you are a child again. Be very aware of the fullness of Jesus as you walk along with the kids, laughing and chatting. Sing. Let God give you His best!

PART TWO – CHAPTER SIX

Relating to God

WITHOUT EXCEPTION, the respondents all claimed to believe in God. Although 82.2 percent of them had accepted Him into their lives, and had made a personal commitment to Him, yet only 62.5 percent felt that they were totally committed to the Lord, and that they had been tremendously affected by their decisions. However, this is very exciting in view of the fact that 66.6 percent of the P.K.s went through a period of rebellion.

In discussing their understanding of spiritual things, I concluded that those people with the clearest understanding of the function of the Holy Spirit in their lives were the most deeply committed. None of the respondents who had not accepted the Lord had any clear perception of the living reality of the Holy Spirit. All of them came from denominations where the teaching of the work of the Holy Spirit in our world has been largely neglected. They had been taught about God the Creator, and Jesus who died for us, but the teaching had not been brought to life for them through teaching about the Holy Spirit.

Without giving names, here are five examples of people who have made no commitment to the Lord, and how they relate to the Holy Spirit. The question was, "What is your concept of the Holy Spirit?"

Person No. 1: "I guess it manifests itself in your conscience. It is part of the Trinity. I don't really feel any involvement nor any concrete concept of the Holy Spirit."

Person No. 2: "I don't know ... and the Holy Ghost and all that. I'm afraid I really don't know much about that. I guess it's just God and that's it. I'm very confused about all that."

Person No. 3: "The Holy Spirit is not just in people who believe. He's also in people who don't believe. If you don't believe, then I think He's going to give you evidence to try to make you believe. It's a spirit, but I can't really describe it."

Person No. 4: "Now there you're going to get me. It's something that God created within us that is lying dormant. Some stimulus may bring it to activity. I don't read too much literally into the Bible."

Person No. 5: "That is vague. I don't know if I can put that into words. Three in One. It is so hard to put spiritual life into words. The Holy Ghost. I don't know. I really can't answer that very well. It isn't anything tangible."

Two years ago, I would have answered in much the same fashion. To me, the Holy Spirit was just a dusty something tacked on to God the Father and God the Son. I had no understanding of God's supernatural power being at work in our world today. It was not until I began to search and discover the power of the Holy Spirit, that Jesus was made real to me.

Sandy, age 42, says: "The Holy Spirit was never mentioned when I was a child. Now with the Holy Spirit, I know peace, for the first time in my life. That is what kept me searching – the search for peace which I found through the Holy Spirit."

In the last three years, Sandy's life has been revolutionized. Her businessman husband has come to the Lord, and their marriage is being restored. Her two teenage sons, one of whom was tremendously rebellious, are showing serious interest in spiritual things as a result of the changes they have seen in the lives of their parents.

When Bob Wells was a very young boy, he gave his heart to the Lord. At the age of twelve, he received the baptism in the Holy Spirit. Although he grew cold and did not follow the Lord in his adolescence, he rededicated his life to the Lord when he was eighteen. He says: "I feel the Spirit with me. It's funny though. Feeling the Spirit with you is so intangible. It's like saying, 'I love my wife,' but I can't show you. I can't force you to believe what I say. Jesus sent the Spirit to take care of things down here now. When I received the baptism in the Holy Spirit when I was twelve, it was really a deep experience for me, and I felt really close to the Lord. But with all of the peer pressure, I rebelled, and was spiritually dormant for several years. None of my friends had experienced what I had, it seemed. There was really nothing to solidify my experience after the camp meeting, to really reinforce it at all. For years, it almost seemed like a forgotten experience. I became like an eight-cylinder car running on four cylinders. But during all of that time, I do not feel that the Holy Spirit ever left me."

Karen Gamble is nineteen-years-old. She says: "The Holy Spirit is a very distinct personality. When I accepted the Lord as my Saviour, I knew I was a Christian, but I didn't have the guts or whatever it takes to witness for Him, and I remember like it was yesterday the night that the Lord filled me with His Holy Spirit. I was saved when I was twelve and filled with the Holy Spirit when I was almost fourteen. When the Lord saved me, He took all of that gunge out of my life, but when He filled me with His Spirit, he filled up that hole and made me a complete person. I always felt that there had to be more, and when He filled me, I've never backslidden since, nor had the desire to. Oh, I've done some dumb things, or sinned, but I've never turned my back on the Lord. At that time, I spoke in tongues, but it was a very minor thing. It wasn't what I did, it was how I felt inside. The Lord showed me that I needed something in me that was greater than myself, and that was it. It is beautiful. Now when I don't have words to express how I feel to God, I can just speak in the Heavenly language, but that's for my own personal purposes, when I pray and have my own devotions."

Tanya Marshall, age 29, says: "Sweet Holy Spirit. He is leading me into all truth indeed, and showing me a much truer picture of Jesus, and of God than I ever had before. The Holy Spirit is beautiful. Without pointing at all to Himself, He shows you truly how God and Jesus are, and how the three of them relate in love. He is the Comforter, and that means so very much to me. He is the Helper, He doesn't have high expectations of me. He is there to give me power, not to demand power of me. He doesn't demand that I have courage on my own. When I was about thirteen-years-old, I decided in a very logical manner to accept Jesus. It was so matter-of-fact, that it was comparable to doing Latin homework. In making the decision, I felt that my duty had been performed, but I sort of said, 'Look Lord, as far as this peace, love and joy stuff is concerned, I really don't understand it, but You can teach me all that later.' That was about fifteen years ago, and that was about as far as I had gone spiritually, until a few months ago, when God Himself came to me in such peace. And then after the peace came love, and then I realized that there were alternatives. My further experience with the Holy Spirit is radically changing me. It has entirely affected my life. It has affected the way I behave, what I will accept at work, and what I will do. I feel that I am really growing spiritually now, for the first time in my life, I am growing with real direction. I feel that I am getting to know the Lord myself. I am not relying on anyone else's prayers for me, or on being good or anything. I'm experiencing more joy and peace than I've ever known. I am experiencing true recognizable growth."

Jennifer Holmes, age 39, says: "The Holy Spirit gives gifts to those who are willing to accept them. In order to receive these gifts, it is necessary to let Him dwell within. The gifts offered are the gift of wisdom, the gift of knowledge, faith, gifts of healing, miraculous powers, prophecy, the ability to distinguish between spirits, the ability to speak in different kinds of tongues, and the interpretation of tongues. To some He gives one gift, to others He gives more. I was seven-years-old at the time of my first spiritual commitment. I was in the car with my dad, and we prayed together. From adolescence until my late thirties, God was not of primary importance to me. Then I began a search for truth, and came to the point where I made a second commitment to Christ. I will continue to search and grow as long as I am here. My first experience made me aware of the choices I had. The most important thing in life to me now is the 'peace that passeth understanding.'"

B. J. aged 21, says: "The Holy Spirit is God's power at work within me, and other Christians. I guess He is sort of 'God in action.' I received the baptism in the Holy Spirit about two or three months after I became a Christian. Before that I had a lot of hard struggles that I don't have now. I feel now that I have more understanding of how God works in people. I accepted the Lord when I was just three. In spite of the fact that I really rebelled, I never lost respect for Christ and the truth He stood for. It was the organization of Christianity that I rebelled against, not against Christ Himself. When you see the human aspects, you see imperfections, that was all I was looking at. I went away from the church completely at the time of my rebellion, and I got into dope and even started dealing it. At that time I had lots of friends who invited me to parties because I had the dope, but as soon as it ran out, it was a different story. Instead of them phoning me up, I'd phone them and they'd say, 'Oh, I have to do some homework tonight,' or 'I'm too tired tonight.' There wasn't any reality in their friendship. I came to the point where it was either suicide or accept the Lord. I had no self-respect left, and life was not a pleasant experience for me, so it didn't make much sense to me to stay here. So I figured, 'Well, I'll give You a chance Jesus. If You're real, You've got to prove it to me in this lifetime.' He did that. I tried very hard on my own to find peace and happiness, and it didn't work. I know that Jesus is real because now I do have peace and happiness. As soon as I asked God to come into my life, I knew that He was real. Over the past two years since I did that, my life has completely changed. As soon as I invited Him in, I knew that I had a friend who I could talk to. I tried life without Him, and it didn't bring me satisfaction. Now I know that my life has direction, and I know that each day has a purpose. I have peace about everything, because I know that all circumstances are ordered by God's will when I submit myself to Him. So there is a purpose in everything that happens to me."

Paul Timpany, age 42, says: "The Holy Spirit is the Third Person of the Trinity, who is given to us by Jesus as promised by the Father. The Spirit is the One who teaches us, enables us, and empowers us so that we can live with Christ. I was converted at the age of seven after reading a book about a young man who tried to get away from God. Kneeling down beside the bed with my mother, I asked Jesus to come into my life. That was a real experience that I have never forgotten, and it has deeply affected my life. God is the control, the authority, and the master of my life in every area. I have since been led into the ministry, and am at peace with God. This has given me freedom from doubts and worries, and fears. It has given me an ability to relax, and know the joy of the Lord at all times, and in every situation."

David Harris, age 28, says: "The Holy Spirit is the One who is in contact with us. We cannot separate Him from Jesus. He is the One who empowers us. The way He differs from Jesus is that He is the One who empowers us to praise Jesus. The Holy Spirit praises Jesus through us. That is the prayer language, or speaking in tongues. We do not understand what is being said. When I was eighteen, I got fed up with our church. I had never heard the gospel there, and I left and went around to other churches. Finally I heard the gospel, and thought it was terrific. Finally I realized there was more to it than just being a good boy and getting to Heaven, which is what I had imagined. I found that all I had to do was ask the Lord into my heart, and so that's what I did. However, the next Sunday, the preacher said you have to ask forgiveness for your sins, and I thought, 'Oh, I didn't do that. I only asked Him into my life," and so I did that and thought I was saved. But the next Sunday, there was something else, and then something else that I hadn't done and I kept trying to work out my salvation. Finally I discovered that I had truly been saved that very first Sunday. Praise the Lord."

In an interview with Denny Duron, "Youth Profile Magazine"[18] reports: "Denny's is not a "Heaven-to-hell" testimony. He didn't come to Christ from a life of crime or horrible sin. In fact, he came as a child–five-years-old, to be exact. God saved him from the wrong road in life before he'd really travelled very far. Now that he's had 20 years to think it over, he's more convinced than ever that he made the right choice."

The turning point in Denny's life came in a Sunday morning children's service at First Assembly of God in Shreveport, Louisiana, where Denny's dad, the Rev. R.E. Duron, was pastor. Remembering that Sunday morning, Denny says he heard a sad story called "Barney's Barrell," a special presentation of the gospel message direct to children. When an invitation was given, he understood, and went forward to turn his life over to God. At that moment, he declares, "Jesus just became the best friend I had."And since then, "All my life He's been my constant companion." That night, Denny was filled with the Holy Spirit, the experience described in the second chapter of the Book of Acts which gives Christians power to spread the gospel.

[18] Youth Profile Magazine, Volume 5, Mo. 3, July-August 1978

Through the years, many felt he was missing out on life because of his strict religious convictions, saying things like, "Denny, you're young – you've got a lot of living to do. Here you're a football player and the sky's the limit as far as opportunities. What's wrong with you? Why don't you do the things we do?"

But Denny doesn't feel he's missed a thing. He replies, "There's a lot of things I haven't done, a lot of places I haven't been. But I've never had to search for something to fill a vacuum in my life. I've always known what the answer was; it was Jesus. And whenever I've felt a hunger in my life, I just filled my life with more of what I already have. And that is my relationship with the real Christ." Denny credits his success as an athlete to the Lord. He views football as an avenue for working for Christ, a vehicle God can use for His glory, and his faith has made him a leader on and off the field.

Believers in Christianity claim that Jesus can help us to be better people, to do better at our work, and to feel better about life. But does a personal relationship with Jesus really accomplish that, or is it really just a crutch, as so many nonbelievers claim?

When I came back to the Lord, I was in bad shape. I was on the edge of a breakdown, I believe, and I admit that I needed help – call it a crutch or whatever you like, but I needed something to strengthen me and reveal purpose in my life.

Some people say Christianity is for social cripples. Is that true? I wanted to know for my own satisfaction. I knew that something supernatural had happened to me for sure. I knew that I was a changed person inside, and that it was not I who had changed myself. But why did it happen to me? Was I really a social cripple? I thought not. Did I need a crutch more than anyone else would? Why would I? On the surface I appeared to have a lot more going for me than a lot of non-believers.

I took a look at the respondents for my answers. I compared the committed Christians with those who had not yet made any commitment to the Lord. Were the non-Christians a group of happy people with their lives confidently under control? On the contrary. The non-believers generally tried to assume an air of bravado, but were confused about many things. They did not give the impression of 'having it all together.' When we got into deep discussion about the realities of life, I felt them reaching out, hoping that there really was more to life than they were experiencing. They were crippled, incomplete people, missing a part of themselves. They needed help and most often, couldn't put a finger on their need. It was just a vague feeling that something was missing. They were like blind people who had never seen light. They had no understanding of what they were missing. They were groping blindly, just hoping that their schemes and plans would work out for them. Generally there were a lot of loose ends in their lives.

The Christians, on the other hand were different people. It was as if they had had lights turned on inside. They had problems too, but generally had a clearer view of their direction. It seemed that they were 'wholistic' people, most of them getting all parts of their lives working together in synergy. Their ideas and their beliefs had shape. Even though they were still 'in progress,' they were whole people. I felt comfortable with them, perhaps partly because they were comfortable with themselves. These were not homely, shy, uneducated people. They were a cross-section of society, vibrant and positive. They were certainly not social cripples. How could anyone say that born-again Christianity was just for misfits, when many, many celebrities, idolized by secular society, have experienced spiritual rebirth?

My conclusion is that everyone has need of something else; that no one is complete unto himself. The something that is missing from everyone's life is God. Only when He is accepted into the person, is that God-shaped hole filled up, making the person complete. Even though all Christians have a lot of growing to do, they are complete in the sense of having all the necessary elements and potential within them.

Anything genuinely spiritual that is going to be worthwhile and lasting involves not only an emotional response, but an intellectual search as well. You have to feel deeply about it as well as intellectually accept it.

It was interesting to me to see how many P.K.s, made decisions for the Lord when they were very young, and how deeply they feel those decisions have affected their lives. Many people feel that a four-year-old child is much too young to be trusted with such a monumental decision, but the evidence from my respondents would suggest otherwise. There may be a period of rebellion, but the scripture holds true that promises, "Train a child in the way he should go, and when he is old, he will not depart from it."[19]

---

[19] Proverbs 3:6

PART TWO – CHAPTER SEVEN

Preacher's Kid to Preacher's Kid

ONE OF THE MAJOR PURPOSES OF THIS BOOK is to touch other P.K.s and other kids from Christian homes who may not understand their parents, their beliefs, and their positions. I want to bring hope, assurance and deeper understanding.

I discovered in my research that I am not the only one who feels that need to reach out and touch others with what they have learned from their experiences. I asked the respondents what advice they would have for other P.K.s. Often, a faraway look would come into their eyes and they would say, "Tell them...." This chapter is devoted to their words for others.

Anita says: "If their backgrounds are like mine, they probably feel they are being centred out, but when they grow up, they will understand that they have been very lucky. In your growing up years, you question a lot; but later, you look back in gratitude."

Elaine Mainse Stacey: "Enjoy it. There's nothing to be ashamed of. We should be proud; not afraid of what people are going to say. To those who aren't enjoying the experience, I would say that you've got to find out for yourself. I can't see why people who know about the Lord wouldn't follow Him. It's all so blunt and straightforward."

Bob Wells says: "I don't feel hard done by. Things could have been better at times in certain ways, but all in all, I view the experience in a very positive light. Don't be afraid of your parents. Look for yourself. Develop a spiritual hunger. Don't just be satisfied with sitting in a pew, and wondering what you're doing there week after week. Are you there because you want to be there, and you're getting something out of it? Or are you just there because you're pleasing your folks? Don't waste your time. Investigate. Try your hardest to build up a good rapport with your parents, and try to understand them"

Diane Osborne: "Some P.K.s are really on fire for the Lord. Others just sort of sit in church and others are totally turned off. It really gets to me sometimes. Going to church can be such a drag, week after week, if you don't understand the reality of Jesus. You get so you don't really care anymore about church and you're just sort of going through life – church Sunday morning, Sunday night, Wednesday night, Young People's, choir practice – it becomes just as dull and meaningless as eating supper. I wish so much sometimes that I could just take someone who's like that, taking the whole thing for granted, who's totally bored with it, and just take him and shake him and show him the reality of all of it. There is something else. It's not just going to church every week and doing the things you're supposed to. There's a reality in there. So many people miss that.

"In our home I think I've been lucky in that way because often we had to lean on God for our bare necessities and as a result we saw the reality of Him very plainly. Often we had to pray food and money into the house and when it came, we thanked Him as a family. Also, the P.K.s have to realize that their dad is human just like everyone else. Although he's a preacher, he can make mistakes just like anyone else. But that's not a reflection on God. Don't look at your father and say 'well he blew it you know,' and think it reflects on God. It doesn't have any bearing on what God is like. A lot of kids think if their parents blow it, they're not going to get into this religious stuff if that's what it's like. And that's not what it's like because that's not what God is like. They're looking at God through their parents, and maybe it should be like that; maybe you should be able to see the Lord in your parents, but still you have to remember that your parents are only human.

"I can think of P.K.s who I know who are not serving the Lord and they are not happy. They know about Christianity – they see people who are living good Christian lives and also they see hypocritical churchgoers. But if you're going to run your life according to the people you see, you've lost it. It's your decision. You can see both sides. The thing is to try it for yourself. Find out for yourself. You can't run your life according to what everyone else is doing or how you see them. Christianity has to be a personal relationship. It can't be according to your father nor the elders in the church nor anyone but yourself.

"I can remember the times I really started finding things out for myself. When I started standing up for Christianity to my friends at school by myself, I started to realize – hey yeah, I am a Christian. I started thinking – I've accepted Christ, – why am I so different from these kids at school? When I started telling them about Christ, I started to grow spiritually. Suddenly this was me standing up in front of my friends and it wasn't connected with my father nor the church anymore. This was me – and God. This is the connection that everybody has to have. You have to forget about everything else – blank everything else out and just talk to God on a personal basis."

Karen Gamble says: "You don't have to prove that you're human, because everybody knows that you're human. When you can get your eyes off of other people, and onto the Lord, you won't have any trouble sticking with the Lord. During all of my high school years, I never backslid. Everyone said, 'Oh it's going to be so hard for you to be a Christian in High School'. I never found it hard because I tried to keep my eyes on the Lord. If you keep trying to hear what other people are saying about you, it's just going to hinder your walk with the Lord."

Tanya Marshall: "Try to be patient with your parents. Try to understand them. Remember, they have their own hurts. Remember too, that you are responsible for your own life. If you were brought up rotten, well, you can overcome that, just as other people do. There are other people in a lot worse situations than preachers' kids."

Denny Duron says: "There's no thrill, there's no honour, there's no experience in life that can compare with the call of God. When God calls, answer, don't hesitate. Don't act as though He's taking something from you. No! He's saying die to your goals and ambitions because I have something better and you'll never know the best in life until you know the ultimate in death of saying God, I die to all that I am and I ask you to take complete control of me. I've looked at the faces of many young people and known God was speaking to them. The choice is with you. You are in control until you're willing to lose control. You control your destiny now, and it's up to you whether you will still be in control of your life or whether God will control it fully."[20]

Dave Lawrenson: "Satan is trying to beguile us from the simplicity of Jesus Christ. All Jesus asks is that we trust and obey. That's all. If you can learn to trust and obey Jesus, you've got it in the bag. We need to realize that whatever comes our way, God is working it out. Some of the worst things that have happened to me have turned out to be the best things. Satan has this world so fooled. I'll tell you, when you lie in a prison cell where the lights have been out for thirty days because of crime, because you thought you were having fun, and you lie alone and come upon a blind alley, a dead end street, then someday you'll say with me, 'I'd rather have Jesus.' If you've been there, then you know it. It's not fun. The things of the world are not fun. Talking back to your teacher is not fun. For me, talking back to the teacher was just a small beginning that resulted in talking back to judges in the courtroom. Then I spent years of my life behind bars. But Satan likes to start small, with things like talking back to our parents. I'll tell you; I'd rather have Jesus!"

In this chapter, it may sound as though I have arbitrarily chosen the advice offered by the Christian P.K.s. The fact is that I went through all of the responses and chose those which I believed would be the most helpful. In this book, I am determined to give solid answers, and I know that Jesus is the solid answer. I've lived life without Him, and it doesn't work. Now I have Him, and He has me, and my life is working. The non-Christians offered advice like, "Just hang in there," and "Forget about what people think of you," and "Do your own thing" and "Do the best you can." The advice was shallow. Jesus gives depth and truth.

---

[20] Youth Profile Magazine, Vol. 5, Mo. 3, July-August 1978

PART TWO – CHAPTER EIGHT

Preacher's Kids to Parents

It is not always just the kids from bad homes who have problems. All kids have problems and difficulties of one sort or another. One of the greatest keys to alleviating the difficulties is communication. But it's one thing to recognize a key and appreciate it's value, but quite another to actually put the key in the lock and turn it. As we have heard the P.K.s point out, there are all sorts of barriers to effective communication, even within a pastor's home.

Often there are things a child would like to say to his parents, but he doesn't quite know how to say it. He may wish that someone else would tell his parents for him, so that he wouldn't have to run the risk of hurting them himself. A family tends to be so emotionally involved with one another that it is sometimes difficult to talk objectively about the situation.

This chapter is an open forum, where respondents who wished to contribute to this issue could speak directly to ministers and their wives with advice on raising P.K.s. No names are used in this chapter. The responses are numbered simply for clarification.

Response #1: "Kids want to do other things besides go to prayer meeting. Playing catch in the backyard usually appeals to them more. It's fun. The parents have to realize that kids need other things besides religious activities. Love in the family is the big thing – being friends in the family, and being a family together. Some parents don't have time for their kids, and it shows when they get older."

Response #2: "How can your children love a God who is just driving and driving a man without happiness?"

Response #3: "When children ask questions, don't make your answers too complicated. A simple explanation is all that is required."

Response #4: "Stick to the directions God gives in the Bible on how to raise children. Don't compromise. When the Bible says to punish, you should not spare the rod."

Response #5: "It doesn't please the Lord for you to serve the congregation before your family. The relationship should be first with God, then with the family, and then with the congregation."

Response #6: "Free the kids. If you can't talk to your kids, give them freedom to talk with someone else. Tell them you love them despite the problems, and let them go to someone who can help them."

Response #7: "Don't shove religion down their throats. Nobody is going to believe unless they want to. You can't say to a kid; 'This is God – now believe in Him.'"

Response #8: "Do everything you can to facilitate an independent life for your children. Love them. Experience things that other people are experiencing. Religion is forced on P.K.s more than on most other children, and somewhere along the line, the child has to be allowed to make a few choices."

Response #9: "Be realistic with your kids. Don't pretend that certain sin areas just don't exist for your family. Teach your kids openly and honestly and scripturally about things like sex and reproduction. God created sex. Don't be ashamed of it and cover it up with a lace doily."

Response #10: "Don't put your ministry before your kids, because they're really important. When you're retired, and you're not working for a church anymore, and your kids aren't working for the Lord, it's not going to be worth much to you. Or even when you get to Heaven and you see all of the hundreds and hundreds of people you've led to the Lord, but your own son or daughter isn't there…"

Response #11: "Don't pretend that everything is great all the time. Let your kids know if you're hurting. Let them know that you need their support and their prayers. If you think that things are the pits, let them know. Don't make the kids walk around on eggshells wondering. Make them know what's going on, and ask them to pray for you so they'll feel involved, and necessary, and important. Don't lie and be phony. If you've had a rotten sermon, admit it, accept it. Verbalize your failures to your kids. Say something like, 'Boy, I really thought I had a red-hot sermon for today, but it was really bad.' Young people need to be used as sounding boards. Let them into your life. Invite suggestions and feedback from your kids. There should be a rallying back and forth in the communication. Let your kids come back to you with a divergent opinion. Let the opinions go back and forth. Don't just deliver your final word or opinion. Your family also has a ministry. Let them know how important their ministry is."

Response #12: "It is very important to enjoy life. It is very important to teach true concepts to your children very early in life, so that they won't depart from truth. They might rebel for a reason, but they'll come back if they've been properly taught. Teach them good habits and get them into the Word. Kids' minds are open. They question a lot. Prepare your kids so that they can answer their own questions. Don't always answer their questions for them. Let them know that you are giving them responsibility in their lives. Aim them in the right direction and don't just pull them all the way. Harness their wills, and interest them in the things you want them to be interested in. If kids have friends in church, then they'll want to go. There have to be things in the church for the kids to enjoy. Don't make church a bondage thing."

Response #13: "Make your kids feel that what they're involved in is really important. Don't make the ministering life look like a negative way of life. Make it exciting. Don't dwell on the fact that you don't have this, or you don't have that. Teach your kids that their lives are special, and that they have a valuable role. Don't put them on an ego trip, but don't belittle their positions, and don't make them feel sorry for themselves. Accept and love your kids. Don't expect them to go to every service. Be open with each other. If you're going to give your kids jobs in the church, make them feel that they have a ministry. For example, if you ask them to pick up hymn books after a service, let them know that they're doing it for Jesus, and that it's not just a joe job. If the teenagers want to go to a different church than yours, then I think you should respect that and let them go. Make the child feel privileged to be raised in a Christian home; privileged that God has chosen him to be part of the minister's family. Help him to see that God has given him a special chance to do something for the Lord. Reinforce that. Don't let him feel like an underdog."

Response #14 "If your child is pulling away from you, and doesn't show any interest in your attempts to develop a relationship with him, pray for him. The main thing is to make sure that your own life falls in line with the Scripture. Spend more time on your own relationship with the Lord, and stop worrying about your child. Leave that with God, and accept the fact that you cannot solve the problem yourself. If your child really wants deep down in his heart to do something, and you stop him forcibly, you're not really helping him to change, because he will still have that thing in his heart, and he will just resent you more for stopping him. When your teenagers are having troubles, don't just look at the symptoms. Look at the root problems that cause the symptoms. If your relationship with God is good, there's more chance that your kids will have a good relationship with Him. When you're just dealing with the symptoms of problems, you can say, 'That's his fault,' but if you get right down to the root of the problem, you might have to say, 'That's my fault.'"

Response #15: "When there is conflict, get the feelings out first, and then get at the problem. Get the steam off first so that you won't be cutting with words. If you let the feelings and the issues get mixed up, then all kinds of bad things happen. Learn to forgive. Choose not to hold the past against anyone."

Response #16: "If your child wants to spend some time with you, and you're busy right at that time, give him hope that you will spend time with him at a certain point."

Response #17: "Stop making moral judgements on everybody's feelings. Don't say, 'You shouldn't feel that way.' The fact is that they do feel that way. Deal with the realities. Don't make your kids give you all the details of their problems. Just pray with them and make them know that you care. But don't pray long prayers with your kids. They feel threatened by the possibility of you praying a long impersonal prayer with them the way you do in the pulpit."

Response #18: "Don't show your kids off as being the P.K.s. They will feel self-conscious and that they have a massively high, impossible grade to reach. If they don't make it, they'll feel like a failure in life. Also, being shown off will make them feel that they've got to be a lot better than other kids."

Response #19: "The Word of God is true. Don't give up. Hang in there for your kids. Show them the positive benefits in being a Christian young person. Make them very aware realistically of the pitfalls they need to avoid. Satan is trying to kill our Christian kids. We are fighting a mighty war, but, 'Greater is He that is in you, than he that is in the world.'[21]"

The comments you have just read would seldom be spoken by a child directly to his or her own parents. Generally these are things children may feel inside but cannot vocalize openly. While children may feel inadequate to confront their parents with some of these issues, the fact is that they have some very valuable things to say.

I believe that relationships would be greatly improved if parents would take the time to foster an atmosphere of trust and mutual respect in which a child can speak openly. The anonymity of a research project is surely not the ideal place for a parent to discover how his child may really feel.

Children, on the other hand, cannot give up and simply assume that their parents will not understand their feelings. Each time a difficulty arises, the child should openly discuss his perceptions. Just because the relationship might have bombed out the last time doesn't mean it will this time.

---

[21] 1 John 4:4

PART THREE

The Preachers Speak

PART THREE

Introduction

AFTER FINISHING "PART ONE" OF THIS BOOK, I knew I could go no further without my dad's blessing. I knew he had to read it before I could continue. This is his story too, and what right do I have to fling his personal life out to the public without his consent? From the beginning, my purpose in writing this book has been to bring more unity to Christian families, including my own. How could I possibly accomplish that by proceeding with something to which my dad might object? In my heart, I knew the outcome of the book rested on his reaction to "My Story."

I was terribly apprehensive about his possible response because most of the content was new to him. Never had I told him how he had terrified me. Never had I told him that I had lived immorally (although I'm sure he knew more than I thought he knew). Never had I told him how his choices had affected my life. Never had I told him who I was.

Until the day that I handed him the rough copy of my manuscript, my dad had seen only my mask and glimpses of the reality beneath. His understanding of me was based almost entirely on assumption. Much of the assumption was incorrect.

Before giving him my manuscript to read, I gave it to seven other people, including my mother, for their opinions. Except for mom, everyone was overwhelmingly positive in response. Aunt Jessie said that not one word should be changed. My husband expressed pride in my openness. Mom, on the other hand, has always tried to protect dad from any hurt, and she was terribly concerned that he would not be able to take my revelations.

I prayed for guidance and direction. I prayed that God would prepare dad to handle the situation in the right way, and that He would give him strength.

One Sunday, Dad arrived as planned, and I handed him the manuscript. It was four p.m. He went up to Todd's room, closed the door, sat down at the desk and began to read. All evening we waited and prayed. We did not know what was happening to him up there. Had he had a heart attack? Had he ripped up the pages? Was he angry? Was he sad? Would he disown me? All of these thoughts and more swam back and forth through my mind as I waited.

At 11:45 p.m., I heard the door open upstairs. Dad came down with the manuscript in his hand. He looked at me and handed me the sheaf of papers. "I think it's going to be a good book," he said.

I could hardly believe what I was hearing! Yes, I had prayed for just such a reaction, but somehow never expected it. I was shocked, and more grateful, more touched, more relieved than I can express. In that moment, he grew about ten feet taller in my eyes.

"I understand why you had to get this out," he said. "As I read, I made a few notes clarifying some of the things you described. There are a few places where my perceptions differed from yours, and I jotted them down. You can read through these notes and see what you think."

It was late, and he and Mom had a long drive ahead of them. They were anxious to be on their way. We were at the door saying goodbye, and he put his arms around me and held me for a few moments. It was one of our deepest moments of communication.

After they had left, I curled up in a chair with Dad's notes. I was feeling very thankful for all that had transpired. I marvelled at the way in which God had prepared him to accept the manuscript.

As I read Dad's comments, I began to realize that the situations I described in the book were not one-dimensional. There was an extra dimension which I had not explored. That dimension was his perception of the situations. I had not investigated his feelings, his attitudes, his real reasons for acting as he did in certain situations. I was as guilty as he was, in lack of understanding. I had accepted his masks as he had accepted mine.

It was not so much that we accepted the masks to be reality, as the fact that we each feared rejection if we attempted to remove the masks. And so we had remained separated by a wall of fear and misunderstanding. The result was that wherever we were involved in a situation which concerned both of us, our understanding was incomplete because of a lack of honest communication. This incomplete understanding led, in many cases, to faulty perceptions.

For instance, on the first page of the introduction to this book, I described a situation where Dad confronted me on the matter of my lifestyle. It was a very explosive situation in which I reacted with bitterness and resentment.

In his notes he said, "Your interpretation of this episode is not mine. I said some things that were much more penetrating than those reported here, but were true. My frustration was not concerned with my control of you, but was a result of your foolish choices. Nor was I opposed to your caring about your friends, yourself, and having a good time. My concern was what you considered a good time, what kind of friends you were preoccupied with, how you curried their favour, and what was becoming of you."

We were both concerned with the same issue at that moment of confrontation – my lifestyle. However, our points of reference differed. I had not challenged his biting observations because I had felt it was useless to try to talk to him. I felt that his preconceived opinions were like a brick wall – impenetrable. My resistance to him was entirely internal. I walled myself off from him as the enemy and made myself impenetrable to him.

He, on the other hand, was unable to get a grip on our relationship because I had internalized everything to the extent that he could not understand what was going on within me and why. Unable to show the loving concern which he felt, he exploded in frustration and rage, which I translated as rejection. It was a vicious circle. The more frustration he showed, the more bitterness I felt. It went deeper and deeper until Jesus broke the chains that bound us up.

Communication is the key to a healthy relationship. It must be a two way exchange of thoughts, beliefs, and attitudes.

In the previous section of this book, the preachers' kids aired their feelings and perceptions of the factors which influenced their lives. I pray that Christian parents have gained a deeper understanding of their children through reading it.

What is the other side of the story? In this section, I have brought together the thoughts of pastors on several issues which concern raising children. My hope in this effort is that the preachers' kids will gain greater insight into their dads' positions, and that other ministers may pick up some valuable tips on child-rearing in the Christian home.

In preparation for this section, I prepared a standard interview to use with each minister. I have included it here for the purpose of general interest.

MINISTERS' INTERVIEW

1. Name - Phone - Address - Age
2. Denomination
3. Number of children - ages of children
4. Is a minister's child unique in some of his problems relating to his dad's profession?
5. When you're a minister, what are some of the unique problems involved in raising children? What sort of things do you have problems with in this regard?
6. What are the unique advantages of raising children as a minister?
7. Which comes first - your family, or your congregation (in honest order of importance to you.)
8. Do you try to be both dad and minister to your kids?
9. Which role takes precedence?
10. Do your children balk at having to go to church every Sunday?

a) If no, why not?

b) If yes, what is the best way to handle this situation?

11. Is there much laughter in your home?
12. Could you relate a particularly humorous incident which happened in your family in relation to this topic?
13. Do you expect your children to be examples to others?

    a) Do they perform in accordance with your standards? Enlarge.

    b) How does their behavior make you feel?
14. Do your children take their problems freely to you?

    a) If yes, why do you suppose they feel comfortable enough to do this?

    b) If not, why not do you suppose? Could you make it easier for them somehow? How?
15. Do you spend time with your children doing any kind of non-religious activity? Doing what? Is this important? Why?
16. Do congregations have any responsibilities to your children? Elaborate.
17. When you feel overworked or tense about your work, do you tend to take out your frustrations on your children?
18. Do you preach at your children?
19. Are your children serving the Lord? How many are?
20. Why do some ministers' children rebel, while others continue to grow in the Lord?
21. Is there a way to prevent the rebellion? How?
22. What would you do differently if you could raise your children again?
23. What are the major pitfalls ministers need to avoid in raising their children?

24. Why did you become a minister?

25. How would you describe your relationship with the Lord?

26. How would you describe your relationship with your children?

27. How would you describe your relationship with your wife?

28. Does a minister's relationship with the Lord have any bearing on his child's spiritual development? Elaborate.

29. Does a minister's relationship with his child have any bearing on the child's spiritual development? Elaborate.

30. Does a minister's relationship with his wife have any bearing on the child's spiritual development? Elaborate.

31. In relation to the publication of this book, may I refer to you by name, or would you prefer to remain anonymous?

Thank you for your time and your contribution to this work.

The following chapters are a compilation of the responses of the ministers to these questions. For the most part, they prefer to remain anonymous.

PART THREE – CHAPTER ONE

The Problems and Advantages of Raising Children as a Minister

THE MINISTERS INTERVIEWED AGREED unanimously that although P.K.s are not inherently different from anyone else, they do occupy a unique position in society. With this unique position, comes a unique set of problems and advantages. However, there was a general feeling that the uniqueness of these problems and advantages rests in the particular combination of factors involved. Some problems are identical to the problems faced by doctors' children. Other problems or advantages are like those of a banker's child, or a politician's child, or a teacher's child, or an actor's child.

In order to have a comprehensive understanding of the situation, it is necessary to identify the problems and advantages. In the preceding section, the P.K.s pinpointed these as they saw them. This time it is the ministers' turn. The following lists are compilations of the positive and negative sides of the issue as seen through their eyes. In most cases, names have not been noted in respect for their desire to remain anonymous.

THE PROBLEMS INVOLVED

1. "Sometimes it is a problem trying to let your children know that you're real and human and you're not a person who can't be touched. A minister needs to be very, very human." (David Mainse)

2. "Being able to consistently ignore the telephone and other de-

mands when it comes time for family devotions can be difficult. As sure as anything, the phone will ring and there will be needs to minister to other peoples' families. In the meantime, you're trying to get some quality time with your own family." (Name withheld)

3. "Ministers are expected to have standards higher than, or different from the rest of the community. The children are generally expected to reflect these standards. Some people are very understanding, and do not expect more, but there are many who say that the minister is supposed to have good control over his home and his children should be better disciplined than other children." (Name withheld)

4. "Sundays are not free for the family. This means that for a minister to go away for a weekend is practically impossible. Thus cottage weekends, ski weekends, etc., are virtually out of the question. The kids go to school five days out of the week while the minister has his heaviest day on Sunday. Saturday is usually taken up in preparation for Sunday, and with things like wedding ceremonies. I feel that there are more demands on a minister and there are more things to keep him away from his family than in almost any other profession." (Al Reimers)

5. "The minister feels very conscious that his children should come to know the Lord. Sometimes he has a tendency to overdo it through his own efforts, I believe. This is sometimes a pressure for the sake of the children in their relationship with the Lord, and sometimes I believe it is a pressure that the minister feels in terms of his family being an example for others in the congregation. Sometimes it is a combination of those two things. In my own case, I felt that I wanted my children to come to the Lord at a very early age. I tried to make them conscious of God without pushing too hard." (Name withheld)

6. "Generally, I believe that ministers' children are judged more severely by the general public than other kids are. When my children have demonstrated behavior that isn't consistent with what is expected of a minister's child, they have been criticized quite severely at times." (Name withheld)

7. "Leaders are readers. A great deal of time has to be spent in study and solitary meditation. The only person who doesn't have problems in raising children is the person who doesn't have any." (Name withheld)

8. "There is not a time in the day when the family can just close its doors and sit down together. When dad does get home for supper, it's just to leave again. This makes it very difficult to establish solid family patterns." (Name withheld)

9. "There are special pressures on the kids, and a minister has to be aware of these, and sensitive to them. There are expectations on P.K.s that are not on other kids. For instance, when we were at a church picnic, my little boy reached out for something, and in the process he knocked over a salt shaker. As the hostess picked it up, she said gleefully, 'Isn't it the truth what they always say – that the minister's child is always the worst?' It's not that the minister's child behaves badly, it's that he's expected not to, and when he does, a different standard is applied." (Name withheld)

10. "In terms of the extra pressure on the child, there is the unavailability of mom and dad to consider. Too often, when dad is at home, the family cannot be his first priority. Most professionals come home from the office and leave their work and career concerns at the office. The minister cannot do this. There was a little girl who told her mommy that she was sick. The mother knew that the little girl was really fine. There was no evidence whatsoever of any illness. The little girl insisted, 'No, you tell daddy that I'm sick.' Of course the mother was concerned about why the child would want to lie to her daddy who was a minister. Finally the child revealed, 'Well, Daddy always visits the sick.' That is an extraordinary story, but there is an element of that type of atmosphere in every minister's home." (Name withheld)

11. "Planning time together as a family is tremendously difficult. We do not have a full day to spent together as a family. For example, for the next three weeks I have three weddings booked which leaves me one day in the whole month that I have to spend with

my children. That could change with a crisis situation such as a death in the congregation. These important external things have a great bearing and influence on our home life and the time we spend together." (Name withheld)

12. "The minister and his family are unable to sit together in church. The wife is left to look after the children and any discipline problems on her own." (Name withheld)

13. "A great problem centers around the expectations which the people in the congregation place upon us and our children. Being constantly watched and placed on a pedestal creates that extra pressure which at times we could well do without." (Name withheld)

14. "The frequent change in locale can be a problem. It means adjustment for the child with school and friends. The parents need to help the children with settling in to their new environment." (Al Roblin)

15. "There is sometimes a tendency on the part of the minister to pressure his children into exemplary behavior for the sake of his position in the community, and for the sake of his effective ministry. This may make the child feel secondary and unimportant in comparison with appearances. This can lead to feelings of inadequacy and low self-worth in the child." (Name withheld)

16. "Ministers have so many things to think about and so many demands on their time that they often feel rushed and pressured while they are trying to relate to their children. The children get the idea that other things are more important than they are to their dads. While that is generally not true, the child's translation of his dad's responses to him have a profound effect on his life. Usually a child who is afraid that he is not loved will react in negative ways, whether externally or internally." (Name withheld)

I found there was a great deal of overlapping in the responses of the ministers who were willing to share their comments. There were certain points noted in the preceding list which were repeated again and again as problems. For example, scheduling of time to accommodate the family adequately appeared to be a problem common to most ministers. I included the repetition to emphasize the commonality of issues.

THE ADVANTAGES

1. "The people ministers meet and entertain in their homes have a tremendous influence on the children. We have people from all walks of life coming into our home, including the spiritual giants of our day, and other people from all walks of life. We also have had people come to live with us who were fresh off the park bench, or kicking drugs, or whatever. Some have staggered in the next night having fallen off the wagon. Our children have seen humanity at all of its levels. They have seen superb demonstrations of the grace of God." (David Mainse)

2. "The children in a minister's home generally have a great opportunity to learn how to minister love to other people. There are so many-people with hurts who come to the parsonage for help." (Name withheld)

3. "The tremendous amount of entertaining that is done in the parsonage is a real benefit to the children in the home in terms of teaching them to converse easily with people from all walks of life. They learn how to entertain in their own homes for later on." (Name withheld)

4. "Ordinarily, the minister and his wife are well-educated people, so that the child grows up in an atmosphere where there is intelligent conversation, where there is good use of the English language, where the thought forms and images are helpful to the growth of linguistic ability. I believe this is a real key to success in our society." (Al Reimers)

5. "Even though the child may have a very restricted life in some senses, yet he has a window on the world with all of the world travellers and missionaries who pass through his home. Far away

places are brought to life for him through the conversations of people who have lived in such places as the jungles of Africa." (Name withheld)

6. 6. "People don't often invite their doctor and his family for a meal, nor do they invite school teachers and their families. However, pastors and their families are invited out for many, many meals. This is a very broadening and helpful experience for the children." (Name withheld)

7. "Socially, there are some obvious advantages. They get a little more attention them the average child does in church. People tend to pamper them and make a fuss over them. That is preliminary to the advantage of social development. That helps them to become socially adjusted early in life, and to be able to converse with people easily." (Bill Crump)

8. "If the children have any desire for public work later on, it becomes easy for them to get into it just by virtue of being a pastor's son or daughter. It gives them instant respectability." (Name withheld)

9. "My kids probably wouldn't see this as an advantage yet, but I do: that is that they have to learn to get along in this world on less than many of their friends have. The clergy are one of the lowest paid professions in the community. In terms of teaching values to children, that's not all bad." (Name withheld)

10. "Although children may go through a time of rebellion, later on they can look back and say, 'Wow, my dad was one of the problem solvers through Christ, and he had what it takes to live.'" (Name withheld)

11. "Along with the problems involved in scheduling, there are also benefits, because the timetable generally allows for greater flexibility. Often, I am the only father present at school events because I do not have a cut-and-dried schedule." (Name withheld)

12. "In terms of the minister's position in the community, it is conceivably possible to exercise authority on behalf of his children." (Name withheld)

13. "I have been able to raise my children in an atmosphere which is rather different from the ordinary. It is a highly spiritual atmosphere. Twice a day we have family devotions. We open and close our meals with prayer. We have all of our meals together and have Scripture reading morning and night. The children read and pray along with us. We are pretty well consistent about that." (Name withheld)

14. "In talking with so many parents about their children's problems, I gained greater insight into my own family." (Name withheld)

15. "A minister is in a good position to see the spiritual as well as the physical needs of his children. As you see the lives and needs of others and minister to them, you can better understand the needs of your own children, in relation to what is missing in the lives of others. You therefore have a resource that is not open to all other people, because you are dealing with more families on a personal level." (Paul Timpany)

16. "One great advantage that any Christian has in raising children is that the standards are already set, and he doesn't have to grope around for values and standards to teach his children. Also, he has the help of God whose Spirit is strong and helpful in this matter of raising children." (Al Roblin)

There are problems with any job that will affect the family of the worker. The interesting thing about the problems and advantages of a minister's work is that they are so great. Few work situations are so demanding and yet can be so rewarding if approached in a positive, constructive way.

Yes, God made mud puddles, but I don't think His plan was for us to get mired down in them. He called Christians "overcomers," and He has given us precise guidelines not just for getting through the puddles, but for actually using them to our advantage. What kind of an overcomer sits in a mud puddle crying about the rain and his dirty condition?

I believe that if a minister and his children keep open, honest communication alive, and if they deal with problems in the light of scriptural guidelines, they will reap tremendous benefits. It is simply a matter of living scripture.

When I say, "simply," I mean that the solution is straight forward. I don't mean it will always be easy. The word "overcomer" implies a certain amount of struggle. God's way is not the natural way of man. It is not always easy or natural to forgive. It is not always easy or natural to love. It is not always easy or natural to trust. It is not always easy or natural to pray. God's ways are not our ways, but they are the only ways that work.

I believe that if people care enough, they will struggle to overcome problems. David Mainse, the famous Christian talk-show host, cared enough. When his children were small, he desperately wanted to know how to guide them most effectively in the ways of the Lord. He wanted to keep them from being deceived and drawn into rebellion. He searched out parents within his own congregation and other ministers whose children were all grown and faithfully serving the Lord. He went and sat at the feet of these people and pumped them with questions. He says, "I don't learn things by stacking them one, two, three, in my brain. I get things more by osmosis. I soak things up, and then I begin to find those attitudes coming forth from me. For instance, the attitude of a joyous lifestyle comes mainly from being with Jesus, but it also comes from being with others whose children are serving the Lord. I found these people have a joyous lifestyle that isn't all chopped up into sections. Talking about Jesus is as natural as breathing to them. Jesus is a consistent thread that runs through their whole lifestyle."

Discovering principles, and putting them into effect in one's own life are two different things. It takes an overcomer to do both. A joyous lifestyle is not always the natural way. But it is God's way. David cared enough to overcome and to struggle for his children. He cared. The result is an unusually close family built on God's principles. His four teenage children are all strong Christians serving the Lord joyously. David says, "If one of my children were to go away from the Lord, I would be absolutely crushed. I haven't had it happen, but I think that would be the very worst thing that could happen to me in my whole life. I would rather die myself. I would rather suffer, or do anything I had to, them have one of my children go away from the Lord. I know my wife Norma Jean feels the same way."

David was a church pastor for many years. He had all of the same problems with scheduling etc., as any other pastor, but he chose to be an overcomer. Together, he and his wife and their four children victoriously overcame the difficulties with God's guidance, and took full advantage of all of the advantages He offered.

PART THREE – CHAPTER TWO

The Minister's Role as Dad

"I WAS TRAINED TO BE A SAVIOUR. At home I can't be a saviour, or at least I don't feel like a saviour. I have a real problem with my identity at home. I feel as though I have to be out saving people or I won't be earning my salary. I can't justify my existence at home." (Name withheld)

Does the family have a legitimate right to a place in the life of a minister? Yes. Ministers need to have a clear view of where to 'put' their families in their lives. They need to establish a firm understanding of their priorities. If the order of importance of their responsibilities is not in line with God's teaching, then things will be out of kilter. There will be problems.

According to Ken Lucas, "The family should always be ahead of church responsibilities by a thousand miles. My personal relationship with the Lord comes first. That is what sets the tone for everything I do. Then comes my family. The family was the first institution ever established by God. Therefore, it must be God first, then the family, then the church, the community, and the world at large. We have to keep that order very clearly in our minds. If the family falls apart, then the church will fall apart, and following that, the community will fall apart. God has given us our families, and they are our first responsibilities after Him."

David Mainse agrees. I asked him, "Which comes first, your family or your congregation?"

He replied, "I think there is a big judgement here that has to be made constantly. That judgement has to do with the seriousness of the situation. If a member of my congregation were dying, and my son had a hangnail, obviously, my congregation would have to come first. My son would have to understand that he would just have to grin and bear it with the hangnail. The order that I have tried to maintain is the Lord first and the family second. That is basically because the family was the Lord's idea long before the church. He made man in a family. My work in the church would be next. In my life and ministry, however, there has been a tremendous amount of overlapping of the two. The church became like an extended family. I tried to make a point of disciplining myself to give the children quality time. When I began to travel as an evangelist, I would take one child with me on each trip. All four of them took their turns. That continued until they got into their teens when it became more interesting for them to be with their friends, than it was to be with Dad. They didn't want to miss out on the Young Peoples' activities at home."

While the majority of the ministers felt that the family should ideally have priority over the congregations in their attention, things sometimes worked out differently. For instance, in response to the same question, one fellow noted that: "This is a difficult question because it is so hypothetical. If it came right down to making an ultimate decision, I hope that I would choose my family. The problem, however, is never that clear. If it were a choice between dealing with a family in grief or of dealing with my child who was having homework problems, I would think that my obligations lay with the other family. What happens is that most of the prioritizing is in that kind of decision process, simply because the demands of the congregation tend to be more visible and more urgent. The result is that while my family comes first to me, yet in practice, they usually get second-best."

Another minister who encountered the same problem lost his wife through separation and has suffered estrangement from two of his children. Putting the congregational needs before those of his own family was not the only reason for the problems, but it was a contributing factor. He says: "Ideally, your family comes first, but it's very very easy to deceive yourself into thinking that doing the work of the Lord requires you to serve the congregation first, and into forgetting that your family is part of the congregation. They have certain demands and rights, not only because they are part of the congregation, but because they are your family. I unhappily put the congregation first too often."

As I spoke with this respondent, my heart went out to him. He is a well educated person with an unusually colorful history. In the eyes of the natural world, he has every right to pride and vanity, but he is a humble man. He is totally open about his faults and his humanity. He reminds me of the apostle Paul, who wrote, "For it is not I who live, but Christ in me."[22]

Following the problems with his family, this man experienced a transformation in his relationship with the Lord. He received the baptism in the Holy Spirit. I believe God will heal his relationships with his children because restoration of relationships is the heart of the Gospel.

Reverend Fisher is a very dear, elderly, retired gentleman who has served God faithfully for many years. He sees changes in the climate of parsonage life. "I am afraid that only too often the congregation came first, as I see it now. I had heavy duties because I was also on so many presbytery and conference committees. This took me away quite a bit. I worked very steadily on congregational work with meetings in the evenings that I had to go to. Then there was always visiting to do in the afternoons. I didn't give enough attention to the children. I didn't really realize what was happening at the time. But now, as I look back, things are in clearer perspective. I see other ministers who limit their time in church activities, but in my day, that was not the practice. We devoted ourselves to the church work and the family just tagged along."

In these days of prevalent deterioration of family life, people in general are becoming more attuned to the factors which affect family life. Much is being written on the subject. As ministers study this material for use in counselling other families in distress, I believe, with Reverend Fisher, that they are becoming more aware of the needs within their own families. However, becoming aware of a certain phenomenon is only the first step. Action must be applied to effect a remedy.

It is at times difficult to know which line of action to take in response to certain needs. For instance, given the fact that members of a

---

[22] Galatians 2:20

congregation need the services a pastor has to offer, and given the fact that P.K.s are members of the congregation, who is to be their pastor? Is it wise for a minister to attempt to fill his child's needs for a pastor himself? Should he try to blend the two roles, or should he leave the pastoring to someone else?

I asked the ministers, "Do you try to be both dad and minister to your kids?" The response was rather evenly split. Some felt that while they tried to put the emphasis on being a father, they were necessarily their children's pastor as well.

One minister responded, "Since the minister's children are generally members of his congregation, the father is usually the only minister the family has. This is a difficult, yet rewarding role, because he can look at his children more from a ministering point of view. I've tried my best to be both dad and minister to my children, and it hasn't always been easy. The role of dad does take precedence, although it may not always appear so to the children. This is often because the dad may seem austere in that the pastoral side of his life is part of his entire life, and it is part of his dad role. His knowledge as a minister must be felt with regard to his own children as well as to other children."

From my perspective as a minister's daughter, I believe this man is making a mistake. I do not believe that a minister should try to be a pastor to his children. I believe he should concentrate exclusively on being their dad. This of course includes the responsibility of being the spiritual leader of his own home, but not on a professional level. My dad did try to fill both roles, and with most honourable, admirable intentions, but it caused a lot of problems in our relationship. My attitude toward God became all tangled up in my attitude toward my dad. When I rejected the church for a time, he assumed I was rejecting him. I felt at times like a cog in a wheel, rather than someone uniquely important to him.

As Al Reimers points out, "I think it is very hard for a minister to pastor his own family. In the case of a doctor, he will not attend his own family, and a lawyer will not handle his own case. You really have to depend on friends. Other clergy and their families who the children get to know are often the ones who can best minister to your family."

Bill Crump, of Fairhavens Ministries, tries to be just dad to his children. He feels that in a secondary sense he is their minister, but he has consciously avoided playing the role of their pastor in the home. He says, "I am their dad, and hopefully their friend. In our case, we have had other Christian friends who have been close at hand, and who have been able to do what I could not do in ministering to our children. In the case of my son, he got straightened around spiritually at a youth camp where someone else said the same thing I had been saying, but from a different perspective. Things suddenly clicked with Laird, and he got things straightened around in his mind. When my oldest daughter got married, I participated as her father, and I did not take part in the wedding for that reason. I wanted to be her dad on that day – not her minister."

As far as David Mainse was concerned, "I was their dad, not their minister. Of course all dads have the responsibility of ministering to their children, but I ministered to them as their dad; not as their minister. That had absolutely nothing to do with my relationship with my children."

A minister who prefers to remain anonymous sums up the situation well. In his view: "I don't want to be the minister to my kids. They deserve more of dad. Too many of my colleagues who had ministers for fathers appeared to have relationships which seemed to be more that of member to pastor than that of child to dad. I suppose that I intentionally decided against that for my children. The problem is that the kids do need a minister. Pastors' wives also have a real dilemma in this area. They often can't get past their husbands' egos. A lot of the problems with manses stem from the fact that we are notoriously without pastors because of our own egos. We can't be both husband and pastor. The problem is to find someone who will be pastor to us. That ultimately has to be the choice of the individual wife or child. Very few pastors actually lead their own children to the Lord. They can receive tremendous ministries from someone else. Our responsibility is to put our children in the position where they can receive that. Who they choose to be most influential has to be left up to them. Other children can go to the minister if they disagree with their parents over a spiritual matter, to see what he will say. With a P.K., the highest spiritual authority is already in the house. Therefore, there is less chance of instinctive sharing. The child feels he is totally inadequate in discussing spiritual matters with his dad, because his dad is the absolute authority. If a minister is aware of this problem, he can do something about it, again being first dad. It is sad if a child's father is up on a pedestal far removed from the child and his problems."

A child needs to be able to feel comfortable with his dad. This does not necessarily mean that he should want to take every little area of his life and share it with his father. It simply means that he needs to be able to relax in the presence of his company and feel a warmth in being together.

This atmosphere of ease does not just happen naturally in most homes. It has to be conscientiously fostered and nurtured. David Mainse says of his family: "I'm open to their problems. When they were little, they came to us with all of their hurts, and they have always been received with love and understanding. Children need to know that you're there when they need you. Very often, when they know that, they don't need you. They just pray about it and then they find that they have the answer themselves. It's there already. But they need to know that you are there and are supportive of them. They need to know too, that you're not going to compromise on your moral standards or whatever. I don't spend a lot of time on the problems with my children. I think I spend more time on the answers. From the teaching they've had, even when they're in the midst of a problem, they know inside what the answer is. Of course they have heard my wife Norma Jean, talking to people by the hours, who had more problems than you could shake a stick at. Everything was a problem with some of these people. Our kids have watched this since they were just so high. For example, we've had teenagers actually come and live with us who have talked and talked about their problems to our family, and I think our kids have just resolved within themselves, 'Hey, I'm not going to have those problems.

A minister deals with so many life and death situations, that there is a danger that his children may feel that their cares are not important enough to share with dad. Ministers need to listen to their children and give them a sense of having worthwhile things to say. No matter how ministers view the situation presented by the children, they must realize that to the child, they are very serious. Each response a minister makes to his child is a brick in building a relationship with him. The bricks must be placed with attention and great care in order to ensure a strong structure which is able to weather difficult storms.

Bill Crump says: "I have worked hard at trying to be objective rather than just seeing things through the eyes of the congregation. I have tried to think, 'What is the right thing to do here? Should my kids be denied this simply because I'm a minister and the congregation might frown? What is the real situation here?' Sometimes it is hard to sort things out and retain your honesty and integrity. We tried to retain a certain degree of elasticity in our home, rather them being entirely rigid in every area. This helped the kids to feel that they weren't overly restricted. I have offered them freedom to make many of their own choices. Often they bring their problems up in the form of family discussions around the dinner table. We have an openness where nobody feels threatened or afraid to share their problems. We sort of always knew where the kids were at, and they knew where we were at. Things weren't hidden around our house. There was a transparency about our family life. There are times, however, when I do get frustrated with my work and can tend to take out my frustrations on the kids and my wife. I like to get alone for a while and get away at those times. My wife senses those needs."

One vital key in raising children successfully is recognizing the importance of a moment in a child's life. Each time they are ignored or pushed aside as unimportant, another brick is being laid. Poorly laid bricks will weaken the structure of the relationship.

Ken Lucas says: "Communication will stay open for as long as we keep it open. We must never ignore the children. We must consistently respond. Children must be taught to wait if you're doing something important, but it must be made clear to them that as soon as you're finished the job, they will have your attention. Then follow through. Don't let the child think that you really don't care. So many people promise to pay attention to the child 'in a few minutes,' but then go on to something else forgetting about the child's needs. If you ignore the kids when they're little, then they'll ignore you when they get older."

It is easy to underestimate the importance of a moment in a child's life. It is easy for a minister to deceive himself into thinking that he will have more time for the child later on. Later on will be a busy time too.

I spoke with a lovely retired couple who had worked hard in the church for many years. The old minister said: "Our children came to us with some of their problems, I guess, but we didn't always realize what was going on with them. We were very busy. My wife, too, was very involved in organizational work, and we thought at the time that the children were old enough to handle their own lives pretty much."

His wife added: "Maybe I was more involved that I needed to be, but I just felt that I was expected to do all of those things. There wasn't really a conflict between my role as mother and minister's wife; I simply put my public life first most of the time. However, we loved them, and they knew that. They really didn't seem to have any major problems."

Unfortunately, supposing that a child knows that he is loved is not enough. I spoke with one of the daughters of this couple. She has turned away from the church. Whether she showed signs of major problems at the time she was growing up or not, she has a major problem now. Would things have turned out differently if she had been given more time and attention at home?

The beautiful thing about this elderly couple was their honesty. They made mistakes and they admitted their difficulties. They were able to bring them out into the open where they could be dealt with. It's much easier to forgive someone who admits fault.

Unfortunately, I talked with a good number of ministers who were very defensive about their actions and attitudes. These were generally men whose children were rebellious and could not communicate honestly with their fathers.

One such minister said, "My children say that I am real and that I am not putting on an act. I feel confident that when they can't handle a problem they will bring it to me."

That man's four children are now adults living far from the Lord. One is even in prison. The father tried to elevate himself during our interview in defense of his inadequacies as a father. He was full of pomp and obviously terrified of being toppled from his pedestal. He is fooling himself thinking that his children will come to him with their problems. They won't because they can't relate to his act. He oozes unreality. If that man could get out from under his ego long enough to say to his kids, "Look, I love you but I don't know how to handle myself with you, so please pray for me," things would start to happen in that family. Honesty and transparency are vital factors contributing to healthy relationships. Throughout the interview, he was nervous and rushed. He accepted absolutely no responsibility for his children's rebellion. His whole attitude was bombastic. If I had a problem and he was the last person on earth, I wouldn't take it to him. How often have his children felt the same way? How very sad.

PART THREE – CHAPTER THREE

Life and Rules in the Rectory

A FREQUENT COMPLAINT OF MINISTERS' CHILDREN is that their homes are too restrictive.

When Bill Crump's children were very young, his two little girls were playing outside. Janice said to Beth, "Beth, let's play house. I'll be the mother and you be the little girl. Whatever you want to do, you can't."

I doubt very much that things were really that bad, but ministers' homes are notorious for being restrictive. Is this good or bad? On the surface, it would appear to be a negative factor in manse life. However, 82.2 percent of the P.K.s who responded to my interview believed that being raised in a minister's home speeded their acceptance of the Lord.

We have heard how the P.K.s feel about the subject; now let's take a look at the other side. Why do ministers set the rules they do in the manse? What are their feelings surrounding the issue of lifestyle in their homes?

I asked the ministers what they felt about church attendance for their children. Is it necessary for a child to go every Sunday?

Dr. Ralph Wilkerson of Melodyland Christian Centre in Anaheim, California, says, "If I lost my kids the way Mary and Joseph lost Jesus, I think I'd go and look in the church as they did because that's all my kids have ever known. I was brought up in the church too. If you look on the back of my head, you'll see a ridge, because we had pews made out of slats. I used to sleep on those benches, and they were the hardest things you've ever seen in your life. They were separated just exactly the width of the ridge down the back of my head. As a kid, I'd lay there, and once in a while I'd find a song book called "Hymns of Praise" to sleep on. I made it alright. I don't think I was too damaged. Some people feel sorry for the poor kids who go to church. I think they're blessed of the Lord if they've been brought up in the house of God. Paul writing to Timothy said that it was the scriptures that he learned as a child that could give him the wisdom that leads to salvation through faith in Christ Jesus. I think that you've got to pour the word of God into the hearts of those babies when they're just little tots and let them learn the scriptures. You'll be surprised how the Word will come to life and they'll understand it."

Dr. Wilkerson's children are strong Christians. Compare his position on the issue with the following excerpt. The minister whose opinion I now quote has four children, none of whom are Christians.

"My kids say that the church is stuffy, and I have to say to them, 'Well, I know you're right, but we need you there.' When we had to start forcing the kids to go to church, we quit forcing them. Our son stopped going when he was eleven or twelve. By that time, he had a pretty good understanding of the Gospel, and we left the choice up to him."

If the church was stuffy, and the minister himself recognized that fact, why didn't he do something about it? Where were the challenging, exciting youth groups? I believe that if a minister expects his children to go to church on Sundays, he had better make sure there is something there for the child. I hate to think what is going to happen on the day of reckoning when the ministers who have been sloppy and lazy stand before God. These men have been entrusted with flocks which they have allowed to stray.

I was talking today with a minister whose church is dead. He can't understand why his people seem so blasé about the Lord. Has he really involved the Lord in his services as the living Holy Spirit who longs for people to hear His voice, or has he organized God out of the church? Is he leading his people in free praise and worship of God, or does he have them chained in tradition and ceremony? Is he truly preaching salvation and the full Bible to the people, or is he treading on tiptoes afraid of offending people?

If a minister is doing his job properly, he will be offensive. To many people, Jesus was offensive. The Gospel is offensive. It is offensive to Satan and it is offensive to anyone listening to him. Many people filling the pews don't want to be confronted with straight Gospel. Some preachers are afraid of losing them and their pocket books. I say let them go if they don't want to hear truth. Maybe the church will be emptied if a minister starts to preach the Word of God, but it's God's work, and He will fill the church fuller than it was before, with people who are hungry for truth. God promises His Word will not return unto Him void.

Children and teens are turned off by phoniness and unreality. They can spot it a mile away. In the vast majority of cases, it is not the Gospel which turns them away from the church, it is the way in which it is presented.

Too often, people expect their children to balk at going to church, and when it happens, they just assume that the children don't like church.

Ken Lucas says: "Find out the root problem of why they don't want to go. Deal with the root problem which could be something entirely different that what appears on the surface. I expect my children to go to church as long as they live in my home."

W. Nelson Hooper gives a clear example to illustrate Pastor Lucas' point. He says: "Recently, our little boy informed us that he didn't want to go to church on Sunday evenings. As we chatted about it, we realized that the reason for his resistance was that we were asking him to have a sleep Sunday afternoons. This was so that he would not be cranky staying up later on Sunday night. Often, when you sit down and discuss the problem, adjustments can be made to the satisfaction of everyone."

Ed Bentley says, "Children should be simply expected to worship together with the family as part of the natural family function. However, there is a point in adolescence where a child should no longer be told that he must go to church. At that point, we must rely on what they have developed as their own lifestyle and faith relationships. There comes a point where we have instilled most of what they will absorb from the parents. Then we have to let go so as not to damage that which we have built."

The ministers were in unanimous agreement that building a spiritually healthy child takes more than family devotions and church every Sunday. It is vitally important that the minister and his children should spend time together in activities unrelated to the church.

They felt it is very important, particularly for a minister's child, to see his dad in ordinary situations where he is just a natural human being – approachable and removed from his pedestal.

Pastor Lucas says, "We have to get things in common with our kids. If a child enjoys playing ball, then the father should get out there and play ball with him. We expect kids to do so much that we want to do, and we must do some of the things that they want to do. We must help them to feel that they have some valuable input."

According to Al Reimers, time spent with the children away from the church is of absolute importance. He says, "Working on the lawn or the garden together, fixing things together, doing household chores together, even taking things to the dump together is important. There is a whole lot of incidental learning that goes on in activities like that. The children learn what kind of tools to use in certain situations, how to deal with a clerk in the store, etc. These are casually learned activities, but very important."

Frank DeVries does not have a television in the manse because of his beliefs. For most children these days, that would be considered a fate worse than death. Reverend DeVries says, "We sit around together and talk a lot. There is more opportunity for that without a television. There is no problem with the children in this regard. In our activities we try not to separate the religious from the non-religious. We try not to separate Christianity from life. When we camp, we camp as Christians. Then all of life becomes spiritual. We do everything to the glory of God. We must be involved with the children in all areas of life, because they need to be developed in all areas. Physical and mental development are important as well as spiritual development if we want our children to be effective people of God."

Paul Timpany is another who feels the importance of a unified life. He says, "Everything we do can be done in the name of Jesus. God does not forbid us activities that are not specifically religious. I believe it is important for my children to know this – that God can be a part of every aspect of our lives, not just the so-called religious aspects. That again is a learning experience for the children as it was for me as a child."

Ed Bentley stresses the importance of spending time with the children away from the church activities particularly for a minister, in order to build up the separation between the roles of pastor and dad. He says, "The greatest spiritual growth in a child occurs in a natural setting. Most of our religious settings are not natural. Look at the way a family sits around together at home. Then look at how it is structured in a worship service. Kids learn best in a natural environment. When I want to provide an opportunity for spiritual growth in my children, I'm more likely to take them to the zoo where we can talk as we walk. They are more open when they are doing things they enjoy, and when they're in an area where they feel that they have as much to offer as you do. That changes the atmosphere from one of teaching to one of sharing. The child will get much more out of a situation if he is given a chance to put something into it. He needs to feel that he has an important contribution."

From his experience, David Mainse says you can't force the Christian way onto children. In his view, it's a lifestyle, and it happens by being together. He says: "It happens by example. For instance, when children sneak past the door and they see you in a room praying, and you didn't know that they were sneaking by, you've shown them something real. They know this is not just something you're putting on. They know that it is just as important as eating three meals a day, or going to bed at night. Then the odd time they may get a glimpse of it being even more important to you. Everything you do is important. We did everything as a family, whether it was fixing things around the house or taking vacations, cutting the grass, or tussling on the ground. We did all kinds of things that people would say aren't religious, but in a sense they are. They are all part of the lifestyle."

One of the chief complaints of the P.K.s was that their dads and others expected them to be examples in the church and in the general community. In his book, *Jesse,* [23]Jesse Winley observes: "Through the years, I

---

[23] *Jesse* by Jesse Winley with Robert Paul Lamb, pub. 1976 by Whittaker House,

have learned that because a child is a minister's son, he's not necessarily going to be an ideal person unless he walks in the ways of the Lord. Even so, as preachers, we're sometimes guilty of imposing certain conditions on our children because we have to uphold our reputation. As ministers of the Gospel, we want to keep our status high. We don't want the kids to bring any reproach on us, and as a result, we tend to push a lot of things on them to enhance our image in people's eyes. And we can make mistakes with them that only God in his faithfulness can redeem. For when kids aren't "born again," and don't have God in their hearts, they have no power in their lives to live the kind of life we demand of them ... even though they may be preachers' kids."

I asked the ministers how they felt about this problem of their children being expected to be examples to others, and how their children's behavior made them feel.

Frank DeVries responded, "I expect them to be examples to others in the sense that they are Christians. They should behave as Christians, but we must always keep in mind that they are also human. We cannot deny our humanity. We should not expect our children to be on a higher plane that we are ourselves. We must realize their weaknesses and shortcomings and that if they miss the boat at times, there is forgiveness."

Paul Timpany feels much the same way. "I don't expect my children to be examples any more than any Christian parent would expect his children to be examples. This is particularly true of my older children who profess Jesus Christ. We share with them that because they have given their lives to Jesus, they are expected to live up to certain standards, according to the Word of God. But no, I do not expect them to be better than other children. I just expect them to be an example if they claim Christ. Sometimes the behavior of my children upsets or discourages me, but I realize that they are no different than other children, and that they are quite normal. They will naturally do things that are wrong, and they will make mistakes. That is just taken as a part of their normal life."

Bill Crump admits that his children don't live up to his standards entirely. He found that as his children grew up, he and his wife Ruth made fewer and fewer decisions for them. Bill says: "We discussed decisions with them, and in most cases they have accepted our value system simply because they're all Christians. But we do not totally agree on every matter. We allow them freedom in their decision making."

Al Reimers is another who recognizes the value of guided freedom. He taught his boys what he could, and is now trusting God to do the rest. "I don't expect them to be examples right away. I believe that they will be eventually. I've already had evidence of them going through a period of rebellion, and I don't know whether that's going to be a short period or a long period. But I look at my own experience, and the experience of those around me, and I expect that sooner or later they will come to their senses and choose the right way. Then they will be examples to others. Right now, they are not doing what I would like to see them do, but they're young, and I'm not really performance conscious at this point. I'm much more concerned about their character. I know that the Lord is going to use whatever situations they are in to help form their character. He is going to reveal something about themselves to themselves. I keep praying that their responses to His revelations will be self-correcting, so to speak. If I am looking at a map, and I see that I am off course, then the sensible thing to do is correct my course. I think that the boys will do this."

Compare that father's prayer to the prayer of this father whose son is deeply hurt and deeply rebellious: "Lord, just let my boy have another miserable day."

That father reasons that when we get most miserable, we're more likely to seek God. He tells his kids, 'Wherever you go and whatever you do, just remember the Lord is watching.'

If my dad had said that to me, it would only have served to widen the gap separating us. That minister thinks he is presenting a picture of courage in the adversity of his children's rebellion. In reality, he feels guilt because he knows he has contributed to their confusion. Nevertheless, he refuses to accept one drop of responsibility for the difficulties of his children, and remains aloof from them on his self-righteous pedestal. We will take a deeper look at rebellion and the responsibilities of ministers in the next chapter.

As far as Ed Bentley is concerned, the pressure to be an example to others is not a burden that can be fairly put on a child in any situation. He says that the problem is that very often, other people expect them to be examples. Ed says, "Sometimes our children make us feel very proud. Sometimes they disappoint us, but I try not to let my ego get into the picture in terms of letting myself be embarrassed by them. My anger is directed more at the child rather than in relation to the expectations of others."

The fact is, that the children of ministers are on display by the very nature of their positions. As long as there are ministers, there will be congregations watching P.K.s and their families.

In one of Ralph Wilkerson's sermons at Melodyland, he was speaking to the congregation about the family and raising children. Of his own family, he said: "I get kind of disgusted every once in a while when people decide it's their business to get into my business. It always upset me when anyone would say, 'There are the preacher's kids. ' Hey – they're not the preacher's kids; they're Ralph Wilkerson's kids. I want my kids to be raised just like anybody else's kids. I don't want you picking on them. I don't want you saying they've got to be better. They don't have to be worse, but they don't have to be better. They would have been better if they hadn't played with your kids!"

There was laughter, and everyone took his words in the loving, jovial spirit they had been given, but there was truth in his message.

Generally, there is a warm relationship between the congregation and the P.K.s. The problems are not unlike the problems encountered in any extended family situation.

The words of one minister summed up the expressions of many. He said: "A lot of people have contributed to our kids' growth. They have been available when I haven't been, and they've covered for me to some degree when I've been busy. As the pastor, my congregation has certain responsibilities to me, and my kids come as part of the package. However, I take it as part of the responsibility to see that my time is not so filled that I don't have time for my family. We all have a Christian responsibility to one another's children."

Life in the parsonage is a fishbowl existence. However, if the big fishes keep their eyes on the little fishes as well as on the things outside the fishbowl, there will be less chance of collisions.

PART THREE – CHAPTER FOUR

The Rebellious Child

MY GREATEST PURPOSE IN WRITING THIS BOOK was based on the whole issue of the rebellious child. I loved my own little boys so dearly that I wanted to find out how to raise them in a Christian home and keep them from straying from the Lord. I knew many of the principles involved in raising children in a preacher's home would apply to any Christian home. I wanted to find out why some ministers' children rebelled while others continued to grow spiritually. Could the rebellion be averted? What are some of the factors important to a child's healthy spiritual growth?

I asked David Mainse what he thought. He said: "Everyone is an individual. I would say that there are many cases where you could put it down to the responsibility of the child himself, who has simply decided of his own free will, to have a fling, and to rebel, and to go his own way. He does not choose the lifestyle of dad and mom. There may have been absolutely nothing wrong with that lifestyle. It may be a totally independent, individualistic decision of that child.

"On the other hand, there may have been something wrong with the lifestyle of the parents. There may have been inconsistencies in the home. The parents may have constantly ripped other people apart. They may have constantly torn the congregation apart, in front of the kids, so that the kids get the impression that there isn't one decent Christian in the whole church. They wonder what is the use of being a Christian if dad hasn't got any. The parents may make things so distasteful for the child, that the child doesn't want to be a Christian.

"The child may find friends at school who have homes where there is love, and happiness, and no backbiting or fighting, or cruelty. These may be people who are filled with the milk of human kindness, but who are not Christians. They may not even go to church. The child will say, 'Hey there is more love here than there is in my own home.' This would be an instance where rebellion would be the fault of the minister and his wife."

Al Reimers gave me an understanding of rebellion that I had not previously grasped. He said it was his guess that we all rebel. I asked him to expand on his thought, and he continued: "Rebellion is in the nature of us. We are all born in sin, and sin is rebellion. It is putting the self first. But putting the self first can take many different forms. In some cases, it is externalized, or more visible than others. Some rebellion is internalized. The externalized rebellions are the ones that gather all of the attention. But you can have a person growing up whose external behavior is quite appropriate, but still is rebellious in the sense of putting his or her opinion above that of God's. I think that all of us, and certainly every minister's child, is going to go through a period of rebellion, more or less open, and it's going to take either external or internal form, or both. Sooner or later, the minister's children, just like everyone else, have to come to the point where they say, 'Lord, I'm sorry.'"

I would say, therefore, that there is no way to prevent the rebellion. We are all sons of Adam and daughters of Eve, and it's a natural inborn thing. We all go through a wilderness period, which may be a matter of a short time, or a matter of many years.

A well-known evangelist who prefers to remain anonymous continues this thought. In his opinion, a great deal depends on the personality of the individual. Some people keep their rebellion all inside so that no one sees it. Others are much more open about it. He says: "Personally, I'm like a doctor, and would far sooner deal with an illness I can see and diagnose. Then it is easier to treat. The danger is in illnesses that you can't see. Everyone has a right to choose whether to do right or to do wrong. In spite of what God did in sending His Son, and what the Son did in sending the Holy Spirit, and in spite of what I've done as a father, my children have the right to choose. C.S. Lewis said that Hell is the greatest compliment God has ever given to a human being. We have the right to choose to go to Hell or to Heaven. God does not coerce or shove us in, in any way. But He does say that man must come on His (God's) terms."

I believe that the root of rebellion is generally pride. It is pride both in the parents and in the children. Frank DeVries says: "The children will copy what they see in the parents. They respond to what they see. As parents, it is necessary to give the example of humility. That would prevent to a large degree the growth of rebellion. The Lord requires us to humble ourselves. Children must realize that parents are aware of their own failures and shortcomings."

According to Bill Crump, "There is an awful tendency to yield to the pressure to have your kids conform to a certain pattern that really involves your pride as a minister. These pressures push you to have your children as models and examples. If you don't approach that thing very cautiously, you can get so warped that without even being conscious of it, you are imposing on them a lifestyle that they're not ready for at all. Preachers don't often anticipate that as a problem, and so they run into it headlong. Also, the preachers are dealing constantly with problems of behavior and morals on the front line, so to speak. They are wrestling with these kinds of problems and so the kids are bound to hit it headlong; whereas with other families, the issues tend to sneak up on them. In a pastor's home, the issues are drawn and laid out more distinctly, mainly because of the vocation involved.

"In our home, we tried to retain a certain degree of elasticity, rather than being totally rigid in every area. When the kids were young, we guided their decisions, but there came the time when I had to give them the right to make their own decisions. There were cases where I didn't approve of the decisions they made, but when you offer kids this freedom, you run the risk of them making a decision that is not consistent with yours. But that's the risk you run, and when they make it, you can't come back to them and say, 'You did the wrong thing.' You can't give them the right, and then criticize them for using it. The Scripture says, 'Train up a child in the way he should go, and when he is old, he will not depart from it.'[24] Therefore, if he does depart from it, somebody has failed along the way. I must say that all of us fail in some respects, but if there's a negative

[24] Proverbs 22:6

pattern developing, then you'd have to go back to square one, and say, 'What is happening here? What am I doing wrong? Why is it not working? If the product is not right, then something is not right in the process. That is often attributable to human beings just being human beings, and being weak, and getting off balance. It is often a failure to see things as they really are. Rebellion is a result, and should be dealt with in terms of prevention rather them cure.

"In the final analysis, we are all responsible to God. We stand as individuals before God, and I'm not prepared to judge any preacher because he has to answer to God. I think that there comes a time when the responsibility for rebellion is transferred from the father to the child. There comes a time when the child has to stop blaming the parents. At that point, he can no longer use his parents as a cop-out, and he has to say, 'Okay – my parents did some dumb things, and my dad as a minister did some very unwise things, but here I am at this point in history and what am I going to do about it?' It's like reality therapy. I think that there comes a point in a teenager's life where he can no longer say, 'Because my father was such-and-such, therefore, I am so-and-so. Obviously there is a strong influence there. If the father is doing a lot of dumb things, then he is going to reap the results in his kids, especially in boys.

"With boys, there is the masculinity factor at work. Often he resists being like his dad lest his friends say that he's going to be a preacher just because his dad is. It's very important to let boys take their own initiative in choosing to go to Bible School, if they do. At many times, a boy's rebellion is not so much a rebellion against God as a seeking for individuality and his own identity. He does not want to be just a replica of his father. There comes a point of pride in individual conviction. The point is that the rebellion may be more a seeking after individuality than a turning away from God."

In his book, *Jesse*,[25] Jesse Winley tells of how God dealt with him through his children. One time he was in Virginia preaching when he felt God was telling him to cut the revival short and go home. The next day he flew back to New York. At six in the morning, detectives and police-

---

[25] *Jesse*, by Jesse Winley with Robert Paul Lamb. Published by Whittaker House, Springdale, P.A. 15144, 1976.1

men surrounded the house and arrested his son. The boy was taken into custody and charged with armed robbery. Jesse recounts: "God said to me, I brought you home so Maria wouldn't have to face this alone.' And I understood the reason for being back in New York.

"That same day, the boy was released in my custody. When we got home, Maria and I sat down to talk with him. 'Why did you do it,' she asked sorrowfully.

"He wouldn't look at us. I didn't want my friends callin' me chicken,' he murmured.

"Maria sniffed and blew her nose into her handkerchief. 'But that's not much of a reason,' she said.

"He was embarrassed for us and himself. I just didn't want them calling me names so I went along with them,' he answered."

Although the boy was only involved in one armed robbery, the police had him charged for several and the defence was unable to convince the judge otherwise. Jesse's son was sentenced to twelve and a half years for armed robbery. Almost immediately, he began serving his time. Jesse continues:

"Maria was hurt. Heartbroken. I was too. I began to search myself to see what, possibly, I had done to put him in such a place as prison. Maybe I had failed as his father ... but I remembered the time right before I came to New York when a buddy and I attempted to rob that Syrian merchant back in Georgetown. And I tried to do that in spite of all the help and church training papa had given me. I simply wasn't 'born again' then, and neither was my son now. That was the key to the whole problem.

"But I determined that I wouldn't turn my back on him. 'This is the time a boy needs his family,' I told Maria. And we began taking the entire family to Comstock to visit him almost every weekend. We made the trip just like a family outing for seven years, until he was released on good behavior. The walls and bars didn't bother us. We were there to help our son whom we loved, and whom God loved.

"When he first entered prison, he was bitter and resentful. In his anger he turned to philosophies of the Black Muslim and Black nationalist groups he came in contact with. But, through the strength of the Lord, we continued to visit and to show him the love we had for him. In all that time, we never rejected him or gave him reason to believe we were ashamed of him. Slowly, things began to change. His heart was melted by the agape love that God shed through us, and I began to receive letters which brought tears of joy to my eyes.

"'Dad, please come up to Comstock. I need you to pray for me.'

"And one day those prayers led my boy directly to the throne of grace and a confession of Jesus Christ as Lord and Saviour.

"I could see the Lord's hand at work as He was dealing with me through my children. Often it was painful, but the victory through Jesus always turned our mourning into joy."

It was the kind of unconditional love that brought Brian Ruud and Dave Lawrenson, and the Lord knows how many others, back to the acceptance of God's love. Children have to know they're loved in spite of their actions.

Dr. Ralph Wilkerson warns: "If you tell your kids long enough that they're mean, they will be. Kids need to be picked up and loved and hugged and prayed over. Tell kids that they're bad if you want them to be bad. I tell them they're good even when they're bad because then they'll be better!"

I believe that is a very important key in raising children. When a child's behavior is bad, that doesn't mean that the child is bad. Instead of saying, "Timmy, you're a bad boy!" as he hits his brother, the message should be, "Timmy, that was a bad thing to do!"

The teenage years are the times when rebellion is most common. According to Ed Bentley, teenagers are never satisfied with the expectations that adults have of them. "They are too confused about their own self-images. He feels that sometimes the rebellion has nothing to do with the fact that the child was raised in a minister's home. Ed says: "Kids will at times hurt you where it hurts most. Where could you hurt a minister more than at the point of spiritual life? This is not necessarily hard and cynical; it's just kid-like. Our children are still very young. I hope that keeping the communication lines open is the key. There is of course a difference between rebellion and non-acceptance. I expect by the law of averages that some of my kids are not going to accept the pattern that I would consider the best one in terms of growing in their relationship with the Lord. But I would hope that the communication between us as a family would be good enough, accepting enough, supportive enough, that my kids could simply tell me about it rather than feel that they had no alternative but to rebel."

Rebellion in teenagers is often a cornered rat type of response. When kids don't see any other alternative, they may think that the only way to get out of this situation is to rebel. The situation may be a discussion, an argument, a career expectation, or whatever. Rebellion is a last resort. I may be naïve, but I hope that the communication lines with my own children will be open to the point that they will never have to reach a last resort.

Ken Lucas has three young children, and is discovering that children are born with sensitive spirits. He says: "They can be hurt so easily. That spirit must be kept intact as you direct the will. In Ephesians, Paul directs the fathers not to provoke their children to wrath. We can be the cause of some of the frustrations of children. The spirit of a person can become bitter and resentful. The key to a relationship is the amount of time spent with that person. When we look back on our own relationships, our best friends were the ones we spent the most time with. A parent has got to be not only a parent to the child, but a friend as well. It is important to spend a lot of time with children doing small things together. Memories are very important. They are stabilizers for later years. These are things which do not cost anything monetarily, but are priceless in the development of the person. We must teach the kids line upon line, precept upon precept from the Scripture. This takes time and effort and work.

"A father must not be just an authoritarian figure who provides food and shelter for his family. He must be a friend as well. A child doesn't look at the roof over his head or his food as gifts. He takes that all for granted, and accepts it all as the responsibility of the parents. We must be a vital part of our children's lives. We must show concern for them – who their friends are, and so on.

"When I go to the church office, we tell our children that Daddy is going to work now. We don't say that I am going to the church. It is important for young children not to feel that the church is always keeping Daddy away from them. We don't want our children to develop resentment toward the church."

Reading through the responses of the ministers to my questions, I found many different points of view, and several thought-provoking, fresh insights. I want desperately to protect my sons from having to endure the consequences of rebellion, but is it possible? I want them to grow strong in the Lord and choose the paths God wills for them. But only God knows how He will have to discipline them and prune them to make them strong and tall. Todd is in bed snuggled up to his little stuffed bunny, and Tim is eating crackers and peanut butter in the kitchen. Everything is so peaceful and beautiful at this age. Oh God I pray you will give us wisdom to guide these children through the tempestuous years. Lord forgive the mistakes we make and keep these boys close to Your side. Make their lives count for You. Help us to be consistent in their training, firm in discipline, giving of our time, open in our loving, attentive in our listening, humble in our attitude, and grounded in Your principles. And Lord let us not forget how to laugh and have fun.

PART THREE – CHAPTER FIVE

Pointers from Pastors

LLOYD OGILVIE ONCE SAID, "We can only communicate effectively that which we are learning."

There is no note of authenticity in what people say if they themselves have not learned, or are not in the process of learning that very thing. There are loads of books around on child-rearing, but who can advise ministers on how to raise their children effectively better than other ministers who have learned by experience? Who but another minister can relate to the problems and advantages of raising children in a parsonage?

I asked the ministers to share their thoughts on raising P.K.s with other ministers. One question was, "What are the major pitfalls ministers need to avoid in raising their children?" Another question dealt with what the ministers would have done differently if they could start over again with their children. We will deal first with the issue of pitfalls in the parsonage.

David Mainse feels that one of the greatest dangers is that of setting the children up as some sort of examples to others. He says that they should be allowed to be thoroughly human. "Ministers should be very honest before the congregation concerning their children, and concerning their own faults. They shouldn't try to gloss over things either in front of their children or in front of their own congregations. We are told to confess our faults one to another. If any self-righteous person tries to take the minister to task for not keeping his children in line, then I think he would just have to accept the criticism from that self-righteous person, and say something like, 'Well, I'm sorry, but we're all sinners and that includes me as well as my children. I do my best. I discipline them when they need it, but they're all individuals and they have to find their own way."

"I think it's a mistake also, to force them to witness to others. For instance, you wouldn't want to put a little 'You Must be Born Again' sticker on their school bags unless it was their own idea. Sometimes the simple fact of being a minister's child is pressure to witness to others for Jesus. This can become a horrible, traumatic thing for a child who thinks, 'I'm a minister's child, and so I have to witness.' Whereas that has to be born of the Spirit within. Our kids did witness at school, but I don't think they ever felt that they had to.

"My dad always wore a clerical collar, which is something that I never wore. I don't think that Peter ever wore anything different, nor did James and John and the other apostles. I think that they dressed much like ordinary human beings. I think that the clerical garb puts a heavy burden on children when they're walking down the street with their dad and he's got this thing around his neck. I used to feel that it was a very heavy thing. I also remember feeling absolutely mortified when I was with my father when he took advantage of the 10 percent discount given to clergy for all merchandise. It was the custom in days gone by that the clergy got 10 percent off in all stores. That embarrassed me terribly.

In our ministry, wherever God opens the door, we just naturally share Jesus. That includes street meetings and so on. But I've never said to our kids, 'Okay, you've got to be there.' I would, in fact, even give them opportunities to slip away if they wanted to. I didn't want to embarrass them if they were not spiritually ready to be put in that place. I always tried to avoid putting my children in situations which could embarrass them."

Bill Crump feels that scheduling can be a real trap for pastors and their families. He says: "Sometimes the demands of the congregation are very pressing, while the demands of a family can wait for a few days. Consequently, sometimes it works out that the congregation dictates your schedule to a great degree. It is important to explain to the family, and not to make them feel secondary. It is also important not to be influenced by what your congregation thinks, as opposed to what is right for your kids.

"Being a father first, rather than a minister to them is important. If kids don't see reality in your life, but sense that you are playing a role, then you are in trouble. It's so easy to fall into the trap of playing a role, developing a ministerial tone to your voice, and all that sort of thing. That artificiality just sickens me. Kids hate to see that phoniness, and they see right through it.

"Inconsistency in the home is disastrous. Kids have got to see on Monday morning in the home, what you preached from the pulpit on Sunday. It's very important for preachers to apologize to their kids and to show them they don't think that they're perfect, but that they recognize their mistakes. If you do that, then I think that your kids will tolerate inconsistencies better. They will forgive you readily. But if you give the impression that you're on a plane above everybody else, then they'll always be looking for ways to bring you down. Asking your kids to pray for you is fantastic."

Frank DeVries feels that ministers should not expect more of their children than is realistic. He says that often a minister's expectations of his children are too high partly because he wants to impress people. We often put higher expectations on our children than God does. God loves us in our humanity. We must not expect our children to be super-human.

On this subject of expectations, Ed Bentley adds: "We need to avoid the trap of considering the expectations of our congregations to be the right ones for our children. We must not always agree with the expectations of others for our children. As young ministers and parents, we are often very hyper and defensive about what we are doing, and it is easy to fall into the trap of agreeing with criticisms and expectations of our congregations."

Ed goes on to say: "We must avoid the pitfalls of being unaware of the effects of our lives and lifestyles on our children. Often we become so tired and want only to be quiet and alone. We fall into the trap of thinking only of our situations, when we need to realize where our families stand, what they need and how they are feeling."

Ken Lucas says: "Don't tag the family on at the end of everything else. Get it up there where it belongs. It is the first responsibility God gives you after your personal relationship with Him. Make your children know how important they are to you. Get down off your pedestal and get down on the floor with your kids. Hug and kiss them a lot. Tell them often how much you love them."

A minister who prefers to remain anonymous stressed the importance of scheduling time for the family. He says: "The pastor could be on every board in the church and attend every meeting. He needs to establish priorities and cut out a lot of meetings. A lot of ministers like to be the 'big chief' with a finger in every pot. It is easy to go from meeting to meeting instead of getting out to reach the people and taking responsibility for the growth of the family."

It was interesting to me that sometimes the ministers I interviewed were doing the very things they decried. They would criticize other ministers for positioning themselves on pedestals, while they themselves were suffering from a love of heights. One minister described to me, in lofty ministerial tones, how his family told him repeatedly that he was such a real person. I think he had a picture of himself which differed tremendously from reality. My impression of him was one of unreality. I found that evangelical ministers were less apt to have aspects of phoniness in their personalities, perhaps because they have learned more about real Christian principles. They are more apt to be honest and humble.

What would the ministers have done differently if they could have raised their children all over again?

An article appeared in the December, 1979 issue of the Reader's Digest. It was a condensation from, "If I Were Starting My Family Again," by John M. Drescher, a pastor for twenty-five years. He and his wife have five children aged fifteen to twenty-five. Mr. Drescher offers hard-earned advice on the parental arts which I feel are worth reprinting here.

"The words burst from the man sitting across from me, his eyes pleading for help:"What should I have done differently? If your children were young again, what would you do?" He was suffering the empty, deathlike feelings of a man whose children have strayed. He felt that he had failed as a father.

His questions stayed with me. What insights had I gleaned from my own experience as a parent and from my years of counseling others? If I were starting my family again, what would I do to improve the relations with my children? After some reflection, I jotted down the points I considered most important.

1. *I Would Love My Wife More.* In the closeness of family life, it is easy to take each other for granted and let a dullness creep in that can dampen the deepest love. So I would love the mother of my children more – and let them see that love. I would be more faithful in showing little kindnesses – placing her chair at the table, giving her little gifts on special occasions, writing her letters when I'm away.

A child who knows his parents love each other, needs little explanation about the character of God's love or the beauty of sex. The love between father and mother flows visibly to him and prepares him to recognize real love in all future relationships. When mother and father join hands as they walk, the child also joins hands. And when they walk separately, the child is slow to join hands with anyone.

Sentimentalism? Then we need a lot more of it. Often there is too much sentiment before marriage and too little afterward.

2. *I Would Develop Feelings of Belonging.* If a child does not feel that he belongs in the family – and that loyalty and love flow to and from him there – he will soon find his primary group elsewhere. Many who live in the same household are worlds apart. Many children see their father only at the dinner table; some don't see him for days at a time. Father-child time together may be only a few minutes a week.

"I would use mealtimes to share happenings of the day, instead of hurrying through them. I'd seek to make bedtime one of the most delightful hours of the day. I know bedtime can easily become a time of tension, because all are tired. Yet, in response to the question 'What makes you feel you belong to your family?' one young fellow replied,'The happiest moments of my boyhood were the times my mother read to us children before bedtime.' I pity the child and family in which the children are hustled into bed. I'd find more time for games or projects in which all could join – a great opportunity for learning attitudes of fairness, consideration, mutual respect and appreciation.

When a child feels he belongs to the family, he has security that nothing else can give, a stability that can stand against the taunts of the gang and the cries of the crowd.

3. *I Would Laugh More With My Children.* It has been said that the best way to make children good is to make them happy. I see now that I was, many times, too serious. While my children loved to laugh, I often conveyed the idea that being a parent was only a problem.

I remember the humorous plays our children put on for us, the funny stories they shared from school and the times I fell for their tricks and catch-questions. It is the happy experiences that enlarged our love and opened the door for doing things together – and still bind us together.

4. *I Would Be a Better Listener.* To most of us, a child's talk seems like unimportant chatter. Yet, I now believe, there is a vital link between listening to the child's concerns when he is young and the extent to which he will share his concerns with his parents when he is in his teens.

If my children were small again, I'd be less impatient if they interrupted my reading. There's a story about a small boy who repeatedly tried to show his father a scratch on his finger. Finally his father stopped reading and impatiently said, 'Well, I can't do anything about it, can I?' 'Yes, Daddy,' the boy said.'You could have said "Oh."'

I was once with a father who did not answer when his young son called to him again and again.'It's only the kid calling,' the man said. And, I thought, it will not be long before the father will call the son and he will say, 'It's only the old man calling.'

5. *I Would Do More Encouraging.* Probably nothing stimulates a child to love life, to seek accomplishment, and to gain confidence more than sincere praise when he has done well.

When Sir Walter Scott was a lad of fifteen, he happened one time to be in a home where some famous literary guests were being entertained. Robert Burns was admiring a picture under which a couplet was written, and he asked who the author was. No one seemed to know. Finally, young Scott named the author. Surprised and delighted, Burns is said to have exclaimed: 'Ah, ye'll be a great man in Scotland some day.' From them on,

Walter Scott was a changed lad, set on greatness.

I know now that encouragement is a better element of discipline than blame or reprimand. Fault-finding and criticism rob a child of self-reliance, while encouragement builds self-confidence and moves a child to maturity. Deep in human nature is a craving to be appreciated.

So if I were starting my family again, I would persist in daily praise, remembering Goethe's admonition to see not only what the child is now, but also what he can be.

6. *I Would Seek to Share God More Intimately.* We are not whole persons when we stress only the physical, social and intellectual. We are spiritual beings. And if the world is to know God and His will, parents must be the primary conveyors. For my part, I would strive to share my faith with my children, using informal settings and unplanned happenings. I would pay more attention to the things my child notices and to what concerns him, and find in these a natural way to discuss spiritual truths.

A famous British schoolmaster was once asked, 'Where, in your curriculum, do you teach religion?' 'We teach it all day long,' he replied. 'We teach it in arithmetic by accuracy; in language by learning to say what we mean; in history by humanity; in geography by breadth of mind; in handicraft by thoroughness; in the playground by fair play. We teach it by kindness to animals, by good manners to one another and by truthfulness in all things.'

I remember a little fellow, frightened by the lightning and thunder, who called out one dark night, 'Daddy, come, I'm scared.' 'Son,' the father said, 'God loves you and he'll take care of you.' 'I know God loves me,' the boy replied. 'But right now, I want somebody who has skin on.'

If I were starting my family again, that is what I would want to be above all else – God's love with skin on."

Dr. Ralph Wilkerson of Melodyland admonishes; "Don't you ever point your finger at someone and say 'Aha, they must have failed somewhere. They must have done something wrong or else their children would be serving the Lord.' Don't do that, because you don't know where it may strike. You don't know how it can hurt. By the grace of God, and only by the grace of God, do we hold our families in the house of the Lord these days."

No parent is perfect. There will be problems in every relationship. However, most problems are not necessarily permanent. Very often, ministers will feel tremendous anxiety if their children are expressing negative attitudes toward the church.

Bill Crump advises: "It would be very distressing to me if my children were not Christians. Three times in the New Testament it says than an elder must rule his own home; and if he cannot rule his own home then he is not equipped to rule the house of God. However, I think that there is a difference between a permanent problem of that sort and a temporary problem of that sort. Many kids go through a period of rebellion where they're in the process of discovering their own faith. If every pastor left the ministry during those temporary periods, there would be very few of us left. However, if all four of our children were turned off of the Gospel and were living as non-believers, then I would be distressed, so much so that I would probably leave the ministry. If it doesn't work at home, is it worthwhile and is it working?"

The ministers were unanimous in their feeling that in order for the Gospel to work at home, relationships have to be right. They feel that the relationships of a minister with the Lord, with his wife, and with his children, all have a profound effect on the child's spiritual growth.

As they mature, children are in the process of sorting out whether the Gospel is real or not. They sense reality or phoniness in the relationships their parents have with the Lord. Children may not verbalize their impressions, but they know when their parents are sincere. If they see their dad crying over the needs of people, weeping with his arms around an alcoholic or around a little family that is broken, they will read the reality like a book. They will know whether their dad is a true shepherd, or just a hireling, "whose own the sheep are not," as Jesus said.

If the minister has a loving, considerate relationship with his wife, the children will feel security in the relationship. As they see love expressed, they will be more able to express love. Things feel a whole lot better in a child's life when he sees mom and dad mush it up a little.

A child needs a good relationship with either his mother or his father, and preferably with both. Ralph Wilkerson says that the greatest joy in the world is planting your life in a child and watching that germination take place. He believes that whatever he is, his children will be. Children soak up attitudes and values from their parents.

Too often, parents just see their children as humans rather than eternal souls. They get all concerned with the child's hockey, or education or whatever. Very often, these interests will take precedence in the parent's eyes over the spiritual development of the child. There must be a balance. Children are spiritual beings as well as human beings, and as such they need healthy spiritual nurturing.

If a minister stops growing spiritually, his children who see him day by day will notice that very quickly. There must be growth in his life. The older the children get, the more they will see what is happening. If they see obedience and trust and forgiveness in their father, it will help them to have a balanced, ongoing spiritual development with the Lord.

David Mainse says: "Sometimes I think children will blame things on their own particular denomination. Perhaps they will meet someone of a different denomination who is also a Christian but who has a different way of expressing worship. Quite often you will fund that ministers' children end up in a different denomination from that of their parents. This may be difficult for the parents to accept. But if a minister really loves the Lord then he'll know that it is first and foremost that they are saved and they know the Lord. He will be glad that they are going on with God."

Many families appear to do everything right and seem to have all the proper ingredients – and yet their kids turn their backs on God. That is why I emphasize the reality that in many cases, it is simply the will of that child that determines the rebellion. I believe that it is important for the self-will of the child to be broken by their parents. If at some time in the child's life, his will is not led into submission to his parents, then it is going to be very difficult for that child to ever break in submission to the Heavenly Father.

"I never hovered over the kids trying to make saints out of them. For example, my young son Ronald was about eight or nine when he was baptized in the Holy Ghost and spoke in tongues. It was five years before I mentioned it again. We were having a conversation where it just came up naturally, and I said, 'By the way, Ron, do you ever pray in tongues anymore?' He said 'Sure.' 'When was the last time?' I asked.'Well, this morning Dad.' It was just a natural trusting thing. We did not attempt by our own human efforts to create saints out of our children.

"There is a lot of hugging in our house and my sons have never been embarrassed to hug Dad. While I'm hugging them I pray, 'Lord Jesus bless them and keep them safe and give them a good night's rest. Cover them with your precious blood Lord Jesus, Amen.' That's a little prayer I've prayed for them ever since they were just newborn babes first home from the hospital. There's a protection I believe a father can bring over his children against the powers of the evil spirits and the influences of the world. We need to help them as much as we can in that area without forcing them to do anything, but just taking our role and the authority we've been given in the name of Jesus to trample on those serpents and on all of the works of the devil. We need to take that authority daily for our children. After all of these years that is just as natural a part of my life as breathing. That is probably the most important thing that I've ever done for my children as a parent."

I believe that the prayers of a parent have a tremendous effect on the life of a child. Over and over again I have heard the life-changing results of a parent's prayers.

Johnathan Goforth was a missionary to China. He had a daughter, Mary Goforth Moynan, who is now 76-years-old. His daughter married a Presbyterian minister and travels all over the world now, spreading the Word of God and telling excitedly about His goodness. She had four sons. Two of them were very rebellious. One refused to have anything to do with his mother. He wouldn't even allow his children to go to hear their grandfather preach. That did not stop Johnathan Goforth's daughter from praying. She prayed faithfully for her boys for twenty years. In October of 1979, her one son called her and asked her forgiveness for all the heartache he had caused her. He said he wanted to devote himself to making it up to her. Just previous to that, another son called who had been far from the Lord. He had really messed up his life, separating from his wife and drinking too much. After twenty years of his mother's prayers he called her and said, "Mom, I've come back to God."

Pastor Robert Richardson of the French-Baptist church in Marieville, Quebec, tells the story of his son, an air-traffic controller. The boy was married and went on a holiday trip to Israel. His mom and dad were back home in Canada and were convinced by God that they should focus persistent and prevailing prayer on behalf of their son. And there he was, geographically following in Jesus' footsteps, but with a heart that for many years had been far from the Lord. Suddenly the prayers of his parents and the convicting power of the Holy Spirit converged on him. There by the Sea of Galilee he was overcome, conquered by the Christ he had professed but failed to obey, and he knew that this time, nothing short of total commitment would do. In the days that followed, his unconditional surrender so transformed his life that his wife, a nominal Christian, saw her own deep spiritual need, earnestly sought the Lord and was born again, joining her husband in the grace and love of Christ. Since that time, at least one other relative has been saved through their testimony and others are keenly interested, including several of the young man's colleagues in air traffic control.

Prayer changes things. God is not dead. He is very much alive, and is in fact the very source of all life.

My own parents did all they knew how to do and more for me. There was nothing left to do but pray. For fifteen years, I rebelled and they prayed. God heard.

PART FOUR

God's Answer

PART FOUR

Speaking Victory Through Faith

OUR TONGUES ARE POWERFUL INSTRUMENTS for action. We speak things into existence. We keep our problems through talking about them and accepting them as problems. It is through the words we speak that our conditions in life either improve or deteriorate.

When children say, "My parents won't let me do anything", they accept that as fact and expect the parents to continue to be overly restrictive. They watch for and act on the negative aspects of the relationship.

When a parent says to a child, "You never do anything right. You are always so messy," the child takes his cue from his parent. He thinks, "What is the point of trying to clean things up? I am a messy person. I am expected to be a messy person. My messiness is a fact. It is an unacceptable and yet accepted trait of mine." He is likely to incorporate that concept into his self-image – much to the dismay of the parent.

The tongue is far more powerful than we realize. In the third chapter of James, we read, "When we put bits into the mouths of horses to make them obey us, we can turn the whole animal. Or take ships as an example. Although they are so large and are driven by strong winds, they are steered by a very small rudder wherever the pilot wants to go. Likewise the tongue is a small part of the body, but it makes great boasts. Consider what a great forest is set on fire by a small spark."

Proverbs 18:21 says, "Death and life are in the power of the tongue."

Victory over life's difficulties starts in our mouths and then miraculously transforms our hearts. Victory is a decision. First we speak it, and then we see it. This may not be an immediate thing. It may take years, but it will happen if we continue to speak victoriously.

In Mark 11:22, Jesus says: "I tell you the truth, if anyone says to this mountain, 'Go throw yourself into the sea,' and does not doubt in his heart but believes that what he says will happen, it will be done for him. Therefore, I tell you, whatever you ask for in prayer, believe that you have received it, and it will be yours. And when you stand praying, if you hold anything against anyone, forgive him, so that your Father in Heaven may forgive your sins."

What a phenomenal promise! That word "whatever" includes everything – even difficulties in relationships. The way I read it, it means that if I think my parents don't understand my feelings, I can just pray, "Father, please bring understanding into our relationship." Then I can accept in faith that He has given the understanding, and I can pray, "Father, thank you for straightening things out between us," even though I may not see the immediate results. God has to have time to work. All I have to do is wait and expect to see the results.

That is a fabulous promise. However, God's promises generally are accompanied by conditions. Immediately following this promise, Jesus said that when we stand praying, if we hold anything against anyone, we are to forgive him so that God may forgive us. Thus our act of forgiveness frees God to work in answer to our prayers. Our act of obedience to His will puts us in a right relationship with Him and allows Him to pour out His blessings on us.

Therefore, if I pray, "Father, please bring understanding into the relationship between my parents and me," I must first forgive my parents for anything they have done which displeases me. My decision to forgive them looses them from my bonds of condemnation and frees them to God's healing. It also clears the way for me to be forgiven of my sins and be put in a right relationship with God. God's laws are full of cause and effect.

If a parent has a rebellious child and continually says, "Someday that boy will end up in trouble with the law," he most likely will spend time at least in a courtroom, if not in jail.

If, however, the parent prays, "Lord, I forgive my child for all the wrong he has done. I give my child to You, and I pray that You will work in his life that he may bring glory and honour to You," then the results in the child's life will be dramatic.

Parents must loose their children to the Lord. No one can make anyone else into a Christian. The Holy Spirit will reveal Himself to each one, but acceptance of the Lord is always an individual decision.

Not long ago, I heard a young man give his testimony in a Full Gospel Business Men's meeting. He had a background of deep involvement in drugs. Now he is wholly committed to the Lord. During the time he was involved in drugs, his father was aware of the problem. Rather than throw him out of the house, however, he continued to love and support his son. The message the son received was, "I don't approve of what you're doing, but I approve of you. You are my son, and I love you. I hate the things that you are involved in, and I will never approve of them."

That father made a very clear distinction between his son and his son's behavior. He accepted his son without accepting the behavior. I believe that this is a tremendously important point. So often parents muddy the issue by combining two very distinct things. That father realized that shoving religion at his son would just drive the boy further and further away. And so he developed a formula of love, patience and prayer. He combined massive doses of each, and the result was his son's conversion to Christ. Too often, people mess up relationships by condemning the person for his behavior, rather than loving the person and condemning only the behavior.

I had a beautiful friend who was killed in a car accident last fall. Four years ago, she was born again and entered into a loving relationship with Jesus. At that time, she was so full of delight in her newly discovered truths that she wanted desperately to have her husband and her five teenage children find the Lord as well. She prayed and prayed for them for two years, earnestly pleading to God for their salvation. She saw no sign of any change in them and became frustrated in her pleading with God. One day, she was lying across her bed sobbing over her family. As she lay there, convulsed in great heaving sobs, God spoke to her. He said, "Don't you believe me? I told you whatever you ask for in prayer, believe that you have received it, and it will be yours. I have answered your prayer. Accept the salvation of your family in faith and begin to confess it with your mouth."

My friend was overjoyed! Whenever anyone asked her about her family, she responded excitedly, saying, "They've all been saved!" People who knew the family began to tell her that she shouldn't be telling people any such thing, because it was obvious that her family hadn't changed. "Well," she replied, "the Lord told me that they were all saved because I asked Him to save them in prayer. Now I'm just believing Him and thanking Him and waiting to see the evidence." Within six months, one by one, her husband and all five of her children were saved and filled with the Holy Spirit.

What a glorious testimony! How often do we really pray in belief? Or do we pray just wishing or hoping? It is time to stop fooling around with God. Either we believe Him or we don't. If we do, then we have to grab hold in prayer and hang on tight, not allowing ourselves to be separated from His promises.

I don't have very many times of doubt in God now, but when I first got serious about Him, I did have a lot of times of doubt. At those times, I felt that there was a very slender silken white cord that connected me to God. For some reason, I often found myself struggling with God in my laundry room. I would hang on to that cord with every ounce of spiritual strength I could muster. I would say, "God, I'm not going to let You go. You are the only possibility for reality and purpose in my life. I'm hanging on and I won't let go. You talked about faith the size of a grain of mustard seed, and mine is pretty small Lord, but please lift me out of this doubt." The reason that my times of doubt are getting further and further apart, is that He always comes and reveals His reality to me afresh.

I believe that He allowed those times of doubt in order to strengthen my faith in Him. I discovered through those times that even if I couldn't feel His presence, He was there. I couldn't trust my emotions. After I decided to put my faith in Him blindly, then He allowed me to sense His presence. We must trust God and His promises in order to be able to receive from Him.

Had my friend trusted God and His promise from the beginning, she would have saved herself two years of needless agony and weeping before the Lord.

As the time passes, God opens up His Word more and more to our understanding. There is a verse in Matthew 18:18, that reads, "And I tell you this – whatever you bind on earth is bound in Heaven, and whatever you free on earth will be freed in Heaven."

What does that mean – binding and freeing? During my years of rebellion, I felt very uptight about religion and my parents' beliefs. Whenever I thought about Heaven or hell or Jesus, I felt a tightening around my chest. Call it crazy if you will, but I believe that my parents had me bound up in their worry. Finally, they saw that my life was such a mess that it would take a miracle from God to lift me up. They got really serious with Him and instead of worrying, they took hold of Him for me. When they freed me to Him on earth, He moved in my life.

I am not saying that my parents' worry was the whole reason for my problems, but it was a factor. It is through experiences and lessons like this that God reveals the meaning of His Word to us. One of the exciting things about the Bible is that no matter how long we study it, God still has more and more to teach us. And the more we open ourselves to Him, the deeper the truths we find.

What are the most valuable lessons I learned from my research? Well, one thing that stands our particularly is the importance of open communication in a healthy relationship. Both parties need to feel secure enough about the relationship that they can comfortably voice their honest opinions. The atmosphere for this openness has to be patiently groomed with acceptance of the people involved, no matter what their behavior, attitudes, or supposed opinions. The element required for effective grooming is unconditional love. It is the only guaranteed medium that can insulate a relationship from tempestuous changes.

Another thing I learned is that there are only two basic emotions – feeling loved, and not feeling loved. All other emotions arise out of those two basic ones. If a person feels loved, his attitudes and reactions to life will be positive. If he feels not loved, they will be negative. You might say,

"What about hatred? I can feel loved and still feel hatred for the despicable things that happen in the world." That is true, but in that case, hatred is a positive emotion arising out of your feeling of being loved. You feel hate because there are things that happen and exist in this world which seek to destroy love and the possibility for all people to find and know love.

Parents and children constantly send messages to each other, whether verbally or non-verbally. No matter what else the message may say, it always includes a communication of love or non-love. People react to these communications – positively to positive communications, and negatively to negative communications.

The difficulty is, that unless there is a great deal of open, hearty, verbal communication, the messages can be misinterpreted. For example, suppose a father loves his son very much, but spends little time with him. He appears to be preoccupied with his thoughts, and shows little patience with the boy's mistakes. Will that boy receive the love message that the father feels? No. He will receive a non-love message and will react negatively to the father.

On the other hand, if a child acts rebelliously toward his father, the father will receive a non-love message and, unless the father is mature enough to see with spiritual eyes and follow scriptural directives, he too will react negatively, and there will be problems.

I believe that the primary onus is on the parents, to make sure that their children are receiving tons and tons of love messages all through their formative years. These need to be physical and verbal and behavioral communications of love. It is a case of the chicken coming before the egg.

The generation gap is a myth. The gap, when there is one, is a communication gap. It is a cop-out to say that it has anything to do with age. Since an age difference is impossible to change, people imply that it is impossible to rectify a relationship when they speak of a generation gap. The simple fact is that parents and children lose touch with each other through lack of active effort.

Perhaps my most important lesson learned through my research was something I had already seen in my own life. However, it was revealed to me over and over again as I delved into the lives of other people. That lesson is the ability of God to heal relationships. I talked with some people who had had seemingly impossible relationships with their parents or their children. Then, when God revealed Himself to these people in a sovereign act of grace, they were brought together by a love that miraculously mended differences. No matter what the circumstances, God can overcome them if people just turn to Him.

I know. No one can dispute the experiences of my family in this area. We know what happened to our family when we looked to God.

I explored every other possibility in life available to me in searching for reality and purpose. It was all futile, satisfying to a point, but never complete.

In Matthew 7:7, Jesus said, "Ask and it will be given to you; seek and you will find; knock and the door will be opened to you. For everyone who asks receives, he who seeks finds; and to him who knocks, the door will be opened."

I was desperate and I asked, "Where is reality?"

I felt lost in life and I sought purpose.

I knocked on the door of hope and God answered!

The Beginning.

Books and Booklets
by Diane Roblin-Lee

Available from **website:** ***www.bydesignmedia.ca/store*** and on Amazon.com

Predator-Proof Your Family Series - #1-#8 – $9.99 ea.
(also available as e-books at $2.99 ea.)

Booklet #1 – *Why All the Fuss?*
Prevalence, Effects and Trends of Child Sexual Abuse   Quantity _____   Total _____

Booklet #2 – *Who is the Predator?*
Identification – Warning Signs   Quantity _____   Total _____

Booklet #3 – *Predator-Proofing Our Children*
Recognizing the Grooming Process   Quantity _____   Total _____

Booklet #4 – *Predators in Pews and Pulpits*
The God Factor - Forgiveness?   Quantity _____   Total _____

Booklet #5 – *The Porn Factor*
Are You Raising a Predator?   Quantity _____   Total _____

Booklet #6 – *It's all About the Brain*
Does Child Molestation Affect Brain Development?   Quantity _____   Total _____

Booklet #7 – *When the Worst That Can Happen*
Has Already Happened – Healing for the Victim   Quantity _____   Total _____

Booklet #8 – *Smart Justice*
Community Response to Predators who
Have Served their Time   Quantity _____   Total _____

Predators Live Among Us – $20.95. softcover
Protect Your Family From Child Sexual Abuse   Quantity _____   Total _____

The Husband I Never Knew - $12.95 softcover
Kari's story – Includes an interview with her husband   Quantity _____   Total _____

```
Name     _____
Address  _____
City     _____  Province/State _____
Country  _____  Postal/Zip _____
E-mail   _____
```

Please order from Amazon.com or Amazon.ca or from website:
www.bydesignmedia.ca/store
or call 905-852-6349 for assistance

Legacy Series

To My Family...My Life – $20.95
Ethical Will Workbook – Faith Edition   Quantity _____ Total _____

To My Family...My Life Legacy – $20.95
Ethical Will Workbook – Generic Edition   Quantity _____ Total _____

To My Family...My Life Legacy – $19.95
CD Workbook – Contains both editions   Quantity _____ Total _____
Available on Amazon.com

The Funeral and Estate Planning Guide – $4.99   Quantity _____ Total _____
**A tool to organize the events necessitated
by one's death**

Some of the Other Books by Diane Roblin-Lee

My Father's Child – $19.95   Quantity _____ Total _____
Ministers and their families
Best-seller also contains Diane's personal story
Also available on Amazon.com as an e-book

Growing in The Spirit – $19.95   Quantity _____ Total _____
The spiritual growth of an ordinary Christian
Also available on Amazon.com as an e-book

*The Wisdom of Grace
– Proverbs for Living a Lovely Life*   Quantity _____ Total _____
Ancient Principles for Today
Available on Amazon.com

Into All the World - Hardcover - $40.00   Quantity _____ Total _____
75 Years History of the People's Church

The Family Blessing Initiative – $22.48   Quantity _____ Total _____
52 Days of Prayer for the Rebuilding of Your Family
Also vailable on Amazon.com as an e-book

I Love to Tell the Story   _____   _____
100 Stories of 100 Huntley Street
Available on Amazon.com as an e-book

                                                     TOTAL   _____

Prices include taxes, shipping and handling.

www.ingramcontent.com/pod-product-compliance
Lightning Source LLC
Chambersburg PA
CBHW071337080526
44587CB00017B/2870